ONE PERCENT CHANCE

A MOTHER'S STORY

BY
HELEN SUE WEAVER

Thank you!
Helen Weaver

N&P
LEGACY

ONE
PERCENT
CHANCE
A MOTHER'S STORY

BY HELEN SUE WEAVER

www.OnePercentChance.com

Copyright ©2011 by Helen Sue Weaver

Published by N&P Legacy

International Standard Book Number: 978-0-9895148-0-4

This book is dedicated to:

Evan

CONTENTS

Acknowledgements

Evan, I thank you for your willingness to openly share your story so that future parents and kids, who experience roadblocks in life, will find inspiration in you, as I have. I so admire you! You are my rock.

I would like to thank my daughter, Jenny, for helping me and guiding me through rough waters, for a thorough reading of the first draft with enormous encouragement, and for never doubting that I would be able to complete this book.

I would also like to thank my daughter, Staver, for reassurance that this book was a worth-while endeavor. Thank you for cheering me on during the many lunches we shared on the spur of the moment during the three summers I lived in the city. You are an inspiration to me, teaching me that the important thing is to follow my passion and the rest will fall in to place.

I give whole-hearted gratitude to Tim who offered to work countless hours on marketing and editing, for creating the cover of the book and for laboriously researching the topic of publishing. You had a vision for the book from Chapter 1 onward and offered unconditional support, excitement and praise. And thank you for your criticisms when needed, always delivered in the most sensitive way. You continually validated my emotional investment in the book and I will forever be grateful for your energy, your effort and your endorsement.

Thank you to Boyd Spencer. You are such a gift to St. Jude Children's Research Hospital and to me.

Thank you to Audrey Moss, Denise Melchior and Vivian Bias for laboriously transcribing tapes.

Throughout this journey, I have been uplifted by so many ... too numerous to name individually. I sincerely thank friends and teachers and Dr. Fox at Charlotte Latin School, my 30-year friendships through my Sunday School class at Myers Park Presbyterian Church, my close friends and neighbors, our caring physicians and medical staff in Charlotte, at St. Jude Hospital, at Duke, at Chapel Hill, but specifically Dr. Golembe, Dr. Swetenburg and Dr. Murphy who were willing to read the manuscript and offer helpful suggestions. Thank you to Dr. Kun and Dr. Pui at St. Jude for meeting with me recently and sharing the great strides that have been made over the last 50 years. This is the pinnacle of celebration that we all feel! Thanks to my advisors, mentors, and "mom friends" from waiting rooms to medicine rooms. I am so grateful to my walking group, my friends and co-workers at The Fletcher School, Marlon, and Sherree, all of whom were behind me all the way. A special thank you goes to my insightful friend and college roommate, Pat and my childhood friend, Carolyn, for ongoing support. I will always miss my dear friend, Ruth, who offered understanding and encouragement but will never have the opportunity to read the final product.

Lastly, I will forever have deep appreciation and gratitude to my extended family, also known as "the beach week clan": Mary Jo and Al MacCracken (a special thank you to Al for his excellent editing), Trip and Beth MacCracken, Joel and Barbara Weaver, John and Jamie Weaver, Scott and Laura Ryan, Jon and Jenny Stillman, Evan and Kelly Kaufman, and Staver. Your love and caring have kept me afloat and sustained me.

Thank you, dear Nana and Pop.

CHAPTER I

I Just Knew ...

His appetite had been poor for so long, that it didn't seem strange to me that Evan's food was auctioned off as soon as dinner was served. "I'll take his hot dog." "Can I have his soup?" "I'll take his orange slices." As Evan, age six, sat there and picked up a couple of crackers and munched on them, his whole supper vanished from beneath his very eyes. It had become commonplace for Evan to have no appetite whatsoever and, after a little coaxing, his food was usually thrown away. In the past, the children would wait for the end of the meal, and, if anyone were still hungry, our little scavengers would help themselves to Evan's untouched food. But after a while, the kids would ask Evan during the meal, "Are you planning to eat your sandwich?" And from there, it was just a short jump to reaching for any food on his plate, even before the meal began, all of it up for grabs, because Evan simply didn't eat. At this particular meal, the talk centered on Easter eggs, the anticipation of the Easter bunny and the candy that would surely appear. Neither eggs nor candy would appeal to Evan.

The dinner guests were familiar: Evan's sister, ten-year-old, Jenny; Sara, Jeffrey and David, who were the children of Pat and Steve Bone. Pat is a close friend and my former college roommate at The College of Wooster. Purely by serendipity, both families overlapped living in Charlotte, N.C. in 1982. "Aunt Pat" and I would get the children together at least twice a week for dinner and call it a party for the children. Because both our husbands worked late, it seemed like a smart way to combat the "no-husband, no-daddy-home-for-supper blues." It was a win-win arrangement ... for the kids and for two adult-conversation-hungry-moms. A quick clean-up and short hour of play and our little group would split for home, ready for baths and bedtime.

After two years, Pat and Steve made a career move to Columbia, S.C. and my husband, Mike and I made the leap to buy our "final house" close to his work.   However, the two families made every effort to spend a holiday together here and there. Both families were looking forward to Easter break in 1984. We had chosen Gatlinburg, Tennessee, of all places, where Steve was engaged in a business deal. It really didn't matter what city. Everyone was looking forward to that "everyone-together" feeling. The kids couldn't wait to see one another, the husbands, ready to play a few sets of tennis, and, of course, a time to connect with Pat.

Jenny and Evan in happier times.

The "wake-up-call night" came when we adults planned to go out to dinner. Pat and I were making supper for the children. The menu consisted of hot dogs and applesauce, homemade soup and crackers and orange slices. It was soothing to watch these five children around the table eating together again. There was a fast chatter among the children while Pat and I stood around the perimeter, ready to serve, like waitresses in a restaurant hoping for a big tip. Enjoying observations of the children and listening to their interaction, we anticipated a very nice meal later on with just the adults.

At the adult dinner that night, after recent news was discussed, a strange and uncomfortable silence fell at the table. Pat had a very serious look on her face and finally turned to me and said, "Helllll-ennnnnnn, (drawing out the two syllables in my name for emphasis) I cannot stand this anymore. What has happened to Evan?" "What do you mean?" I asked with a strange feeling in my stomach. "Well, he looks pale. He looks tired, and well, frankly, he just simply looks sick." Had Pat not been my best friend, I would have become defensive, but as it was, I knew that her observations were always given out of love and concern. I wondered what she was talking about. A serious discussion ensued and the four of us spent a great deal of time talking about Evan, his poor eating habits and his tired-out appearance. (*Have I been too close to this forest to see the trees? Has his poor appetite become so commonplace and accepted that I have talked myself into believing that this was a developmental stage? God! Pat was right! There's something going on here. But oh how I've tried! Had Pat not realized how many screaming fights we have had around food? How many edicts have been handed out concerning a clean plate? How many times we had begged Evan to please try green beans? Had she forgotten so easily how many times we had bribed Evan into trying a salad? Evan simply had no appetite! Oh God! It was true! We were down to cereal and peanut butter.*)

The rest of the Easter weekend was fairly uneventful. However, I clearly remember the drive back to Charlotte and reviewing Pat's observations about Evan: all the things that she said made so much sense. I was beginning to be sick with worry. (*I wasn't doing my part to raise my little boy to grow up to be healthy and strong. It was time I decided to get help. I had tried everything I knew to try, and nothing had worked. I needed a plan. Please God! Show me how to help Evan. Help me find the right help. Just let Evan be OK!*) I sorted out the facts and realized that my intuition had grown into a grapefruit-sized worry in the pit of my stomach. This would not be the last long drive with two children in the back, asleep; a husband, a million miles away, listening to a medical tape, and I, riding along, and fighting off nightmarish demons in my head about my precious children.

As soon as Jenny's school let out in May, we had decided to take an "educational" trip to Williamsburg. In our family, it was important for Jenny and Evan to learn about history, and what better place to start than Jamestown and Williamsburg. In case there was too much moaning and groaning, there was an amusement park nearby called Busch Gardens, and the children were told that it would be their prize, if they patiently and diligently walked around Williamsburg with an inquisitive attitude. I loved colonial architecture and antiques, so this was a perfect place to immerse myself in history, and, at the same time, create an educational experience for the children.

A Williamsburg vacation was intended to be the perfect comination of education and fun ... but something wasn't right.

I remember Evan wore his usual Adidas outfit -- blue with a white stripe down the sides of his shorts and the V-neck rimmed in white. The weather was very hot and the humidity was high.

Evan was out of sorts; too tired to walk around and look at "junky stuff." *(Did not ALL the children there look tired and dragged out?)* I remember when he winced as he stepped off the curb in the parking lot of the Holiday Inn. It was odd that this memory would become etched in my mind. Evan constantly asked to be carried. Both Mike and I tended to baby him, to respond to the whims of our only son and youngest child. It was always difficult to refuse Evan's requests that he delivered with a mixture of love and humor. Was it "normal" for six-year-olds to wince like an elderly person with arthritis? Then, I started to think about arthritis. (Mike has ankylosing spondilitis, a type of arthritis that affects the spine and that has caused Mike much pain over the years. So rare is this inherited disease that Mike actually diagnosed himself -- and his mother -- in medical school.) *(Could this be Evan's difficulty? Perhaps Evan had inherited ankylosing spondylitis, and I have been too stupid to put two and two together. I will call a friend of ours, Dr. Box, a rheumatologist, tomorrow.)* I felt sick to think my sweet, innocent child might have to deal with arthritis for the rest of his life like his Dad. And, I admit to feeling smug to think that a mother's instinct might be superior to a husband's medical degree.

We had not been back in Charlotte more than 24 hours when the all-out offensive began. I made an appointment with our pediatrician and the rheumatologist. In addition, I sought out the name of the most capable psychologist in town, one who specialized in food and eating disorders. We spent the next months, hip-hopping to various doctor appointments and, disappointingly, always ran into a brick wall. Neither the pediatrician nor the rheumatologist found any problem. Dr. Warren, a psychologist and member of our church, met with the whole family once a week. Though it was difficult to "buy into the plan," we all tried. The plan went something like this: Jenny agreed to be a good role model. Mike and I would make decisions about what foods we would try that week and in what order. The plan included one new vegetable each week. We decided what portion to put on the plate before it was served. Evan was told all the rules ahead of time so that he would know exactly what was expected of him. For emergencies, a paper bag would rest on the chair next to Evan. As I retell the story, it sounds extreme (even ridiculous), but we promised the psychologist that we were onboard and willing to take any necessary steps. I thought we were making progress and called Pat with updated reports. I credited her with the jolt needed to jump start our eating plan, and I appreciated her concern for my children.

The summer months were upon us and it was more difficult to make progress around the table. Late afternoons at the Olde Providence swimming pool turned into early evenings, and with them came begging and pleas to have supper at the pool snack bar. My un-air-conditioned kitchen did not lend itself to heavy cooking, and the whole family had less of an appetite during the hot weather. Even if I agreed to the pool snack bar, Evan would "order and toss" the meal. I always tried to strike a balance between what was "normal" and "reasonable" and what was "accentuating" the problem.

At the end of the summer, there was a mad rush at Eckerd's for school supplies and to the mall for new school clothes. One evening, Evan was playing as Mike and I watched him in the back yard, and casually, Mike turned to me and asked, "How come he is limping?" "Gosh, I don't know, maybe he just hurt himself." I added, "I've just been to the doctor. I'm sure it's nothing!" I began to feel "haunted!" (*Was I ignoring a problem that is connected to his limp in Williamsburg? Should this be evaluated?*) I called Evan to me and asked him if his leg hurt. "Why are you limping, sweetie?" He said that he couldn't remember, but he thought that he had fallen out of a tree at the birthday party he had attended that day, and that he was all right. I thought the answer rather strange and later in the evening, after the kids were in bed, I called the birthday mom to ask about the fall. "No." She couldn't remember his falling from a tree (that many of the kids were climbing) but she WAS glad I called because at the party, Evan's entertainment consisted of sitting on the grass and watching all the other children have fun. When encouraged to join in, he just said "I don't feel very good." Bam! ... a hit to the stomach. *(Dear God! Wrap us in your arms. I'm scared!.)*

Back-to-school day at Charlotte Latin School was always the most exciting day of the year. We always got up early in the morning and dressed in pre-agreed-upon outfits. Breakfast was fast, and then we jumped in the car for the long drive down Providence Road. On the way, I always gave the proverbial speech on how NOT to be disappointed should a best friend not be placed in your homeroom. After all, sometimes it was the best thing, because it enabled one to make more new friends. And one would still be able to see old friends on the playground. The postscript always included an impassioned speech about how hard it must be for new students and how it was their job to befriend anyone new and introduce new students to other classmates.

There was a mad dash to the lower school lobby, where teachers' names headed lists of students in their classes. Kids ran up to Jenny and excitedly screamed "We're in the same class!!!" Parents and students alike asked eager questions about summer vacation. This particular year, Jenny was entering fifth grade and had been assigned to Eva Mitchell, and Evan was entering kindergarten, and his teacher was Diane Totherow. I couldn't believe our good luck! Each child had gotten the very teacher I would have chosen for them, had I been given a choice. Diane had been Jenny's kindergarten teacher and was already a family friend.

Diane, a teacher with many years' experience, exuded confidence. She was also a mom whose two children were students at Latin, as well. She had wonderful rapport with her students. She was insightful, while watching developmental milestones, and intuitive to their personalities. I remember that she swore that she could predict, as early as kindergarten, who would be the class president twelve years hence and who would star in the senior class play. Unbelievably, one of her astounding feats was her ability to remember the birthdays of each of her students, not just the present year's class, but for years after a child had moved on. She was a creative teacher and masterminded the special day when all the dads go through the kindergarten day with their child to see what kindergarten was really like. In the spring, she started a tradition called "Mother/Daughter Tea Party," a day when all the girls, young and old, wore hats and gloves and sipped tea at the same time, learning manners and social graces. Diane cared about getting to know each student and his family. She set the stage for Latin's reputation of being a family school. I knew immediately that Evan was going to have a wonderful year.

After the parent and child inspected the list of teacher-homerooms in the lobby, it was time to go to the classroom, take a seat and hear the teacher talk about what an exciting year it was going to be, give out the class list, the school rules, the school directory, have us fill out milk forms, volunteer to drive, volunteer to be the room mother, meet the other children and their moms, arrange car pool, and the list went on. I sat there with such relief and joy! I was a working mother (the office manager for Mecklenburg Neurological Associates that Mike and I had founded together four years earlier). The last two years had become most difficult to juggle the different schedules of Jenny's school with Evan's preschool. Everything would be so simple this year: both children in the same wonderful, caring school. Both would have the same hours and ride in the same car pool. Both children would have the same holiday schedule and, most of all, both would be in the perfect setting to advance both academically and socially to the fullest. And, oh yes, both of them would have a lot of fun. To this very day, whenever I feel satisfied that life is nearly perfect and things are going well, I immediately get the old, familiar knot in my stomach, for I have learned how tenuous life is and how it can change in an instant!

It had been a week since the birthday party and Evan's "fall from the tree" story. I began to notice that his limping was worse. I decided, just to be on the safe side, that I would make another appointment with the pediatrician to decide if there was anything that we were overlooking. It was a little embarrassing, since this was the second time in a week that I was taking Evan with the same complaint. I brought up the arthritis idea. I guess the very fear of going to the doctor straightened the limp out, because when we got there, as predicted, the pediatrician studied Evan's walk and could see nothing out of the ordinary. Evan could also bend over and touch his toes and, after a few more similar tests, the pediatrician assured me that it was nothing but if it were to persist, come back, and he would take another look. I left the office that day, as I had left the time before, thinking how lucky we were to have such good medical care, but also, quite perplexed. (*Perhaps Mike knows more about ankylosing spondilitis than the pediatrician does. The pain remained confined to the back. Why don't they listen to us?*) In fact, we began to refer to Evan's complaint as his "back problem," that Evan pronounced as "back ploblem" due to a persistent immature speech pattern. Bless his heart, I hated to correct his speech, since it was so endearing. We assured Evan that we would find the right doctor, an assurance that would become a recurrent theme. This was a comfort to him.

In the meantime, Mike and I were forced to make a stupid decision, one that we made, despite the fact that we knew better. We felt dismayed that Evan was still in pain. We could not persuade our pediatrician "to work this up" or to take this complaint more seriously. After we returned to the pediatrician for the third time, and coupled with the fact that Evan was limping every day, we convinced ourselves that we needed to take the situation into our own hands. This was NOT a figment of our imagination. One of the pitfalls to having a doctor in the family is that sometimes the urge is too strong to handle a problem yourself. And that is EXACTLY what we did. Together, Mike and I decided that we would start a treatment plan with a high dose arthritis medicine to determine if the pain would be helped. Then, armed with our own, albeit unorthodox, unproven research, we could take our results to the doctor in an effort to justify our actions.

Two days into Evan's "new treatment," Jenny ran to me yelling "Come! Evan is throwing up in the garage." Another trip to the pediatrician yielded a stern reprimand. I had to disclose our new regime of medication, explaining our hopes of helping the back pain. Rightfully, the doctor gave us an ultimatum. Our doctor HAD to be in charge. Only HE could prescribe medicine. If we could not follow these two rules, we would be discharged from his practice. Actually, I admired his courage in taking such a staunch (but reasonable) stand. (*Does he not understand that I have had five appointments so far within the last month? Why doesn't our doctor recognize two desperate parents and one obviously sick child? Why does each visit end in "If it gets worse, come back!" God! I keep coming in! What now?*) Evan continued to "pull it together" enough to be able to mask the pain for the 10 minutes while he was in front of the doctor. The x-ray that was ordered two visits ago had come back "normal." (*God! Give me patience! Help our doctor help Evan.*) "Yes, of course, you are in charge. We will not jump ahead again, I promise. Please understand that I feel there is something very wrong. Can you please do some blood work, or another x-ray or SOME diagnostic procedure?" (*Is it possible that because I am "only a mom," that no one is taking me seriously? Surely not! Is it possible that if Mike were with me, they would work this up? Would that make a difference?*)

On the first day of school, Evan was very excited about going, but at day's end I received a call from his teacher, Diane, saying that she had noticed his limp and he seemed to be quite uncomfortable. I was very surprised that she would notice this right away. I told her my dilemma: my intuition was that something was wrong, but no one else thought so. We agreed to keep in close contact.

Diane's call prompted a return to the pediatrician again. This time, the limp was apparent, but it seemed to the doctor that it was ever so slight and definitely nothing to worry about. This series of appointments was the most frustrating experience of my life. (*I know that I have made a pest of myself. Perhaps the doctor thought to himself, "Oh, here she comes again!"*) I remember feeling sick upon leaving, and began to visualize in my mind our trip to Jamestown and Williamsburg, and then "falling out of a tree at the birthday party" episode. After work, while standing in front of the elevator on the fourth floor, our secretary, Carolyn ran out to me and said, "Thank goodness you are still here ... Evan's teacher is on the phone. She's very concerned about Evan." To this day, I can still think of that sentence and it sends a chill up my spine.

Diane called me again and described a special outing. It had been a beautiful day and she had decided to take a field trip, as a class, to the school's football field some distance away from the lower school. At the beginning of the walk, that entailed going down some steps and up a slight incline on a grass pathway, Evan winced on each step, almost going on tip-toe, in order to stand the pain. He then told Diane that he didn't feel as if he could make it all the way to the football field. He wondered if it would be all right if he stayed behind with Mrs. Wohlbrook, the school secretary, as the trip would "hurt too much." He even apologized for the request. This really concerned her, because the whole class was quite excited about the outing, and so was Evan, that is, until he realized that he would have to walk a long way.

Hearing this story, my intuition was fed further. Something was wrong, really wrong. My husband kept pushing for the explanation of arthritis in the back. He felt like it coincided with the symptoms. I just knew it was something ... serious. The pediatricians all felt that Evan had anxiety symptoms and made a good case for school-itis. But, again, my sickening suspicion wouldn't leave. Were we dealing with something complex, something rare, something very bad? When the puzzle pieces did not point to juvenile arthritis; when they did not support school-itis, a sick feeling in my stomach became permanent. I just knew ...

I hung up and called the pediatrician immediately. I was pleased and surprised to learn that they had office hours in the evening and that we could bring Evan in that same day. I insisted that Mike join me. He needed to experience this ordeal first hand. We did not see our regular doctor, as he wasn't on call that night, but

Evan was worked up very thoroughly by his partner. (*This was such good news... after all, this surely meant that we would get a fresh set of eyes and a new opinion. I thought we were getting somewhere!*) The partner watched Evan walk up and down the hall and asked him to bend over and touch his toes. It seemed as though they were evaluating how limber he was. Having answered a million questions, he told me that he really did not feel that there was anything significant going on, but since we had been in to the office so many times, (*What does THAT mean?*), he would order another x-ray and another blood test. Evan began to look very worried, because it sounded like this would involve a needle. As we left the office, the doctor assured us that we should continue to watch the limping, and if it became worse, to call, or if there were anything wrong with the blood test, he would call me. When I asked what this could be, he said that he thought it was simply growing pains. Mike thanked him. (*I KNEW this was not growing pains. Intuitively I knew. I recognized that they are doctors and that my only experience was having one older child. I was not over-reacting! Oh God! Am I crazy, like they must think? God! I hope they are right.*)

A pattern was beginning to form. Evan would wake in the morning, crying because he did not want to go to school. He would say that he didn't feel well and that it hurt all over, but mostly his back. He did not have a fever, his appetite was as usual, and I would launch into my speech. Daddy had a job to take care of patients. My job was to manage the office. Jenny's job was to go to school and to learn, and that Evan's job was to go to school and learn, too. It was okay to stay home from school or work if a person were sick, but otherwise, one needed to go and do his best.

By the time Evan got home from school, he was unusually tired. Mornings became worse and worse. He would awaken, hurting terribly and begging not to go to school. I tried to be very stern. Finally, I placed a note in his lunch box to ask Diane to give me a call to give her opinion as to whether she thought we were dealing with a bad case of "school-itis" which contradicted his enthusiasm for Charlotte Latin. The expected call came while the children were at recess. She told me that he seemed to be limping more at the beginning of the day. He seemed very well adjusted and very well liked by the other children. She also noticed his general malaise. She was willing to put her reputation on the line: this was not school-itis.

Mike and I were beginning to have long discussions about the "back ploblem." It felt good to have him onboard. Again, he began to sing the juvenile arthritis tune. I felt then that Mike couldn't get past his own experience with severe back pain associated with this crippling disease, and his mother's before him. He worried that Evan was the recipient of the gene that carried this trait, and that perhaps Evan would have it even worse than he had. Though my opinion was worthless, I disagreed silently. The rheumatologist had already ruled out juvenile arthritis.

Back to the pediatrician's office, I saw another partner who was beginning to wonder why I continued to come back so often. I carried Mike's "suggested" written order for another x-ray to be taken from another angle hoping that an arthritis diagnosis could still be made. During this appointment, I learned that both the x-ray and blood test results from last week came back normal *(was that supposed to make me feel better?)* Even though Evan's symptoms did not manifest evidence of a child with arthritis, the doctor was accommodating and wrote out the order for another x-ray to be done. He sat down with me in private, and we discussed "school-itis," and how Evan was starting kindergarten, and that it was very common for children to develop real anxieties about going to school. This discussion prompted a long letter to Diane when I got home concerning the "school-itis" diagnosis and the anxiety that some children feel when they first get to kindergarten. *(Can I buy in to this???)* Perhaps it was too hard for Evan to contemplate filling Jenny's shoes, and I felt sorry for him if it were this difficult to make the transition from preschool to kindergarten.

By mid-September, when the carpool arrived to pick up Evan and Jenny one morning, Evan had big tears in his eyes when it became apparent that he was to sit "in the way back" of the station wagon, on the floor of the fold-down seat. (This was before the 'everyone-must-have-a-seatbelt rule.) He whispered to me that it would hurt too much to sit there from our house all the way to school. Plus, he wasn't sure he was even able to crawl back there. Despite the new skirt that Jenny was wearing, and without my asking her, she hopped in to the "way back," giving up her seat to Evan in the more comfortable middle of the second row. It turned out that all four of the other drivers, each day of the week, had been rearranging the children to give Evan the most comfortable seat in the car. Everyone recognized that he seemed to be in a great deal of pain. The other children could tell this was not a ploy, and Evan was always appreciative for their consideration.

Two days later, on Friday, it was my turn to drive the car pool. When I pulled up to the covered walkway, the doors of my Chevrolet station wagon flung open and the children all hopped out, as if we had just arrived at Baskin Robbins, all except for Evan and Jenny. I watched as Evan ever so slowly got out of the car, wincing, and carefully moving in a guarded way. Jenny seemed to know just how to hold out her arm to steady him. Instead of pulling away, instinctively, I sat there, holding up the line of cars behind me. I watched Evan and Jenny midway to the kindergarten door, stop and sit down on the bench with Jenny at Evan's side. Causing the long car-pool line to pile up 10 cars deep, I got out of my car and ran up to them. "What is the matter, Jenny?" I asked. She explained that for about a week now, Evan would hold on to her arm and she would walk with him, stopping at the same place each day, the halfway point to the door. Evan needed to rest and then would gather up the strength to make it the rest of the way. Diane had planted a chair right inside the kindergarten door, his final destination. How PROUD of Jenny I felt, and then, so incensed that my child was experiencing this much pain, and no one was helping us! This was NOT (*give me a break!*) school-itis, and I was not going to let the sun set one more day without getting specific questions answered. I remember feeling like I would need SOMEHOW to get SOMEBODY to take me seriously, even if I have to lie down in the middle of Providence Road.

I thanked my sweet "Jenny-girl" for being a compassionate big sister and then told Evan to come back to the car with me. The time had come that we would find a way to make his back better. Evan became quite worried, because my voice sounded "mean" (*that's code for determined!*) Even Evan asked, "are we going back to the doctor AGAIN?" In a very calm voice I "therapeutically explained" that he was right: we had certainly gone to the doctor a lot recently. I told him that the doctors were very puzzled about his back pain. I assured him that I knew that his back pain was very real. I comforted him by explaining that there were some special doctors at the hospital where Daddy used to work (Duke Medical Center) and that we would be going there today, where the doctors would know exactly what to do. At this point it sounded good to Evan to be able to get his back "fixed up," but he was worried and scared at the same time. (*So was I, Evan. So was I.*)

When we arrived at the pediatrician's office, I calmly told the receptionist that I was sorry that I did not have an appointment. I apologized for not having called ahead, but we came straight from school. I also told her that I was willing <u>and planning</u> to sit there all day, if necessary, in order to be seen. My son was in a great deal of pain, and we needed to be seen by any one of the doctors in the group one last time.

The real reason was that I knew that patients could not just "show up" and that I needed a referral from our Charlotte doctor. With any luck at all, our pediatrician would have some connection at Duke, since most of them did some part of their training there, and he would be able to pave the way for an immediate admission and subsequent work-up. We were in the waiting room a surprisingly short time when Evan's name came across the loudspeaker. "Evan Joel Kaufman, please proceed down the left hallway" and were ushered into a familiar room. (*We had seen them all in only a few weeks.*)

Luck was on our side. This time our wonderful friend and neighbor, Ray Swetenburg, walked in to see Evan for the first time.
After reading the chart, he seemed genuinely concerned. He was
surprised at the nine previous visits with no diagnosis and did not
fight my idea of leaving for Duke immediately. Given his sympathetic and supportive demeanor, my mama-bear, fierce attitude
gave way to difficulty speaking, and a quivering voice. To this
day, I remember Evan turning around and looking at me quizzically, wondering why tears were streaming down my cheeks. I
explained to him that I was sure this was not school-itis, as was
Evan's kindergarten teacher, Diane Totherow. He was more than
familiar with Diane, since his own children attended Charlotte
Latin, too. Secondly, we have already been to Dr. Box, a competent rheumatologist, and he had ruled out ankylosing spondilitis. To underscore our desperation about Evan's pain, I admitted
once again that Mike and I had even resorted to putting Evan on
medication for a short time to see if it would do any good. *(Why
do I cry at the most inopportune times?)* I was tired of leaving the
office with a child who was still in a great deal of pain and with
nothing being done about it. He listened to me with patience. He
did not make me feel like a hysterical mother and told me that he
agreed that something was going on. *(Oh God! Please keep Evan
safe!)* I proceeded to tell him that I was going to go to Duke that
very day, in order to get to the bottom of this. "Don't even THINK
of discouraging me." I was quite surprised when he agreed that
it was a good idea. He reminded me that it was Friday and that,
perhaps, it was the wrong day of the week to arrive at Duke Hospital. In a calm and persuasive voice, he promised that he would
review the chart over the weekend and that he would call a pediatric professor-friend of his, and he would pave the way for an
arrival early the following week. I apologized for seeming to be
unreasonable, but I would not wait another day. I had made a
resolve to get help for Evan, and I didn't care if I were arriving on
Christmas. I would pitch a tent on the lawn of Duke Hospital if
I had to. I was GOING to go. Dr. Swetenburg didn't argue. He
asked me to wait in the exam room once again, while he called his
Duke colleague to prepare her for our arrival today. *(God, thank*

you for this doctor. Just keep Evan safe.) Dr. Swetenburg entered the room. "I have spoken to my colleague at Duke. She has asked that I order a bone scan here in Charlotte. She wants you to bring it with you. If you leave Charlotte now, you won't arrive at the hospital until late afternoon, and it will be Monday before they can do the scan there. You will save time by going over to the hospital right now." With one step forward, I thanked him.

I drove the short two blocks to Mike's medical office, and took the elevator to the fourth floor. I was a familiar sight there, but the staff was surprised to see me carrying Evan in my arms. I whisked him straight through the waiting room to the long hall of examining rooms and ducked into one of them. I lay Evan carefully on the examining table. Mike was alerted and came in immediately and asked why I was there. With a quivering voice and tears still on my cheeks, I told him that we were on our way to the Radiology Department for a bone scan and after that, I was driving to Duke. I recounted the car pool line and my conversation with Dr. Swetenburg. Mike assured me that he would join us as soon as he saw his last patient. We talked about the cancellation of our weekend plans (to attend a church retreat in the mountains), and that he would cancel his patients for Monday in order to accompany Evan and me to Duke. (*Oh God! I think we are making progress! Please Lord, I pray that you hold Evan in your arms and keep him safe!*)

I whisked Evan back through the waiting room as fast as I had come in. The Hospital was across the street, so I left my car. By the time I carried Evan across the street, in through the emergency room and down a maze of hallways, I was out of breath. The minute we arrived at the Radiology Department, there was no waiting. (Dr. Swetenburg or Mike must have called ahead.) Evan was very clingy and really quite frightened. I had not had the time to explain to him about the visit to the pediatrician, the visit to his Dad's office, or the return to radiology. I could only imagine how it felt for Evan. I would have time to prepare him, once we undressed him for the x-ray. Removing his clothes for a hospital gown was laborious and painful. As long as I held him in a special way, his back did not hurt as much, and he kept telling me how much he wished that he were back in school. It was difficult and painful for Evan to lie on the hard-surface table and remain still for an inordinate amount of time. But he cooperated like a trooper.

After x-ray set #1, we were told to wait in the holding area and not get dressed, until the radiologists were satisfied with the quality of the scan. The technician returned to us and explained that they were unhappy with the angle of the pictures and that they would like to retake a whole new set. *(Are they inept? Why can't they get this right?)* Although irritated that this needed to be redone, Evan cooperated and held still for the second set of pictures. I was amazed at how many needed to be taken. *(MY! This is going to cost a lot!! I hope our insurance is willing to cover this.)* Again we waited for word that the scan was good and that we could leave. But this time, the radiologist, himself, came down the hall and asked me if Evan had ever had an injury to his lungs or rib cage. Had he ever had a bad fall or an operation? Had he ever been seriously ill? He was nonchalant, but I felt that he was trying too hard! *(Lord, what is it? Why would he be putting on this front? Obviously, he is looking for a reason for something he sees ... how I wish I could come up with a reason!)* "No, he has never been hurt, never been injured or seriously ill." He smoothly smiled and said that he was only wondering. He assured me that there was no problem and would I mind please waiting just a little longer to be sure they had "seen everything?"

I looked at my watch. Jenny would be coming home from school soon. The same familiar technician came down the hall once again and asked us if we wouldn't mind bearing with them one more time for set #3. The machine was giving them some "problems" and they needed to repeat the set one more time." *(Do I LOOK stupid? Do they not realize that I KNOW that something is wrong ... they need to TELL me! ... God, what is it? Please Lord, keep Evan safe.)* Even Evan, age six, wondered if this were a game. He began to guess how many more times they would make an excuse. Evan was so patient and so good. I wanted to hug him and protect him and keep him safe forever.

A short time after round #3, the technician came back and said that we could get dressed now and go home. The radiologist appeared, making an obligatory appearance, and explained that there was a very, very benign-looking "spot" on one of the x-rays, and told us that they had taken extra care to take many pictures and promised that they were not missing anything. Not wanting to "deal" with an hysterical mother, he assured me that everything looked fine and then apologized that it had taken the entire afternoon. He further explained that he had asked other radiology specialists to read the films and they would be ready for me to take to Duke on Monday. *(My reputation had obviously preceded me. How did he know that I was heading to Duke?).* He suggested that we consider continuing our plans for the mountain weekend getaway. *(That's strange! How had he heard about that, anyway?)*

There is something about a hospital that is exhausting. Is it the air? The smell? Is it the automatic stress that one feels? Is it the knowledge that this is a serious place---somewhere that no one wants to be? Though the floors were "clean", one could almost feel the millions of germs crawling on everything. Is it the uniforms that everyone wears to further identify "the people in the know?" Is it the machinery that looks so intimidating? Is it the holding area with matching chairs lined up in a row that makes one feel like cattle being herded through? Is it the generic hospital blue that is repeated as a reminder that an effort is being made to make one feel the sterility of the place? Or, is it the feeling of being out of control? And for those of us who like to control situations, maybe it is exhausting to realize how OUT of control life is.

At about this time Mike showed up. The radiologists were somewhat uncomfortable with Mike's arrival. As a parent/physician, he might be a time-consuming obstacle to the tight schedule of the department. Perhaps these doctors were more comfortable dealing with technology than with patients' feelings. Mike asked to speak to the radiologist who had read Evan's films. He had many questions but was easily dismissed with the assurance that everything looked OK. Mike firmly gripped my hand. The radiologist said that he had taken extra care with Evan. Everything looked fine. He told Mike not to worry and that, as an extra precaution, he was going to have a specialist come down to look at the films when he could. We should go and enjoy the weekend. Not wanting to insult anyone, Mike did not insist on looking at the films himself.

Evan could no longer walk due to the severity of the pain. This was a long afternoon and Evan was exhausted and asked us to please LEAVE! With relief, Mike gladly carried him out of the radiology suite, back across the street to our parked car. This was the beginning of Mike's becoming Evan's legs. Mike carried Evan everywhere, and the two would grow to become interdependent. Evan would depend on Mike for transportation and Mike would depend on Evan for constant assurance that his spirits were still high. Through trial and error, Mike learned how Evan needed to be carried, and Evan would cling with his arms around Mike's neck. Evan's long, dirty-blond, Beatle-cut hair fell over his eyes, showing a little fright, but still mirroring our confidence that this was nothing more than a temporary interruption in his life. On the way home, we discussed what we should do about the weekend.

Jenny met us in the driveway, worried that our trip would be called off, and the look on her face convinced us that our choice was already made. The two-hour trip to the mountains was uneventful. When we stopped on the way to get something to eat, it seemed like second nature for Mike to go around to the back door and carefully pick Evan up in the special way in order not to hurt him. Everyone ate fast food for dinner that night except Evan. He wasn't hungry.

Montreat is a beautiful Presbyterian retreat and college near Asheville. It is no wonder that Billy Graham chose this beautiful mountain for his home, and one could easily believe that one is a little closer to God when staying there. It's a perfect place for rejuvenation. The town is quaint and small. I loved the double stone archway that leads to Lake Susan and the various buildings owned by The Presbyterian Synod. I wondered if a similar-looking building to the large stone walls of Assembly Inn may have been the inspiration for the hymn "A Mighty Fortress is Our God." The Inn sits high above Lake Susan and, in October (always the month of our church retreat because of the change-of-leaves) the beautiful color quilt of yellows, oranges and reds were brilliant both above the water and reflected by the water. The lower level of the Inn was the drop-off point. There were rolling hotel carts available to haul an entire family's weekend possessions to the room in one trip. At the first floor, newcomers were welcomed by a mountain-esque, straw-stuffed, life-sized farmer couple sittin' on a country bench. Handmade quilts decorated the walls with reasonable price tags pinned to the bottom. The artwork displayed was always local mountain scenery painted at different seasons of the year. The family retreat planned by our church always included family hikes of different ability levels, family baseball games near the Inn, and a family square dance on Saturday night with a local "caller." For the more sedentary guests, there was bridge in the lobby, a shopping trip to Asheville, antiquing in the town of Montreat, and interesting nature trails and bird watching. There was something for everyone. There was always family fun in the expansive first floor lobby that included big glass windows with perfect views of Lake Susan and the mountains beyond. Roaring fires filled two fireplaces in the evening. The fireplaces were large, with five to six feet openings. Two grand pianos, albeit out of tune, were on opposite sides of the room, with many comfortable chairs and sofas arranged in conversation groupings. The ceiling was high, perhaps around thirty feet, and the walls were spectacularly made of huge stones. There were large plank floors and beautiful old area rugs covering them. Even the check-in desk was nestled among the stones, with old-time open mail boxes holding old keys from the past that were still being used.

Evan could no longer be carried with one arm around Mike's neck. It was simply too painful to be draped over Mike's shoulder. Rather, Evan now needed to be lifted from under his upper thighs with his weight evenly distributed in order to tolerate movement. It was dark when we arrived. As we finally pulled up to the bottom floor of Assembly Inn, I remember getting out of the car and taking a big breath, filling my lungs with that fresh, cold mountain air. What a long day it had been, and I was happy that it was almost over. What I didn't know was that we were facing the worst night of our lives.

I admit that I am a compulsive person and unpacking meant that the entire car had to be cleaned out and organized before we left it. It also meant that, upon arriving in our room, the suitcases needed to be unpacked and the drawers filled, our toiletries placed in the bathroom. As the children were doing their part of this routine, Mike appeared in the doorway. He looked sick, pale, and frightened, and without a gesture, I left what I was doing to come out to the hall to see what had happened, a little annoyed that he had mysteriously disappeared, leaving all of the unpacking for me.

I first asked him where he had been. His voice quivered while he told me that our dear friend, Ray Swetenburg (the last of the pediatricians to see us and, coincidentally, one of the members of our church who was also attending the retreat with his family) called back to the Radiology Department when he arrived at Montreat. Having a queasy sense himself about Evan, he was worried about the bone scans and x-rays that had been taken that afternoon. He learned and subsequently told Mike that the entire radiology department was abuzz after we left that afternoon. Various other physicians had all gathered around Evan's films. Sadly, he related that a large tumor was pressing on Evan's spinal cord and another tumor was seen on his left shoulder. Evan had cancer. Hearing this was like having your heart ripped out, and you are standing there bleeding, and nobody can make you whole again. Mike took my hand and said that the best we could hope for was Hodgkin's disease. *(GOD! Hold me up. PLEASE let this be a mistake. This has GOT to be a mistake. Please let Evan be OK!)*

Jenny ran out to the hall and said, "Hurry up, they are beginning to roast marshmallows in the main lobby," and Evan begged, "Please let us stay up longer than usual." I am now totally numb. Is that my voice answering him? Are those my feet that are walking? Are Mike and I now discussing our children's bedtime? Perched at the top of the steps, I can look out and see everyone mingling around in this very large room, the enormous fireplace on one side. The fire is crackling. The children are running around, each with a stick in his hand and a marshmallow dripping from it. Everyone is gay and lighthearted and hugging each other and asking what time each family had arrived. I wanted to stand at the top of the stairs and scream. *(What is happening? Am I going to wake up? Is this a dream?")* I am still numb. There is not a nerve-ending in my entire body that is working. I see the people as if they are talking but I can't hear them. The only thing I can hear is inside me. I can hear my heart pounding, my stomach churning, and I am stiff with coldness. Someone approaches us. I think I hear my voice talking, but I don't know what is said. I wonder if it makes sense. *("Please let me wake up, God. Please don't let this be true.")* What I need right now is to talk with Mike or Dr. Swetenburg. If only I could ask one of them, "What does all this mean? Are they sure? Where do we go from here? What is happening? Is it possible that this is a mistake?" But for now, I am supposed to smile. I am supposed to talk about the events tomorrow. Someone approaches me, "Had I remembered the refreshments for tomorrow?" I don't know what to answer. *(Oh God, I feel so numb.)* Jenny approaches with a marshmallow. She is surely confident that she will be in my favor, for I am known for my sweet tooth, but I explain to her that I think I am coming down with the flu and that I don't care for it right now.

The evening dragged on. It was finally time to put the children to bed. I have always had the utmost admiration for Mike. He is a good person in so many ways: bright, earnest, honest, but what was so outstanding to me tonight was his ability to rope off all feelings for later and play games with the kids, as if nothing were wrong. Somehow, he found the energy to play charades. He looked absolutely fine on the outside; and all the while, he was hurting on the inside. As for me, I had collapsed behind the guise of flu. Everyone had now excused me from helping with the teeth brushing, the pajama change, and the routine story hour. After the kids were in bed, Mike and I both changed, and I seized the opportunity, while he was brushing his teeth, to whisper a million questions. He would only shake his head "No" and mouthed, "Wait." Hours passed, before we knew for sure that the children were asleep. I had never seen Mike cry before, I mean sob. He could barely talk, and it was the first time I had ever seen him incapacitated by emotion. I kept going over in my mind how unfair this was. Wouldn't God take care of us? Mike finally shook me up: "Don't you get it? We would probably lose Evan." BAM! The absolute worst part of the ordeal, until now, was NOT KNOWING! There was no differential diagnosis. There was no speculating as to what he had. There was no way to discuss what we could do about it. Where could we go for this problem? What were our chances and how far had it spread? Silently, we cried and sobbed. We gripped each other's hand. There was only one detail we knew for certain, and that was, on Monday morning, Evan would be admitted to the hospital. There was no use returning to Charlotte early, especially because both of our children had looked forward to spending the weekend at Montreat, and we were not going to rob them of what could be Evan's last Montreat weekend. We were going to show them a good time, if it killed us, and it nearly did.

We heard the children begin to awaken. *(God, is it morning already?)* We quickly jumped up from the floor in the corner of the room and lay down, burying our heads in the pillows, as if we were dead to the world. To make it sound as natural as possible, we drowsily said, "Just five more minutes, kids," for we needed five minutes of transition time, so that we could face the day fighting. Thus began an incredibly long day. It was the start of a sickening journey.

Jenny started to bounce on us in order to wake us up, and Evan, who didn't feel like bouncing, hobbled over to us and tenderly gave us each a kiss, saying that he was hungry and could we please get up. He was such a loving child. Happy to hear about this appetite, we got up quickly and dressed.

Evan has always been a kidder and a teaser and has always seized every opportunity to have fun. In the cafeteria that morning, Mike filled up his little juice glass with the best, fresh orange juice that he had ever tasted and begged Evan to please take a sip because it was so good. As part of a set-up, he purposely <u>emphasized</u> how much he was looking forward to drinking that wonderful juice. Agreeing to be Evan's accomplice, I asked Mike if he would mind getting up to get me a cup of coffee. With Mike's back turned, Evan grabbed Mike's glass of orange juice, gulped the whole thing down and carefully placed the empty glass in the same position it was, before Mike left. When Mike got back, he handed me the coffee and sat down to a delicious breakfast, but when he reached for his juice it was gone! Immediately he ascertained "the game," and decided to play it for all it was worth. "Has anyone seen my orange juice? I could have sworn it was right here, my full glass of orange juice! I don't understand what happened to it." "Well, why don't you just go and get another glass," I suggested. About the time he sat back down, placing his glass carefully in front of his plate, I told him that my coffee was now cold and that I would appreciate a refill of hot coffee. Evan was grinning and silently thanking me, with a gleam in his eye, for helping him out. The minute Mike's back was turned another time, Evan grabbed the glass of orange juice, guzzled it down like a fraternity brother guzzling a beer, and again carefully placed the glass, totally empty, at the front of the placemat. In a very theatrical way, Mike returned, dismayed that his juice had again disappeared. So pleased was he that he was tricking Evan into drinking his juice that his entire plate of warm scrambled eggs, bacon and biscuit had been sacrificed. By the time we finished playing our game, we were the last ones in the dining room. Admittedly, it wasn't as if we were in a hurry to go anywhere. We were not going to be hiking or playing baseball.

While Jenny was hiking the mountain with her friends and their parents, we had decided to spend our day in a more sedentary way, sitting on the banks of Lake Susan, fishing. This activity was perfect for me. I was thrilled with the instructions: to sit quietly on the bank of this very still lake with the backdrop setting of a beautiful mountain, and not scare the fish away by making a sound. I was so relieved that I didn't need to make conversation. Here was an opportunity to meditate and pray, to beg and compromise and to make deals. *("Dear Lord, we are in your hands. Please give me the strength, dear God, just to make it through today. Please let Evan be all right. Dear God, I am so scared, I don't know what's ahead. Take this pure and innocent child and cleanse him of whatever this disease is. Please spare this life. I promise I will work diligently to do your will if you will just spare this life, dear God. I humbly ask for your strength to see me through today and tomorrow. Please be with us, amen.")*

Jenny was anxious to join in on the annual square dance that evening but realized that Evan would be unable to participate. She suggested that we all play charades instead. (*Little did she know that the biggest charade of all was being played out as she spoke.*) Evan was unable to move, so we improvised with making shadow figures on the wall late into the night. We could help prop Evan up against the bed on one elbow, but every time he became too exuberant, he would wince in pain. When the kids happened to turn away, Mike and I would exchange glances of mutual agony. Nothing can pull at your soul like watching your child in pain, not the pain that heals and makes him stronger or the kind that teaches a lesson but the sickening pain that your child did not bring on himself, the kind that lets you know that something is eating away at his body, the kind that you must reassure him about, although you know that what is causing the pain might relentlessly progress.

When we left Montreat on that beautiful Sunday morning, I was relieved to have some active part in what was coming. Putting in the time on top of a mountain in such a passive way was extremely difficult. The church agenda for Sunday was breakfast, church service, free time, lunch and hiking. For us, it was time to pack, drive back to Charlotte and prepare for Monday morning. As we pulled away, looking at the beautiful old stones of Assembly Inn, I wondered whether I would ever return. Would I ever get rid of the enormous lump in my stomach or my numb hands and limbs? Would I ever lose the sickening, nauseated feeling in my heart?

Mike drove and, for some reason, I was downgraded to the back seat. Perhaps Evan needed more room to stretch out. It was going to be a long trip back to Charlotte. I worried that Mike wouldn't be able to stay awake. For two nights now we had taken the opportunity, once the children were asleep, to sit up and talk and cry and sob, and try to comfort one another. We were both in a state of total exhaustion. I never realized how tired being emotionally upset makes one, but I think it is more exhausting than any physical activity.

I sat in the back seat and lectured to myself on how important it was to keep smiling, to keep pretending and putting up a front for Evan. (*"Don't cry Helen, just don't cry. After all, they really don't know exactly what's wrong. We are going to go into the hospital tomorrow to find out. It really could be something quite benign, and it was just premature to start getting this upset. "Dear Lord, just keep this child safe."*) In my very compulsive way I decided to find paper and pencil and start making lists. I needed to get organized. However, all I could find was the roster that was on the floor of the back seat, listing all the families attending the Montreat weekend, their room numbers, and the names of the people in each family. And so, in the margins of this roster, I began listing the phone calls I needed to make, when I got home.

1. Call Frances -- I am going to need some help with car pool until who knows when.

2. Call Linda Dowd from the Girl Scout troop. I will need to give up my volunteer job teaching the little girls in the troop how to sew a skirt from a pattern. We were right in the middle of the project and someone else would have to take over from here.

3. Call Soccer Coach Mileham. Evan would not be practicing or playing in any more games.

4. Call the soccer team mother. I think I was supposed to bring oranges to the next two games, I won't be able to.

5. Call Diane Totherow. She needed to know that Evan would not be able to attend school, and also I needed to resign as room mother.

6. Call neighbors: Adelaide and Hannah.

7. Call Nana and Pop.

8. Call Ann and Carolyn at the office.

My mind began to wander. Oh, how I wish I could call up my employer and say, "I am sorry but my son is unexpectedly ill, and I will not be coming in to work." But as it was, there is no one to call except my very own husband. How stupid I have been that no one else knows my job. This was such poor management. I will have to do the next best thing: start a new list for Carolyn. She will need to go through the mail each day and pile up bills in one stack, insurance forms in another, then go across the street and check the mail boxes at each hospital for the inpatient list. I wondered how I would be able to handle anything more than Evan's hospitalization. Who knows how long and involved this will be? I had always loved my job, but now it seemed like a big burden, and I was angry with myself for not having a back-up person able to step in. I made a promise to myself that, as soon as I could, I would run an ad in the paper and replace myself.

I honestly believe that I have felt God's presence in my life, especially at critical points. When I look back at situations and circumstances in my life and the timing of unexpected events, I somehow feel that God is there walking beside me. My spiritual journey was pretty uneventful throughout my childhood and early adult years. Many people who have been raised in the church as youngsters simply do not question their beliefs as adults. Beliefs are just "there." A hospital chaplain once told me that it is very common for people "to get religion," when they are given a serious diagnosis and may be dying. Embarrassed to admit this, I think that I was one of those people who dutifully went to church because my parents always took me. But when Evan got sick, when I needed God to "come through for me," when I prayed in earnest and didn't feel like it made any difference at all, I became very discouraged ... and very angry at the God that could let this happen! I didn't want any part of a God who would "choose" innocent Evan to have cancer. Through this ordeal, I have come up with my own religious beliefs and my own concept of God. I believe that God's gift to mankind is an "ordered world." If you jump out of a window, gravity will take over every time, whether you are praying or not. We don't know what causes cancer, but whatever it is, the cancer will occur under set circumstances. In other words, I do not believe that God directs bad things to happen to people. I always cringe when I hear survivors being interviewed on the news stating that "God had saved them." I immediately think, "If God has saved you, why not the other people who died? Does God not want to save them, too?" I do believe that God knows what is happening to each of us and cries along with us. I also believe that somehow, in some sort of loving way, God helps us cope with problems, when we have asked for help and strength to endure. I don't know how prayer works. But I do think that God is omnipotent and listens to prayers.

The timing of the sale of my parents' home in Akron, Ohio was a bit eerie. Nana and Pop's home had been up for sale for years. Not only had they had no offers on the house, but no people were even looking at it. They had become quite discouraged, as they were hoping to be able to sell their house and spend summers in Ohio and winters in North Carolina. Akron was going through an economic disaster. It had once been the rubber capitol of the world, claiming the headquarters of General Tire, B.F. Goodrich, Firestone and Goodyear. While I was growing up, Akron was thriving. But the day came, when most rubber was produced in South America, and eventually it became cheaper to build the factories there, too. By the 1980s, after years of union disputes and strikes, the only company to survive was Goodyear.

In 1937, Pop graduated from The College of Wooster. It was during the time that our country was trying to recover from the depression, but before World War II had begun. Only 10 people in his class had jobs waiting for them after graduation, and he was one of those ten. Always describing himself as "lucky-Joe," he could only reason that he had worked his way through school and had many professors recommending him as the most motivated and hardest worker in his class. It wasn't that he came from a "poor family." In fact, his father was a state senator and owned many farms south of Akron. He was the youngest of seven children, all of whom had their various jobs around the farm. He would recount that "you don't know what heat is, until you have spent the entire day at the top of a hay loft in August." He had only one set of good clothes for church and literally walked miles to school. The three siblings closest in age to him were all girls, and maybe he learned to have a sunny and mild disposition because of them. For Christmas, everyone received an orange and a bag of hard candy given out at Sunday school. So, when it was time to go to college, and the registrar asked him how he was going to pay, he simply answered "I don't know." Aside from his sweet disposition, his other outstanding quality was that he was extremely good looking. Tall and slim, his eyes were so dark brown that they were described as black, and his thick hair matched his eyes. Right before Nana and Pop officially met in the library, Nana turned to her friend and asked, "Who are the brown eyes?"

Dad was thrilled to be hired at Goodyear, and he consciously decided to show them just how hard he was willing to work. In fact, he would say that he always set a goal to get his desk cleared off by 11:00 a.m. each day. He kept asking for more responsibility and kept taking on higher jobs. He would no sooner learn his new job than he would be given a raise to the next level. Eventually his job was deemed "essential" to the war effort, since Goodyear Aircraft was then handling military contracts. Dad's work ethic was only one reason for his success. He had an amazing, extroverted, friendly, easy-going personality. He was always smiling, always likeable.

As mentioned before, Pop's family were farmers. Five generations of Weavers lived on the same road in the small town of Manchester. None of his siblings wanted to continue farming, and neither did Pop. But he was the only one to realize the possibilities of developing the farms into subdivisions for new homes. With soldiers coming home from the war, combined with Dad's "ideal salesman-personality," he became very successful. It must be noted that he also had the good luck of having "a silent partner." My Mother earned her Phi Beta Kappa key, easily being the #1 student in her class all four years of college. She diligently worked alongside Pop, keeping the books and paying the bills. This self-taught business woman was the brains of the business. Each needed the other for the unique skills they brought to the table. Because Pop kept his office within our home, Nana and Pop were together all day, every day, for sixty-nine years.

Imagine the frustration they both felt, when this real estate broker/extraordinaire could not sell his own house that he personally had built for his own family thirty years prior. The house sat square in the middle of six lots, best of the farm, and was probably over-built for the neighborhood. Then, out of nowhere, a gentleman drove up and submitted a good offer if Nana and Pop could be out of the house in a month, the very month that Evan entered the hospital.

The replacement troops had arrived in Charlotte! No one could believe their "luck." Years ago there were several duplex houses in my Charlotte neighborhood, randomly scattered throughout Eastover. But one by one, they were bought up and converted to single family houses. One remained. This duplex was one block from my house. It was available. (My folks would spend the next nineteen years there.)

When we finally arrived home from Montreat, Mike carefully picked up Evan and carried him in the house and laid him ever so carefully on the couch, while the rest of us unpacked the car. Despite the mountain of laundry, the stack of mail and bills, and the still-packed suitcases, I announced that it was important that I go to the office. This was really not too unusual, since I would often go in to the office on the weekends to get organized for the coming week. With list in hand, I could barely wait to get out the door, for I knew that I would finally be able to break down in private.

How strange it felt to arrive at the office and discover that everything looked "usual and normal," despite the emotional bomb that had exploded at home. I felt so abnormal and so sick inside, yet nothing at the office had changed. I dialed the first number and when I reached Linda, I simply began to sob. "Helen, is that you Helen? What's the matter, what is going on?" My tongue didn't work, my throat was closed off, and there were no words. I remember thinking to myself, should I just hang up? Finally, I whispered, "Evan is sick. Can't make it." This was the sum total of what I could get out. The last call was finally made. I put my head down on the desk and cried. (*Dear God, please give me strength, I am so sick inside. Please just give me strength.*) Then I noticed my head was buried in a stack of mail sitting on the counter. (*I am so behind, and I won't be coming back to the office for who knows how long. I need to leave more notes for Anne, leave more notes for Carolyn, I have to get organized. I have to make another list. This pile can wait, this pile has to be handled immediately. These forms have to be completed, charts have to be pulled, phone calls made. I can take this pile home. This pile I had better do now. I have to get organized. I have to get home. I have to know how Evan is doing, and poor Mike needs a reprieve.*)

I found Mike in the library playing charades with Evan guessing, but this time only Mike was acting out the charade, since Evan was in too much pain to move. I could tell that Mike was thankful to see me, and he eagerly asked me to join in. On the outside, he looked so jovial and so lighthearted. After the last charade, there was a little bit of quiet and Evan looked up at me and said, "When are we going to the hospital?" "Why, Evan, who said anything about going to the hospital?" He repeated the question, "When are we going?" I had planned that Mike and I would sit down before bedtime and prepare Evan for what he faced the next day. I wanted to prepare a list of "topics" to cover. He needed to be prepared for procedures and hospital rooms and so much more. But it was more important to answer the question straightforward at the time the question was asked, as opposed to waiting for the "perfect time." "Tomorrow morning, sweetie" I said. It was clear that he did not want to continue, nor were there any more questions.

I sat there with him in quiet, as he shut his eyes. He certainly knew that his problem required more than another doctor visit. Instinctively, he realized that the ever increasing pain meant that the problem was getting worse. He discerned we were going to have to do something soon. His intuition was correct.

Jenny was the only one in the family who could truly act normally around him, since she wasn't carrying around a grapefruit in her stomach like her parents, and that was so good for Evan. Suppertime came and went. No one was hungry, and there was no food in the house anyway. Jenny thought it was cool that I allowed her to eat potato chips for supper. Tomorrow was going to be a long day, and I suggested to Evan that it was time to go to bed, even though it was quite early. Mike offered to read a long story to Evan which was very appealing to everyone. And so we went upstairs, Mike carefully carried Evan under his thighs so as not to move his back. Removing clothes and dressing were becoming more difficult because all movement was painful now.

The doorbell rang. When I opened the door, there stood Ray Swetenburg with a very concerned look on his face, his doctor's bag in hand. He told me that he had thought about us all the way home from Montreat. He decided that if he examined Evan tonight at our home, we could eliminate a trip to his office tomorrow morning before checking in at the hospital. I was so appreciative of this caring man who was trying to make tomorrow go as smoothly as possible. He climbed the stairs with me and entered Evan's room on the right. He spent about ten minutes with Evan and then came back downstairs and asked Mike and me to talk with him, while Nana and Pop finished reading the bedtime book. We chose the porch, because it was the furthest from earshot as possible. From the look on his face, I began to feel even more scared than I had previously. He reiterated that Evan's pain was indicative of a very serious problem. He told us that he had a second conversation with the radiologist-oncologist, and upon review of the chest film, Evan had a medialstinal mass (a growth in the center of Evan's chest between his heart and his spine), and most certainly, the bone lesions were metastases (places where the tumor had spread making it inoperable). He made arrangements for us to go straight to the hospital in the morning and had already alerted the Radiology Department that we needed more x-rays and a CT scan. He told us that we would know more after that.

Also, Dr. Swetenburg had already called Dr. Golembe, who was a pediatric oncologist. Barry Golembe would be taking over "the case," though Dr. Swetenburg would be checking in from the sidelines. Quietly he said that the most we could hope for was Hodgkin's disease. This was absolutely no solace to me. I carefully studied his body language. His head was drooping down; his eyes were not dancing as they normally did. His voice was a bit quivering, and tears began to swell in his eyes. This was a hard visit for him, but he put our dire situation above his discomfort. The one sentence I heard ringing in my ears afterwards was: "This is going to change the whole rest of your entire life." He followed that with: "The two of you are going to have to remain strong to get through this for Evan's sake," and that we were about to embark on emotions that most parents never have to deal with. (*My God! He's talking about Evan DYING! That can't be! NO! I won't let THAT happen! No, God! No!*) Somehow the denial mechanism was working on overtime right up until this moment. I wanted him to tell me that he felt like it wasn't time to get worried yet. Let's go back to the partners' assurances that this was nothing! I wanted to hear that things could always be worse. I expected him to tell me how it won't be that bad and there were other possibilities to hope for. Instead, he was gloomy and sad and upset. I remember that Mike and Dr. Swetenburg started talking 'medical lingo,' (*Surely I was going to wake up from this nightmare any minute now and be so relieved. Why don't I just wake up? The alarm clock would sound so good! Why don't I just open my eyes?*)

Dr. Swetenburg asked if we wanted to pray, so the three of us held hands in a circle and bowed our heads. Dr. Swetenburg said a prayer, and I loved him, because he was a compassionate person. He gave us each a hug and left with his head drooping. On the way out, he asked if he could share all of this with his wife, Jan. She knew someone in our church family was in deep trouble but he kept that confidence until obtaining permission from us. He is a prince of a person and a professional doctor of the highest calling.

Mike was beginning to fall apart. He wondered whether Evan was asleep. He wanted to go upstairs, but he didn't want to face him with red eyes if he were still awake. It took all he had to keep up a front. Now, even he was exposed. We waited and waited. The best part of the day was shutting our bedroom door. It was the time that I could let down and cry. It was the time Mike could silently stare at the ceiling. What a relief to be ourselves. The charade was over. It takes energy to smile and think of clever things to say; it is tiresome to put on a front! It was the time to stop dead in our tracks from exhaustion. I was anxious to hear Mike's evaluation of the conversation he had with Dr. Swetenburg. Finally, we just sat there sobbing, hoping for some kind of comfort from each other. Later, people always looked puzzled when they heard that our marriage was never stronger than at this time. But no one else in the entire universe could know how each of us felt. All we had was each other.

Somewhere in the middle of that evening, our bodies, minds and hearts shut down. Prayers were said. Tears flowed. There just wasn't anything left. We fell off to sleep. I kept waking up periodically, and each time I awoke I would notice the sick feeling in my stomach. *(Yes, it was true, it was happening, it wasn't a dream.)* I tried to comfort Mike, whose eyes were open, staring at the ceiling. Getting up the next morning was difficult, not just because of exhaustion but knowing that it was time to smile again, time to be nonchalant and act like nothing was that serious. We carefully dressed Evan, went downstairs but none of us had an appetite. We got in the car, and Mike placed Evan, ever so carefully, on my lap. Sweet boy! I hugged him, and I felt close to him. Mainly, I wanted to protect him, as every mother does.

But, it would be impossible to protect him against cancer.

CHAPTER II

WAITING ...

We arrived at the hospital through the emergency room. The staff person put Evan in a wheelchair the minute we walked through the doors. It looked so unnatural. I hated it. We spent the entire day in the radiology department, waiting, as pictures were taken, and waiting more. Next, we were waiting as CT scans were taken. *(Had they not taken enough, when we were here last Friday?)* The CT scan required Evan to lie very still on a moving table that would be inserted into a large drum. They questioned whether a six-year-old would be able to hold still long enough or would be too frightened inside the drum. I answered that, if I could be given a few minutes to prepare Evan for what would happen, he would cooperate. And thus began the trust-bond between Evan and me.

My years of teaching in a therapeutic nursery school, established by the Department of Psychiatry at Case Western Reserve University School of Medicine, taught me some lasting parenting lessons. Known as Hanna Perkins School, five year-old-children attended the nursery school, at the same time that their parents entered into counseling with a therapist on the staff of the hospital. The concept was to treat the whole family simultaneously. Each week, therapists, psychiatrists, residents in psychiatry from the medical school, teachers and school staff would conference about the problems of parent/child relationships and specific family issues. The real life family experiences that were confronted there would leave lasting ideas about how to raise psychologically healthy children.

And so it was that I would always be committed to "telling it like it was," painful or not, good news or bad news. Hopefully, Evan would receive comfort, always knowing exactly what was happening. Children misbehave because sometimes their world becomes confusing. They have no way to order or make sense of circumstances. Children need explanation. And then trust develops that a caregiver or parent will not surprise them on a moment's notice. A trust-bond/connection forms.

I asked if I would be permitted to sit next to Evan during the procedure, while the technicians and doctors stand behind a large glass window shield. They could give me directions through a microphone. They decided to "pamper" me and let me "talk Evan through the procedure," knowing that in a few minutes, they would be prepared to administer a general anesthetic to achieve the necessary cooperation. Just as I promised, Evan listened carefully to the description of the steps. Without much time to prepare the main points that would concern a six-year-old, I came up with the following: 1) I will be here throughout the procedure and can hear you if you need me. 2) You will have to remain perfectly still while they take the picture that will be similar to Daddy's taking a picture with a camera. 3) Nothing will touch your body. 4) The table moves inside of this drum, like the drum at the playground. Some people feel very nervous because there is not much space, but it is only for a minute (a minute is about the amount of time it takes you to brush your teeth at night). 5) You will hear a clicking sound much like the flint-lock pistol you got at Williamsburg. 6) As soon as the clicking sound stops, the picture is over, and the table will be moved back out of the drum. I will be sitting here waiting to give you hugs and kisses. If you get too frightened inside the drum, just call me and I will ask them to stop, and they will pull you back out. This procedure is important because the doctor needs to see the pictures of the inside of your back in order to know how to stop your back pain. Do you think that you can do it? You can tell me when you are ready. I won't let them move the table until you say so.

This preparation is based on 1) identifying what it is that will be most frightening. 2) Then addressing the fear and acknowledging that I understand it. 3) Trying to give the child some way to be in charge, in this instance, letting Evan be the one to say when he was ready. 4) Finding comparable sounds and bits of reality that the child can relate to. 5) Allowing the child room to opt out if it really IS too hard (in which case, we would be forced to turn to the anesthesia). 6) Lastly, an important step is to "relive" the situation later. By that I mean that the child recounts every step and realizes that it turned out exactly the way he was told it would. (Usually the child is so proud of himself that he automatically wants to relive the procedure.) This builds on the trust bond. He will need this reference for future procedures. Also, note the absence of a list of "goodies" promised for being "good." This has nothing to do with being good (or bad).

Throughout the morning, people we met in the hallway tried to be light, make jokes and be cordial. It sounds atrocious, but I could say nothing back. I knew that Evan was frightened, and I had a full-time job looking at this hospital day through his eyes and interpreting the sights and sounds for him. I explained logically that, even I wasn't sure what would happen next, but that 1) he could count on me never to leave him and 2) that I would always find out first what was going to happen next and then explain it to him in a way he could understand.

Our first day hospital experience was like walking through a maze. Evan traveled by wheelchair with four "propping pillows," since it was more comfortable for him. We kept walking from one station to the next and continually kept running into familiar physician-friends who kept saying, "Helen, Evan, what are you doing here?" and then, taking a closer look at us, wishing they hadn't asked. Word traveled through the medical community and as one might expect, rumors had all but included the funeral. Finally, we arrived at Evan's room that was sunny and inviting as compared to the radiology department. Another cheery touch was the delivery of a few baskets of flowers, plants and balloons that arrived before the patient. Mike joined us around suppertime, and Evan recounted the day with not much displeasure. He had received a lot of attention. He had not had any painful procedures, and gifts were arriving by the hour. The recounting also left room for Dad to gloat and praise his son for being so cooperative and already proving to be the perfect patient. I suppose Evan finally felt a little relief that SOMETHING was finally being done about his back (I felt the same way) and surely all these big machines and smart people would figure out what it was in short order and be able to fix it. Soon, he could get back to his class. In the meantime, he decided that maybe he could have a good time.

Mike informed me that soon we were going to meet with Dr. Golembe, the pediatric oncologist in charge of Evan's case. He would be running the tests and basically "calling the shots." I hated to say good-bye to Ray Swetenburg, our pediatrician, who was the one who started the ball rolling, but I was reassured by him that we needed a specialist. He predicted that we would all love Dr. Golembe. It was Monday night, and I explained to Evan that Dad and I needed to meet with his new doctor and that Helga Rundquist, his former preschool teacher, was coming for a visit and would wait with him, while we talked to Dr. Golembe. I promised Evan that we were not leaving the hospital and that Mrs. Runquist knew where we were, if he needed us. Helga was a favorite teacher and family friend, and Evan was happy to spend time with her.

Barry Golembe met with us at around 8 o'clock p.m. I felt bad that the time of the meeting was so late in the day, and I wondered if his daily hours always extended into the late evening (his poor wife and family). Mike, by his own admission, would describe himself as an "educational snob," and so he couldn't help but check out this new physician's credentials. He was relieved and happy to read that Dr. Golembe had trained at the prestigious New York Hospital-Cornell Medical Center, which is the umbrella hospital for Memorial Sloan Kettering Cancer Hospital, probably the best cancer hospital in the country. Mike approved of our new doctor. My criteria centered more on Dr. Golembe's concern for his patients. He passed my standards in the first five minutes, putting me at ease immediately. He started out telling me that he could imagine how sick and scared and numb I must be. What a validation of my feelings! *(Was this the same psychology that I was already using with Evan?)*

He spoke to both of us, a Mom and a Dad, as opposed to directing the conversation to Mike, another physician. Dr. Golembe was perplexed that the radiologists could not agree on the diagnosis. Basically, Evan had cancer, but we weren't sure of the kind. Additional tests were scheduled for bright and early the next morning, among them, a bone marrow and a spinal tap. As he named the procedures, Mike grimaced, and I felt sick all over again. *(note to self: I needed some details to prepare Evan for this.)* "What was the differential diagnosis?" I asked: How bad is it? Dr. Golembe explained that the most likely diagnosis was Stage IV (widely disseminated) Neuroblastoma. Mike stared at the floor. The other possible diagnosis was advanced, metastatic Ewing Sarcoma (cancer of the bone). There really didn't seem to be a third choice. "Which one are we hoping for?" I asked. His serious face was like being hit with a truck. BAM! "Helen, we aren't crossing any bridges." He could see that the answer did not get him off the hook. "Both diagnoses were uniformly fatal." Pushing him harder, he finally admitted that "Evan had about a one percent chance to live if we were dealing with EITHER diagnosis." Second BAM! to the gut. He planned to do the bone marrow and spinal tap in the morning, and in the meantime, he wrote orders for Evan's urine to be collected over a three-day period in case the bone marrow and the spinal tap did not give us a diagnosis. After three days, he would send the urine sample to The University of Oklahoma where a highly technical analysis would be performed. As each test was completed, Dr. Golembe would keep us updated. *"In the meantime, keep the faith." (God! Are you not a "loving God"? How is it possible that you would let an innocent child die from cancer? Evan hasn't even started to LIVE yet? Are you there, God?)*

I wanted to know chances and percentages. *(I needed someone to prepare me!)* In my mind, I kept hearing, over and over, that he thought we had a one per cent chance. Mike was very discouraged, agreeing that we had little hope. I was not satisfied with this negative thinking! Every person deals with news like this differently. Mike was an "action person." He cancelled his patients for the rest of the week and spent each day calling cancer centers trying to ascertain what hospital had the best success rate with Neuroblastoma, and which hospital had the best success with Ewing Sarcoma. We were going for broke and wanted to improve our chances, any way we could. We needed to poll all ideas and seek opinions of the experts. He did not limit his search. He called San Francisco (UCSF), St. Louis (Barnes), Houston (MD Anderson), Boston (Dana Farber), New York (Sloan-Kettering), Durham (Duke), Baltimore (Hopkins), Philadelphia (Penn), Los Angeles (UCLA), and Rochester (Mayo Clinic). He also called London and Paris and perhaps others that I did not even hear about. I, too, am an action person. But I learned quickly that, as a mother of a child with cancer, I had been rendered totally passive. I couldn't research ways to help Evan. I couldn't work harder to make his path easier. I couldn't suggest drugs to try. Earlier, I couldn't even pull the alarm that he was sick! There was virtually nothing to do but sit and wait and worry. Then, I read an article about positive thinking. The basic tenet was that, if one remained positive, talked positive, and looked positive, that Evan's attitude would follow in a positive way. One study tried to prove that positive thinkers have a better outcome with cancer. And so, I adopted this attitude, and my work was cut out for me. This was harder than you think.

We returned to the room and plastered smiles on our faces and started to explain to Evan that the next morning the doctor would do two different tests. Unlike the x-rays and scans that we had today, these tests were performed with needles. *(God this is hard to talk about. I don't want to scare him so much that he can't sleep.)* I honestly answered every question he asked. The doctor would give him some numbing medicine first. He did that with a needle. Evan needed to hold still, because the next needle had to go into the spinal canal. This was difficult for the doctor, and sometimes, even when the doctor is highly experienced, he misses the spot, and the needle has to be inserted again. "You will be facing the wall and won't even see the doctor who will sit facing your back. I will be there to hold your hand the entire time. I will talk you through the procedure, if you decide you want me to. You can always tell me to quit, and I will. But you can't tell the doctor to quit. The bone marrow procedure will also hurt. The only thing that will help get through this will be to hold as still as possible. Some children cry, because it hurts so much. If you want to cry, you can. I will stay with you and not leave you. You will feel such RELIEF afterwards!" Evan and I acted out the procedure most all evening. He turned toward the wall. Then I would tell him that the needle was about to go in, and I pinched his back very hard and also applied pressure to give him an idea of what it would feel like." I emphasized 'now it is over,' and he truly felt relief during our practice session.

Evan, Mike and I had a discussion about which one of us would spend the night. Evan decided that this night would be his Dad's turn. After all, his Dad was known and respected around this place. His Dad knew where things were (the extra-blanket-closet and the ice machine) and, most of all, his Dad was very special. I stayed until Evan finally fell asleep and then, after some "hall tears," Mike gave me his car keys, and I left for home.

Although exhausted, I knew that some work needed to be accomplished at home. No one had sat down with Jenny and explained to her all that we learned over the past two days. In fact, she was riding solo since our return from Montreat, and she needed some answers, too. When I walked into the house, the dishes were washed and stacked up, the laundry was piled up on the floor waiting for some instruction on how to start the washing machine. Nana and Pop were waiting at the door, worried and wringing their hands and anxious for any bit of information I had. A list of calls from concerned friends was posted, asking for a return phone call. (This was before cell phones.) I felt bad that I had not been able to call even my parents from the hospital. They were trying to keep the house running and Jenny's life as nearly normal as possible, but they were anxious for news.

By-passing the washing machine, the phone calls, and even my parents, I headed straight upstairs and into Jenny's room, where she was lying in bed and wide awake. She was feeling very, very alone. I told her that she could count on me to tell her the truth about Evan, even if the news were bad. I explained how very difficult the rest of this week would be, because Mommy and Daddy were so worried about Evan. I understood that she might feel very deserted at home, and I hoped that she might confide her feelings to her grandparents when she needed to talk. I told her that she would need to have courage to face Evan's problem, and that I understood that it was our whole family's problem. I kept repeating how much I loved her but that I would have very little time to spend with her. She asked about Evan and what was the matter with his back. Honestly, I explained to her that he either had a brain tumor or cancer of the bone. Both were very serious, and that Evan could die. That was the first time those words had crossed my lips.

I was surprised at her reaction and can return to that night in my mind, like it was yesterday. She got out of bed and started to pick up objects around her and throw them across the room. Her large geography book skimmed her desk, taking everything on it to the floor. She was mad and screamed: "It's not fair! It's not fair! How could this happen? *(my sentiments exactly)* It's not fair that this is happening to Evan. I am mad, I am furious!" Nana and Pop heard the commotion and came running upstairs and a conversation ensued among the four of us that lasted hours. We talked about life and death and about how fragile life was. We talked about how Evan must be feeling, and how we still had a lot of hope that something could be done for him. Jenny was really very scared for Evan; she was compassionate and very sweet. But, age appropriately, began to ask other, relevant questions. Is this disease contagious? Is there a chance that she, too, was exposed to whatever Evan has? What would happen, if she were the only child left? As if needing to confess her sins, she thought back to fights that she and he had had and the awful names she had called him. Could these dreadful sentences have anything to do with his being sick now? Why had this happened? Were we not good people? Do we not go to church every Sunday? Is this something that happens to you, even though you are good? The philosophy and religion classes that I took in college were not holding up here. This night I needed the cliff notes from an honors senior seminar ethics course or a value-tales book on childhood questions about death. In the end, all that I had to offer were answers from the gut. Ironically, Jenny had verbalized the very questions I was feeling in my heart, and I was returning to my own anger at God. *(How could God let this happen? Is God a loving God? Is this a God who had this all planned out and who would let such a thing happen to such an innocent child? Maybe life is simply a matter of chance, and prayer makes no difference. Are we Presbyterians who believe in predestination? Is that crazy thinking? If I am to believe that God had this all planned out, then I don't want to be part of this madness, this unfairness!)*

Jenny and I explored every possibility. We ended up hugging and crying and praying, and then I insisted that it was time for her to go to sleep, and I promised her that we would return to the discussion and arrive at some answers. Honestly, at this late hour, I could no longer come up with answers, and certainly no wisdom. I was beginning to feel such total exhaustion that I fell asleep on her bed, still dressed.

I continued to pray fervently. As much as I hated to admit this, perhaps there was a chance that prayer could help, and I didn't want to discount any available assistance. Each subsequent night, I fell asleep while saying my prayers but continued to be plagued with waking up at 30 to 45 minute intervals, always checking reality, to ascertain if this could possibly be a dream. I so wanted to wake up and have Evan in the next room safe and sound. Mike had given me some sleeping pills. I thought it strange, wondering why one would need sleeping pills in an exhausted state. I know why. It was impressive to contemplate the effect of trauma on the nervous system, one's thinking, and one's emotional stability.

I noticed two distinct changes in myself. While I didn't know a name for it at the time, I since learned that I began to experience "magical thinking." One can predict outcomes randomly by playing the game. It goes like this: if you get on an elevator, as the door is shutting, you lay claim to the rules. If I ride all the way to the 7th floor without stopping, which means that we will get through this without complication. If we stop at just one floor, that means we will have just a small bit of trouble but will get through in the end, and so forth. Another example: when you approach a traffic light, you quickly set the rules: if you zoom right through on a green light, you will have smooth sailing; whereas, the yellow offers caution. Red means that the game is over, and you lost *(or lose your son)*. The magical thinking began to ruin my sense of reality. It began to take over. What do zero parking spaces mean? What is the meaning of a grocery bill that exceeds $50 versus a total under $50? I have learned that magical thinking develops in people who find themselves in a world that is spinning out of control. It is a way to get back in control.

Another bizarre (and shameful) thinking pattern began to plague me. A recurring picture began in my mind: our whole family, except for Evan, was sitting in the front row pew of our church. The church was full of our friends and a small casket loomed in the front. Every time my mind would picture this I would get furious with myself and then feel very guilty. *(Stop It, Helen!)* I could not understand why I kept returning to this. It made me feel so bad that I felt uncomfortable admitting it to anyone. In retrospect, I learned that this is a defense mechanism. My mind and body were unconsciously preparing for the absolute worst. Once I pictured a funeral, the worst outcome, I could adjust to the everyday bad news and then more bad news. It was as if once you picture the worst, you can more easily accept the "bad." This is difficult to explain, mainly because it sounds so bizarre and then, because it is associated with so much guilt. No, I was not giving up!

The next morning, bright and early, I arrived at the hospital. I brought Mike some toiletries and a change of clothes, and one last time, reviewed the day's itinerary with Evan. I couldn't help but think of all the books I had read, while I was pregnant, about how to be a good parent. Back then, I decided to start my own personal library of children's books. Most importantly, I wanted books on the shelf that would deal with every child-centered issue; for example, where do babies come from, Johnny and his first allowance, Susie's first day at school, how to be a friend and have a friend. The list is long. I wanted to be prepared for EVERY conversation that might come up, every eventuality. How ironic that, as it turned out, the most crucial subject for my little family was not represented on the shelf: How do you explain to your child that he has cancer? What are the points to cover when your child is facing a bone marrow procedure? How do you describe death to a kindergarten child? *(Dear God! I have to get this right! Help me help Evan. Put the right words in my mouth.)*

For this, I was not prepared; however, what came natural was to treat Evan exactly the way I would want to be treated if I were in his shoes, that is to say that I wanted him to ask questions. I wanted him to trust me. I wanted him to use me as a shield against the rest of the world. I kept trying to put myself in his shoes; I tried to picture what he was imagining. I tried to be his outlet for anger and fear.

The nurse came into the room on time, which was sooner than I expected and told us it was time to take Evan for the two procedures. There was an option for Dr. Golembe to do the procedures in Evan's hospital room, but I did not want Evan to associate his room with unpleasantness. His room needed to be a safe-haven for him. Fortunately, Dr. Golembe felt the same way. The "procedure room" was small, and there seemed to be an inordinate number of people in attendance. Dr. Golembe asked that either Mike or I stay at the head of the table, so that we could be a calming influence on Evan. The energy level was high. Nurses were scurrying around to prepare the tray, while Dr. Golembe positioned Evan and put on sterile gloves. A very nice nurse said to me, "Do you want to wait outside?" and then in a very low voice, "Do you have the stomach for this?" I assured her that I needed to be in the room, that I wouldn't abandon Evan to save my life, and that I was really very strong.

Evan was quite composed. This was probably due to two reasons: 1) He had had no previous experience with a bone marrow procedure and thus was not dreading it like he did for every subsequent one. 2) During this initial hospitalization, he still hoped that this might be the last procedure, a step toward recovery. The initial shot to numb the area was given. He screamed out in pain, realizing from the preparation that the harder shot was coming next. God love this little boy because he started repeating, all on his own, "I can do it, I can do it!" while squeezing my hand and gritting his teeth. Cancer pain has its own signature. It's not sharp for most of the time, but then, periodically, a sudden movement or a needle in the back causes agony. As parents of a cancer victim, we suffered with Evan's pain, as if a hand reached into our abdomen and gave a hard punch each time he grimaced. Evan was getting worse. He was dying, and part of us was dying too.

I was totally unprepared for the next part. My legs started to get weak. I felt my body sway, and I recognized that I might pass out. Still holding on to Evan's clenched fist, I dropped my knees to the floor and my head next to his. *(God! Stay with me.)* Evan and I both made it through. I learned later that this bone marrow procedure was comparatively easy, as the needle entered the tumor-softened bone without much resistance. The spinal tap was much more painful. Evan's muscles tightened when the needle went in, making the pain worse. Probably, we were only in this room for 15 minutes (Dr. Golembe was fast, efficient and facile), but I swore it was two hours. He remarked how proud he was of Evan's cooperation! For Evan, the hospitalization that seemed like a very doable, attention-focused, fun place with lots of toys and balloons, had now turned into a really horrible, bleak, nightmarish Tower of London, and he was ready to get out of there as soon as possible!

Dr. Golembe told me we would have the results of the bone marrow by the end of the day and that he would be meeting with us again around 8:00 p.m. The day dragged on: "I'm going to grandma's house, and I'm taking a toothbrush ..." making flashlight pretend people on the wall, rhyming words, "I'm thinking of an animal and it begins with "O" (only seasoned players know that opossum starts with an "O," not a "P."). Eventually, Evan would say, "Do we really have to keep playing?" as if he were passing the time for me rather than the other way around.

By evening, his loyal teacher, Diane, appeared in the doorway with a large banner, signed by everyone in his kindergarten class. The timing was perfect, because Evan was totally comfortable with her, while Mike and I met with Dr. Golembe down the hall. He looked serious. The bone marrow did not confirm either diagnosis. He was becoming concerned about the large lapse of time between Evan's first symptoms and diagnosis. *(So was I !!!)* Each day that passed extended the growth of the tumor making it more virulent and possibly resistant to treatment. *(Oh God! We needed to DO something FAST!!!)* Here's the game plan: a biopsy was needed (by surgery). Dr. Golembe talked to the pediatric surgeon, Dr. Morton, and together they decided that a rib was the most accessible biopsy site. The operating room would be scheduled for 12:00 noon on Friday. At the same time, Dr. Golembe had spoken to the pathologist at The University of Oklahoma who promised that the urine sample result would be ready by Friday around 11:00 a.m. If the urine results were inconclusive, the surgery would be "go." Everything was happening now with lightning speed. I asked: "Surely there was some other diagnosis I could pray for." I could tell that Dr. Golembe felt sorry for me. I needed a thread of hope. He told me that he had been thinking that, although it was a long shot, there was a possibility that it could be acute lymphocytic leukemia. He continued, "Some patients have been cured of leukemia" and added that, "just recently, different research centers are having very high success rates." *(Please God, this is just the news I have been waiting for. Please, have mercy on my child, God. Just let us have a chance!)*

By noon on Wednesday, Evan had somewhat recovered from the previous day's procedure and was beginning to be perked up by grandparent visits, cards, more balloons, presents and friends stopping in. Reading books and having a remote control to the TV all to himself wasn't too bad! Legos, board games, puzzles, cars and robots kept appearing at the door. Eventually, even Evan tired of opening gifts. His gluttonous lust for toys became satiated. However, he always was appreciative of every visitor. It seemed that the more he rested, the better his back was, and the less activity he had, the better it felt. With no procedures scheduled for two days, Evan was in fairly good spirits. No insurance company today would tolerate such a waste of a room. We were waiting, of course, for the final diagnosis to come in (either from the University of Oklahoma, where pathologists were studying the urine sample, or from the rib biopsy taken at surgery, scheduled for Friday). Then, Evan assumed, his back could be fixed, and pretty soon he would be back at school.

The days became very difficult to put in. By Wednesday afternoon, we were on to more sophisticated games like "I'm thinking of a person who has brown hair and lives in Charlotte," or trivia questions like "Can you name five of the seven dwarfs?" Unbeknownst to Evan or me, Mike continued at the office, not seeing patients, but with his sustained search for our treatment possibilities. Mike was becoming an expert on current research for Neuroblastoma, Osteosarcoma and oh yes, for Acute Lymphocytic Leukemia.

Wednesday night we sat down with Dr. Golembe again. Unfortunately, he did not have a clear-cut diagnosis yet. The pathologist in Charlotte gave Dr. Golembe a convincing argument in favor of Neuroblastoma, but in the final analysis he couldn't be sure. Again I said to him, "Let's not forget leukemia! I'd like it to be leukemia." He laughed nervously, "We all wish it were leukemia. Helen, please believe me, that's such a long shot!" The pathologist at the hospital was very good, and he felt that the possibility had been eliminated; however, by the same token, it was true that neither the results from the bone marrow nor the spinal tap could confirm any other diagnosis. He reiterated that a positive call from Oklahoma would cancel the surgery, and we would have a diagnosis. It was that simple. We kept pushing Dr. Golembe: "OK, there is no doubt that Evan is at high risk and I admit that I am worried about losing him." *(NO! Lord, I know you have the power to make it be leukemia, and I pray, if you will just let it be leukemia, I promise Lord that I will live the rest of my life for You.)*

Evan chose Mike to spend the night with him again, so after Evan fell asleep, in the dark of the night, I went down to the parking lot and drove home to a very anxious and worried big sister and grandparents. Nana and Pop were waiting at the door and anxious for me to sit down with them and tell them about the events of the day, what we had found out, and what they thought the diagnosis was. Nana informed me that she had promised four family members an update call. Sorry! No calls this night. The little time that I had left before collapsing had to be spent with Jenny. I walked into Jenny's room to kiss her goodnight, and she was waiting up for me with tears in her eyes. She was worried and concerned for Evan. She wondered whether our lives would ever be the same again. She asked whether Evan was going to live and what was the name of the disease. I again told her that we weren't sure but she could join me in praying for leukemia because that was something the doctors might be able to fix. She told me how guilty she had been feeling for all the mean things she had done to Evan and all the fights they had. I assured her that all brothers and sisters fought, and that it was absolutely normal. She told me that her constant prayer was that, if only he could live, she would never again be mean to him, and that she would protect him to the best of her ability for the rest of her life. *(God! I have such great kids!)* I promised her that she could see him the next day. She needed to play an active part, and I knew that, like me, she needed to have some hope. Again I fell asleep in her bed, snuggled up to my sweet daughter, rubbing her back, and assuring her that we would get through this together.

Thursday was more of the same: more balloons, more cards, more people, more friends, and more physicians. I am thinking of an animal that begins with M; I am going to Grandmother's house, and I am going to take a toothbrush and a chair and a hat; more plants, more flowers, more TV programs, more trivia, and more books. The only thing scheduled was: waiting.

I had a lot of preparation to do in case the "urine call" revealed no diagnosis (that is: did not confirm the Neuroblastoma diagnosis). We would be off to the OR (operating room) quickly. We had some good luck. By chance, the Dad of one of Evan's good friends was an anesthesiologist at the hospital. Dr. Dave Lennon asked to be on Evan's case. He went out of his way to help me prepare Evan. He was the son of a missionary couple and was excellent with kids. He brought a mask with him, so that Evan could try it on and become familiar with it. He reviewed exactly what would happen and what it would feel like. Thinking it would be far easier to tell Evan that the surgery was off than to quickly prepare him, we proceeded like it was a sure thing. Evan and I reviewed the information all evening long.

My constant prayer was that the urine sample was inconclusive and that surgery would be needed. Strange that I should pray for surgery for my little boy, but the alternative was hearing that the urine analysis was positive for Neuroblastoma. Mike continued on the phone, talking to researchers, or in the library, reading the latest pediatric oncology articles while I was officiating the games-routine. I appreciated each dear friend who came to see us, but at the same time, it required so much energy to smile and relate the whole story from the beginning so many times. This period of time was an emotional roller-coaster for me. Dr. Golembe came by in passing, and I never missed the opportunity to remind him that I was "counting on" leukemia. Poor Dr. Golembe, he must have felt like I was holding him to this diagnosis, and that, he better deliver. I assured him that I was not giving up on leukemia, and that I would "will it to happen, just wait and see." He would always smile a pathetic smile and assure me that "We will do the best we can."

Thursday night, after Evan fell asleep, and in the watchful eye of the head nurse, Mike walked me to the door toward the parking lot. But instead of opening the door, we turned instead into the cafeteria for a cup of coffee. Between his research calls, and my constant vigil over Evan, we had not had an opportunity to really talk together. A whole section of the snack bar was closed off and had already been cleaned for the next day, but we ignored the ropes and walked way to the end corner, where we could talk in private. Mike began to cry. He had done stacks of reading and was sure that we were facing Neuroblastoma. It was traumatizing to hear Dr. Golembe say that if that were the case, Evan had about a one percent chance of living.

Mike was the quintessential scholar, and so, here, too, in between sobs, he talked in metaphor: "It really isn't too hard to be in the top half of your class. And, actually, getting into the honor society, of being in the top 20%, is a little more difficult but still doable. But Helen, Evan needs to be the valedictorian!" We sobbed together. *(God, I know you can make it leukemia! Please, tomorrow, just let that urine sample be inconclusive. Just a chance, that's all we need, we just need a chance.)*

On the way home that night, I hit every green light, four in all! I admit that I had to approach one of them slowly, but unless you apply the brakes, it still counts as "no stops." This means "smooth sailing," "good news." I hated going home by myself. I needed Mike to explain further all the things he had read. I needed to hear all the information. I needed comfort and every time I was alone with my thoughts ...

Mike and I were both at a point of total exhaustion. We weren't thinking straight. Nights were turning into days, and lunches were turning into dinners or, more accurately, no food was appetizing. We now went through familiar motions throughout the day, much like one does when brushing one's teeth at night, without even thinking about it. I drove to the hospital very early but had no memory of getting into the car or making the necessary turns to get to the hospital. When I got to the hospital room, I saw Evan still asleep. Mike was unaware of my arrival. He was standing there, just staring. As I stood there, my horrible vision returned, and I saw the church and the front row. Why can't I get it out of my mind? Is Mike standing over this child, thinking the same thing? I can never ask him. I can never admit to him what is going through my mind because maybe he won't understand.

It had taken a decade to get to Friday. We were somewhat prepared. No matter which way our fate would turn, it was better than waiting. We were supposed to get a call at around 11:00 a.m. from the University of Oklahoma. If the urine sample did not yield the diagnosis, the operation was on go. The surgeon would go in through Evan's back and remove a piece of his rib that would then be sent to Duke University for electron microscopy. The pathologist would finally be able to tell us a diagnosis. The updated O.R. schedule was 1:00 o'clock which would give them about two hours to prep Evan and begin the operation. The results of this one simple urine test would decide our fate: Neuroblastoma or not! If yes, we would travel to Boston the next day to be introduced to a new hospital: Massachusetts General. Maybe, we were headed to New York for a bone marrow transplant at Sloan-Kettering. It was hard to keep up with Mike's research. But we were going somewhere!

I was still praying for leukemia. It was our only hope. Who would ever have thought that a mother would pray that her child had leukemia, but it was my constant prayer, and I was grateful that soon, at 11:00 a.m., the phone would ring, and half my prayer would be answered. We were given no advance warning, when on Friday at 7:00 a.m., orders arrived that Evan needed to be wheeled to radiology for surgical prep. How did that slip by me? Poor Evan had no advanced notice either. Of course, I assured him, while moving through the hall, that I would not leave him. And I didn't. I was not looking forward to this visit considering our dissatisfaction from the week before. Fortunately, Mike was with us this time. This stopover would prove to be possibly worse.

Mike questioned that the wrong rib was marked under fluoroscopy (it was the 6th rib, not the 7th, where they planned to cut). It took an hour to correct the mistake and we gladly left radiology once again. *(Thank you God for Mike and his careful scrutiny!)*

Friday, early morning, Mike and I tried very hard to put forth the effort it took to smile and be cheerful and jovial, and talk "small-talk." I knew that Evan saw through us, but he clearly preferred not to see us crying, so we all kept the charade going. "I am thinking of an animal that begins with O." Evan guesses opossum immediately. "I am thinking of an animal that begins with T." Tyrannosaurus Rex is the answer. I suppose we have played this game until we can't come up with any new animals. Our repertoire had run out. We began, "I am going to Grandmother's house, I am going to take a toothbrush," and Evan quickly added on. But unfortunately, my mind cannot remember more than four items, and the game is over. Evan was the winner! "Shall we go back to: I am thinking of a person?" "No, we have played that too many times." "Well, why don't I get out the Trivia game?" I opened the box and picked a category and started to quiz Evan with multiple choice answers. "I have had that question before, Mom," "I have had that question, too!" "Mom, have you gotten the cards mixed up? Why do you keep asking me questions that we have had before?" I think it is because we have asked all the questions in the entire box within the past week, and so I tried to trick him by asking my own questions. Understandably, my mind didn't work as fast, and Evan decided to go back to "I am thinking of an animal and it begins with M."

It must be nearly 11:00 o'clock and I was getting very nervous. I looked at my watch. Surely it's later than 9 o'clock. I offered to read to Evan which was a wonderful way to escape the present. Evan lay back in a semi-comfortable position that his back dictated, and I began page one, "Where the Wild Things Are." Usually when I read, the time goes by fast. We can easily read an entire afternoon away. But today, I am aware of every minute that is passing. At one point Evan looked as if he was dozing off, so I stopped reading, allowing precious time for meditation and prayer. *(Please Lord, Please spare this life! Please let this test be confusing to the doctors. Please eliminate Neuroblastoma. Please allow the operation as planned and the end result be leukemia.)* But Evan awoke and wanted to hear me read more. It was such an infringement on my need for a precious few quiet minutes.

There was a knock on the door and a big bouquet of balloons arrived from Evan's carpool friends. It put such a smile on his face, and I began to cry again. Evan quizzed me: "Why do you cry every time something good happens?" I tried to be honest: "Every small kindness by someone who cares for you is so deeply appreciated that a feeling of gratitude brings tears to me." We tried to play the game of pushing the balloon up in the air and keeping it there so it wouldn't touch the ground, but Evan's range of movement would not allow him to jerk his arm up, in order to catch the balloon as it falls, so we tied the balloon bouquet to the end of the bed and just appreciated the cheerfulness that it brought.

How can it be only 15 minutes after 10:00? Shouldn't it be 11:00 by now? Nana and Pop arrived at the hospital room. Is this how General Lee felt at Gettysburg with the arrival of more troops? Nana and Pop were famous for making up games and passing the time but best of all, I could meander down the hall in meditation. I needed one last serious negotiation with God.

There had been a steady stream of friends, neighbors, colleagues, church members, Sunday school members, parents of acquaintances, friends of Evan and Jenny, school administrators, former teachers and ministers, all who came, one by one, to be supportive and helpful and offer advice after a cheery visit with Evan. At the end of a visit, these special people often took my hand, and we walked out of the room and down the hall together for a short distance. Together we cried. Upon return, Evan inspected the look on my face and the color of my eyes in order to get an exact indication of how bad things were. But by Friday, there was no energy to get out of the chair, and while I was appreciative and grateful, people came and left without a private word with me. I used up the very last drop of energy. All bodily functions had closed down: my tear ducts had dried up, my stomach had closed down, my intestines didn't work, even my inner ear balance was off. Could it possibly be 11:00 yet?

I must have dozed off while meditating. When I awoke, I was curled up in a ball in a large blue chair in the corner of the room. Nana was still helping Evan put a puzzle together. I looked at my watch. It was a miracle. It was 10 minutes PAST 11:00. Without a word, I jumped out of the chair and walked down the hall to inquire about the call. Had the phone not rung? What was the matter? It was difficult to arouse one of the nurses into seeing the significance of the 11:00 o'clock hour. I begged one sympathetic nurse to page my doctor to ascertain why we had not yet heard. Finally, she returned to tell us that there had been a slight glitch due to the time zone difference. It was only 10:00 a.m. in Oklahoma City and it would be one more hour! (*Please Lord ...*) I said my prayer over and over.

Dr. Morton, our surgeon, came by to apologize for the delay and informed us that, unfortunately they could no longer hold the O.R. for us. He offered to tag us on to the end of his schedule for the day if, by chance, the O.R. were available. Like a miracle, as our surgeon was standing there talking to us, the nurse came down the hall to say, "Dr. Morton, we just received a call from the University of Oklahoma. (*Oh! God! This is it!*) She raised her notepad to read: "Regarding Evan Kaufman, there is no confirming diagnosis from the urine sample." The surgery is on! (*Thank you, God!*) This news was like an electric bolt going through my body. I felt a tremendous surge of energy. I was ecstatic. I ran back to our room, and I reached for Evan first for a kiss and a hug. I kissed Nana and then reached for the phone to deliver the news to Mike. Evan was definitely taking his cues from my reactions, for he too, was smiling despite the need for an operation. Poor Mike was en route to the hospital, so he had to wait an additional 5 or 10 minutes before enjoying the news. (There were no cell phones in 1984.)

Dr. Morton appeared in the doorway: "Good news." Since Evan is already prepped, they are giving us the O.R. now. I reviewed the crash course for Evan again. I explained 1) why we had to have the operation, 2) why we thought it was good news, 3) that they could only let moms come as far as the double doors of the hallway, and then a nurse would have to take him the rest of the way, 4) what it felt like to have anesthesia, (remember the mask), 5) what it will feel like when he awakens. 6) when he first opens his eyes, he will not see me but I will be there, as soon as they will permit it. This time our descriptions are enthusiastic and hopeful. Evan began to feel very nervous, and by the time we got down to the O.R. corridor, they took pity on him or me or both and allowed me to go through the double doors and hold my naked son wrapped in a sheet for a precious few extra minutes while waiting for the nurse anesthetist to come for him. As I held him there, I remembered what it felt like to hold him 6 years earlier as a newborn. I held him tight and gave him hugs and realized, as I stopped time in my heart, that I would always remember this moment between us.

When the nurse arrived to get Evan, she was concerned that she was going to have a screaming child on her hands. Despite the "calming medicine" that they had given Evan 20 minutes earlier, she assumed that it would be difficult to pull him away from his mother. Before she could say anything, I assured her that Evan was well prepared for each step and that he would fully cooperate. Please wait for him to say he is ready. Relieved, she leaned over to pick him up, but she was inexperienced with the way one had to hold him. He winced and then screeched out in pain as she tried to get a better grip. He whimpered and stared at me the length of the hallway. When he was out of sight, I put my head in my hands and had a good cry.

A group of friends and family and our minister were waiting in the waiting room. The conversation centered on how unfair it was that this had happened to Evan and what a good boy he had been, and how was I holding up, and what a miserable week this had been. It sounded as if Evan had already died. Mike seized this small window of time to run up to the medical library to read some more pediatric oncology research articles.

When the nurse came out to say that Evan was in the recovery room, I also learned that Mike was with him. Hurray that Evan awakened to his Dad's face. Dr. Morton came out to the waiting room to tell me that the operation had gone fine. He said that it was remarkable that a mere touch of Evan's rib caused it to break. His exact words were "it just fell off with a tap." As he shook his head back and forth, he further described the rib as looking like "Swiss cheese that had been half eaten away." The description enlarged the already huge grapefruit housed in my gut, and my legs began to feel wobbly.

As I joined Evan on the ride back to his room, he looked up, so sweet, so angelic, so small and vulnerable. The anesthesia made him sick, and when he was fully awake he began throwing up, a difficult maneuver for someone unable to move very well. Each movement would cause a wince. When it grew dark outside, neither Mike nor I wanted to go home and leave Evan. Mike tried to arouse Evan's interest in playing games or reading books, but he simply wasn't up to it and chose, instead, to lie quietly and watch TV. Both Mike and I lay on the corner of the bed with Evan, holding him and each other. I was grateful for this prayer time.

By the next morning, Evan was beginning to ask questions. "When are they going to make me feel better? When are they going to know what's wrong with me? My back still hurts, and I don't feel so good. It still hurts to move." When Dr. Golembe made his rounds early that morning, he explained to Evan, in such a sweet and unhurried way, that a piece of Evan's rib was being flown all the way to Durham as we spoke, and that a very special doctor would look at it under a microscope and be able to finally tell us the exact name of Evan's "back ploblem." *(Haven't we heard this before?)* We were finally at the end. He predicted that it would be three days before the doctor could tell us the answer *(more waiting, ugh).* Meanwhile, he had some very good news. Today, we could go home! I expected Evan to be jubilant, but instead he simply raised his eyebrows with a blank stare. I couldn't help but wonder if he shared my own feeling that it was tedious now to wait <u>again</u> for a new deadline. Could it be that only one week had passed since I retrieved Evan from the half-way mark on the school path and informed the pediatrician that we had had enough and that I was on my way to Duke? One hospitalization later, we were going home, still with Evan's intense back pain and no diagnosis. It was as if they were giving up on us.

I tried to look on the bright side of leaving the hospital. Mike and I would no longer have to play tag-team at Evan's bedside. Evan would love to be at home, and Jenny would be a hug and kiss away. I ordered a hospital bed to be delivered from Winchester Surgical Supply. We would "set up camp" in the library on the first floor. I would finally have the chance to ask Mike my list of questions and hear from him what his thoughts were about our chances, the possibilities, the new differential diagnosis, and the preferred treatment options. I looked forward to going home and being able to have Evan in the next room. Everyone would benefit from this "quiet" family time, but particularly Jenny who need-ed to be able to see Evan, and to work out some of the feelings with which she was struggling. I compulsively began to circle the room, gathering up cards, flowers, balloons and presents, boxing up our many games, toys, crayons and books that we had brought to the hospital. It felt good to be active.

We carried Evan out of the hospital more carefully than when we had carried him in. When we arrived home, Nana had made up the bed with fresh, inviting sheets, and a tray holding the old school bell for Evan to ring for his ever-loyal servants. There were flowers everywhere, and more continued to arrive. Soon the li-brary looked ever so much like the hospital room, transplanted to home. Jenny was particularly thoughtful and sensitive when Evan arrived, and tried very hard the rest of the day to provide some entertainment and fun for him. The doorbell rang over and over, announcing a steady stream of friends and well-wishers. Imagine a six-year-old child announcing that he was tired of opening up gifts, and could we please wait until tomorrow to open anymore? Late that night, after the children were asleep, Mike and I savored a moment alone. He soberly explained to me that, after conversations with both Dr. Golembe and the hospital pathologist, the probable diagnosis was still Neuroblastoma, even though the urine test was inconclusive for it.

"No!" that couldn't be the answer! I refuse to believe that until some test confirms that diagnosis! I remain optimistic! That's my job. Every turn of events kept pointing to another diagnosis, so why couldn't it be leukemia? Pitifully, he could only look at me with tears in his eyes, as if I were an ignorant, naïve, non-scientist *(which I am)*. He told me that he was preparing to lose Evan. That conversation lasted until the wee hours of the morning, and I began to feel hopeless and helpless, too. He dragged me down. We had a few minutes of morning time to discuss the day, and how we could make it cheery and fun for Evan.

Watching Mike cry made me feel more vulnerable and nervous. Wasn't he supposed to be the strong one? Was it not HIS strong shoulder that a wife should lean on? In the past, whenever something upset me, I would always recount the problem to Mike, and he either had an intellectual answer on how to fix the problem, or a nonchalant attitude, puzzled over why anyone would get upset over the problem to begin with. Basically he always had a way of making any problem look small and insignificant. Watching Mike sob and give up made me realize that our situation was worse than I could have ever perceived it.

Had I not complained all these years that Mike never shared his feelings with me and never turned to me to lean on? In the middle of the night, we both needed the same thing: a shoulder to cry on, a sympathetic ear, and an assurance that everything would turn out OK. There was no solace. There was no energy to "talk it through." There was no strength for myself, much less for my spouse. The only comfort we could be for one another was giving each other the I-know-exactly-how-you-feel nod. This deep-down sick condition was reserved only for parents. There was strength in sharing the physical misery; when he described a huge knot in his stomach, I could compare it with mine; and when I described how numb my body felt, he had that knowledge. We both cried. We were necessary parts for each other, and I felt closer to Mike at that moment than I had ever felt before.

The moment soon vanished when Evan called out, and we both sprang to his room. He was sweating and upset. He had had a bad dream and needed help to turn over. He could remember the dream in detail: We had left him alone in the house. When he went outside to look for us, he was all alone, and everything around him was quiet. As he walked to the end of the driveway, the ground opened up, and he fell into a hole from which he couldn't climb out. He awoke as the hole was closing over. We just held him repeating, "We will never leave you." Evan had now realized that he might die, and all we could do was assure him that we would always be there for him.

He was too sleepy to notice our eyes or the look on our faces. He fell back to sleep when we noticed the time. It was the middle of the night. The hours were ticking away, and our precious rejuvenating time was closing in. Tomorrow would be another draining day.

Now that we were home with Evan, we were alerted, after-the-fact, of a tragedy that could have happened, but didn't. During Evan's hospital week, Mike had had a conversation with a pediatric oncologist at Duke who suggested that, on the basis of Evan's pain history, we should consider doing a myelogram to be sure there was no spinal cord compression. No one had thought of this, and Mike ignored the suggestion because he hated to over-react and he thought that Evan had been through enough tests. Jenny was in the library helping to prop Evan up in a more comfortable position. She was trying to be careful, but with the inexperience of a 10-year-old, she moved him too quickly. Evan cried out in pain, worse than we had heard before or since. Describing it to the doctor, it was thought that Evan's thoracic vertebra (that had been weakened by the tumor) had collapsed. Because of this excruciating pain and the oncologist's advice, Mike asked Ron Follmer, a neurologist and good friend, to come to the house and check if Evan's reflexes were "brisk." Both Ron and Mike underestimated the potential gravity of the situation. They sighed and marveled that Evan hadn't become paralyzed right then and there.

In normal households, weekends meant that the office was closed, and it was time for a little bit of fun, or at least a breather before the stress of another week. But when you are waiting for a diagnosis, when you are waiting for a verdict, weekends are cruel. 1984 was a time before email or instant communication. We would be in the dark until Monday morning, when offices and hospitals opened, and people started answering telephones.

My always-can-count-on brother, Joel, left a message on the answering machine that he was coming to Charlotte, fresh from his crash-course on magic tricks. It would prove to be a great diversion. Evan could enjoy the magic tricks from the couch and begged to see the various tricks repeated. Thoughtfully, Joel brought along some magic tricks that Evan could learn to do himself and that required no movement. This was the beginning of Evan's magician stage. Perhaps Evan believed that only a magician could perform the miracle of making him better, since the doctors didn't seem to be having much luck.

Joel was a good listener: unbiased, empathetic, scientific, and logical. Nana would often repeat the phrase "still water runs deep," when referring to Joel's personality. By this she meant that Joel was the kind of person who may not be in touch every day or every week. But if there were any type of family need, he could be counted on, always. For many years, Joel had been a professional student earning a Bachelor of Science degree, Doctor of

Pharmacy degree, and Doctor of Dental Surgery degree. For good measure, he also obtained a Ph.D. in pharmacology. This was followed by a three year residency in anesthesiology. Eventually, he would start the first certified training program for dental anesthesiologists at Ohio State University. His many degrees were not regarded by him as his measure of success, and this is what I admired about him. He felt successful and satisfied in life because of his total commitment to his family. He and Barbara raised two outstanding (and yes, accomplished) children. His priorities were never compromised: first, his wife and children, second, his extended family, and then, everything else. He was quiet and serious minded. Joel became the uncle that spun in and out of Evan's life at important times, becoming Evan's hero. Always thinking of ways he could help, Joel offered to return home to Columbus to talk to oncologists there about our sick little boy back in North Carolina. He feared for the worst.

Jenny invited a few friends over in the afternoon, and they played volleyball in the back yard. The minister also came for a visit. Evan had a permanent seat on my lap, and he seemed to enjoy vicariously watching the children play. Sadly, it was "good enough" just to watch.

For all the preparation and conversation that I deemed absolutely necessary, Evan was reticent to ask some important questions. He knew for certain that he felt much worse than when he went in to the hospital. He knew that his body was deteriorating by the day. He had continuous pain upon any slight movement now. He was unable to turn over in bed. Finally, he asked why it was that the doctors couldn't figure out his back problem, and when was he going to get better? We tried to explain that still another doctor, this one at Duke, was studying a tiny piece of his rib under a microscope. We had faith that he would come up with the answer to what exactly was wrong and how to fix it. Evan never asked what the "fixing" would entail. Perhaps he sensed that we didn't know yet. So much for preparation. So much for following the book-advice of experts. I am flying on my own.

BJ was my next door neighbor who remained thoughtful and involved with our progress or lack of progress. On this day, she brought over a new "box" that had its own case. She called it a VCR or VRC, an abbreviation I could not keep straight. I had never heard of it, and truth be told, she didn't know what the letters stood for either. She swore that we would be able to watch a movie on the TV, just like ones shown at the theater and even included the movie "Annie" for us to watch. This was such a gift! Evan was totally tied to the hospital bed, and daytime TV was hardly appropriate for a six-year-old. B.J. no longer had the directions but tried to explain to this half-brain-dead mother how to "hook the VCR up." All that I could remember was that there were three cords: one plugged in to the wall for electricity, the yellow plugged in to the audio, and the red plugged in to the video. I must have gotten it wrong, because after I plugged it in and pressed "power," all we had was loud, offensive noise and a "snowy" picture. Evan didn't want to give up (his signature trait, even at age 6), so he instructed me to keep turning the channels. When we accidentally flipped to channel 3, Voila! Annie was singing her song in the orphanage. We were awe-struck! We played the movie through three times without stopping and learned that one could even put the movie on hold for a quick bathroom break. On the fourth round, Evan thought it would be fun to turn the volume to mute, and he would provide the words (and song). What an unbelievable machine!

I called BJ to thank her, and she told me that on Park Road, in a converted gas station, there was a "video store" with multiple aisles of "theater" movies, and that one could rent a video and play it at home, an amazing concept. We did not run out immediately since Evan was so pleased with the movie "Annie," and he opted to watch it over and over again. The next day we watched the movie four more times. (It was such a blessing for a child who is confined to bed, that my Dad made sure that an anonymous donation was made to the medicine room at The Nalle Clinic in Charlotte, where children received chemotherapy all day and would appreciate the movies as much as Evan.) It was amazing how many toys Evan received that he was unable to play with, simply because he was unable to sit up and move. The most-used "time filler" would be none other than a simple flashlight that he could use to make designs on the ceiling and walls.

The arrival of Sunday night was a relief, as well as scary. It was a relief, because the phone had quit ringing, and the doorbell had died down, and Evan was asleep for the night, as was Jenny. Mike and I were marveling that we made it through the weekend. It was scary because the verdict would arrive soon, maybe even tomorrow, Monday. Mike announced that, if we needed a bone marrow transplant, he thought we would go to The University of Pennsylvania. He had long conversations with the pediatric oncologist there and was impressed with their program. I wondered if that meant that Evan would be in a sterile environment similar to the story on 20/20 recently. The child lived in a germ-free bubble. His mom would be unable to read to him or hold him. Mike was so sure of our fate that he called a distant relative whom he had actually never met, a physician at "Penn," to ask about the proximity of the Children's Hospital to the Ronald McDonald House. *(Please, dear Lord, please make it be leukemia. That is all I ask.)*

On Monday morning, the October weather was crispy cold, despite a full sunny day. The leaves were turning, and it looked like a picture perfect day. Only God can provide this beauty. It has to be a day of good news! Mike left for work early, and Jenny was picked up by the carpool. As I watched her leave, I wondered if Evan would ever get to that point again.

Evan wanted to watch "Annie". By the time Annie discovered Daddy Warbucks' swimming pool, I could no longer stand by passively. At about 10:15 in the morning, I tip-toed out of the room unnoticed and shut the door behind me. After dialing the main number for Duke, I asked the operator to connect me to the Department of Pathology. A bright, cheerful secretary answered the phone. I identified myself in a very matter-of-fact, businesslike voice as Dr. Kaufman's office in Charlotte, North Carolina. (I knew enough about the system to know that a mere parent would get nowhere!)   I explained to Miss Sunshine that a specimen should have arrived last Friday night from Charlotte for electron microscopy. The patient's name was Evan Kaufman, and I was calling to see if it had been read yet. She asked me to hold, and I began to pray. She returned to the phone and informed me that the specimen had arrived, but that it had not been read by the pathologist yet. YEAH! I have the right phone number and the right department. Business-like, I asked to speak to the pathologist, as if she should put me through without any questions. When she told me that he had not arrived at the office, I had the nerve to continue: "Where is he?" "Well, he is probably on rounds at either Duke North or the VA."   "By the way," I push even further, "what is the name of the pathologist who will read it?" I expected her to catch on, but she complied. YEAH! Part II of the mission accomplished!

I knew all along what I HAD to do. I hate people who pull rank. But I am a desperate mama bear, and the rules of conduct do not apply to mama bears. I disconnected our conversation by pressing the button on the handset of my telephone, not wanting even to take the extra seconds to hang up the receiver and wait for the dial tone. I dialed the same hospital operator again, but this time I asked the operator to page the pathologist whose name I had just learned. I waited an inordinate amount of time, until the operator came on and said in a sing-songy voice: "I'm sorry, but he is not answering." Without missing a beat, I dialed zero and asked to be connected to the VA Hospital. Again, I asked the operator to page the pathologist by name. This was very gutsy, and I was feeling nervous. My God! He's on the phone. It is time to fess up: "Hello, I am Mrs. Kaufman. You may know my husband, Dr. Michael Kaufman, who was on the staff at Duke Hospital just two years ago. The line was absolutely quiet. In one long sentence, I calmly told him that our child was very ill, and that Evan's biopsy report was sitting on his office desk back at Duke Hospital and that I was wondering if he would find some compassion and give us the results, as soon as possible. I am disappointed with the response. "How did you get my name, and how do you know that the specimen is there?" Whoops! I think I have just gotten "Miss-Sunshine - secretary" in trouble! I pictured the pathologist on the other end of the phone as middle-aged, probably never married, and definitely without a family of his own. He was irritated that I suggested that he rearrange his schedule to accommodate our anxiety. And further, that I had interrupted whatever it was that he was doing at the time of my call. He rushed me off the phone, saying that he would get to it, as soon as he could. He added that he would not be able to call me personally because standard procedure had to be followed; that is, he could only discuss a report with the referring pathologist who, in turn, would call me. Whoops! I hope that I have not made him so irritated that he passive-aggressively delays. Perhaps I should not admit this to Mike, because, no doubt, he will reprimand me for jumping the gun. As sweet as I can muster, instinctively I thank him for his time and apologize for the interruption.

I was extremely annoyed that this individual could not see the "humanness" of my situation and was unwilling to make any concession for a desperate mom. I decided that the world was made up of rigid people. This was probably a person who chose pathology because he didn't want to interact with patients (like me).

I checked on Evan. Annie is tap dancing her way down the stairs with Daddy W, to the tune of "Together at Last." "Have I not learned my lesson yet," Mike would probably say. I shut the doors again and returned to the kitchen to call Dr. Farmer, the Charlotte pathologist and friend of ours. (It is so much easier with a name and phone number). I alerted him that the Duke pathologist would be calling him with Evan's results (Evan was famous around the hospital by now, and it wasn't even necessary to explain who Evan was, or the reason the report was so important.) Would he please call us immediately? The response was positive. I asked him to write down our phone number, and he assured me that we would hear within seconds after he had heard from Duke. I am unable to sit. I am unable to stand. My fingernails have been bitten down to the quick and I am now working on the cuticle. There is a big grapefruit in my stomach. I can only pace and pray.

Around noon Mike came home, and I confessed that I had already called the pathologist at the hospital. He just smiled: "you are so predictable." It was time to wait for the phone to ring. Mike found a small spot at the end of the couch and sat with Evan's feet in his lap, content to be Evan's foot masseuse. I admire Mike's ability to compartmentalize: he can exit reality and watch the movie, even enjoys it. After lunch, Evan asked to rewind the movie and start watching all over again. Each time the phone rang, my stomach sank. Running to the phone, I thought: "This is it!" Quickly I interrupted the caller, "I can't talk now, I will call you back." (No caller ID in 1984.)

Finally, I went into the library, or rather our "makeshift theater," and sat down to watch Annie myself. At exactly 2:30 p.m. the phone rang and I was sure this was the phone call we were waiting for. For some reason, Mike must have thought the same thing, because he dashed to the kitchen phone at the same time.

The next part happened in slow motion. I – watched – Mike – pick – up – the – receiver – and – heard – him - say, "Yes, I – have – been – expecting – your - call." (*This is the moment.*) I was "<u>willing</u>" the diagnosis to be leukemia. Mike took my hand and clutched it tightly. I – repeatedly – verbalized - "leukemia" - "leukemia" - "leukemia" – softly – but – out - loud. By mouthing it over and over, I reasoned that I could make the word come out of the doctor's mouth (and Mike's). I found myself clutching Mike's hand even harder when I <u>saw</u> the answer flashing in his eyes before I <u>heard</u> the answer. All of this played out so slowly. With – the – doctor – still – on – the – other - end, Mike – dropped – the - phone, grabbed – my – arms – and - screamed – at – me – from – 8 – inches - away, "It's leukemia!" Out loud I cried, "Dear Lord, thank you." Mike wrapped his arms around me, and he said in my ear, "I believe." It was a moment that I will never forget. I started to scream and cry out loud, "It's leukemia, it's leukemia," as if it were necessary to repeat it so that the doctor wouldn't change his mind.

Mike recovered enough to pick up the receiver to ask if the diagnosis were absolutely confirmed. He needed to know if there was any doubt. He thanked Dr. Farmer and hung up. My Mother heard me scream and came running with my father on her heels. We met in the breakfast room, where they tried to reconcile this ambiguous reaction. We were screaming with joy and crying from emotion. My parents couldn't quite comprehend what had taken place. I ran over to Nana, hugged her and said "It's leukemia! We have a chance!" and we cried with joy together. We ran into the sickroom and told Evan that we finally knew the name of his illness, and that it was a problem that we could make well. Mike was totally dumbfounded. We both ran to the phone together. Cancel the office! Call the airport! I yelled down from the upstairs bedroom, "Where are we going?" Without missing a beat, he answered, "We're on our way to Memphis, Tennessee. We're going to St. Jude Hospital."

Jenny arrived home from school in the midst of this thunder of good news, but she was not quite sure what the implications were. We went from slow motion to fast forward in a few minutes. First, I ran to find a suitcase. My bedroom was a mess, including a week's worth of clothing on the floor. It is hard to concentrate. I grabbed a change of clothes for Mike and me, our pajamas, a few toiletry items. I ran into Evan's room to gather up the same. Mike is at the bottom of the stairs calling up to ask whether we can be ready to go in 15 minutes. The answer, of course, was yes. I tried to find some loose money. Then frequently, I kept stopping in the middle of my tracks in disbelief. *(Oh, thank you God.)* One last thought: I need to find Evan's blanky for security. I found it! Threw it in, and zipped up our one, little suitcase (for the three of us) and ran down the stairs. Mike had already picked Evan up carefully from the couch and taken him to the car. I asked Jenny, Nana and Pop to jump in the car, too, because it would provide us a few precious minutes to talk. No one stopped for supper or gave it a thought.

On the way to the airport, I spent most of the time with instructions for Nana and Pop. "Please be sure that Jenny's homework is done every night. The night before a test, she likes you to go over the chapter and ask the questions, as the teacher would on the exam. She needs to practice her piano at least half an hour every day. Dad, you remember where Mrs. Scoggins' house is on Crescent Avenue, don't you? That's on Friday afternoon. Remember Girl Scouts on Tuesday afternoon. Dad, do you remember where St. Stevens Methodist Church is, on Sardis Road? Nana, my carpool schedule is on the inside of the cupboard door. Could you please call any one of the mothers and let her know that I have left for St. Jude?" Jenny sat next to me, and we held hands. Clearly, she was happy for Evan and was glad that everyone was smiling for once, but she hated to see us leave and wondered out loud how long it would be until we returned. I answered her, "I don't know, but I think we will be back in a few days."

When we arrived at the airport, we learned that the flight had been delayed. While we were all waiting at the gate, I asked Jenny for her spelling words, and we got them "out of the way." It was going to be quite late for Jenny by the time she got home. We moved on, to finish her math as well. I worried that Nana and Pop had not had their supper yet. Evan was tired and weary, and he was in pain. I was extremely grateful that Nana and Pop were right there, and that Jenny's care would be the last of my worries.

(Oh, thank you dear Lord that it is leukemia.)

It was finally time to board the plane. Jenny had a difficult time letting go of me. I assured her that I would be back soon and that she was in good hands. My last words were that I loved her very much. I am sure, as I look back on it, she had many worries herself: "Could this happen to me? Could something happen to Mommy or Daddy? Could this be the last time I ever see Evan? What is happening? Am I left behind?" I thanked Nana and Pop repeatedly for all their help, for all their worries, and for being there. Everyone looked at this moment as the bright hope we now had. The doctors at St. Jude and the possibility of saving Evan's life were now our total focus. It was a morale boast.

It was a turning point.

CHAPTER III

THE INITIAL SHOCK

We were on such a high en route to Memphis. It was as if this whole ordeal had been a terrible nightmare, and we were now waking up. Surely the torment of watching Evan get worse, and not knowing what was wrong, was the low point. And then, receiving a diagnosis of leukemia filled us with such hope! Now, all we had to do was meet the expert doctors, follow their orders, and we'd be home free. My thinking was as innocent and naïve as Evan's.

It had been such a long, hard day for Evan, (and all of us!). He fell asleep, before we reached the end of the runway. Mike, too, was dozing off. But being a night person, I was wide awake. All that I could do was recount the last week's events in chronological order and then compose letters of thanks and gratitude in my mind. In the dark of the plane, one by one, I thought about Ray Swetenburg, Barry Golembe, Diane, my brother and sister, my neighbors, my parents, and finally Danny Thomas, for having founded St. Jude Research Hospital. I was so grateful that we had somewhere to GO, somewhere for a cure! Always a little ahead of myself and onto the next step, I was already planning how I could participate in fund raising for St. Jude at the conclusion of Evan's treatment. Strangely enough, I also remember wanting to compose a letter to Billy Graham (Charlotte's religious icon). I felt so jubilant, so positive, so appreciative. I had just traveled my own faith journey and felt that I should be on some crusade, telling our story. I was assuming that this moment was the conclusion of our road-trip with cancer. Instead, we were just passing through the toll booth to enter the freeway.

Although the airport clock said 10:30, with the time change, we actually arrived in Memphis at 11:30 p.m., Charlotte time. By the time we retrieved our one bag and flagged a taxi, it was midnight. It was quite chilly, and I worried that all I had brought were sweaters. Early on, our job descriptions were set, though unspoken. Mike carried Evan, holding him with both thighs together in a way that minimized his pain. I carried the bag and kept track of tickets, addresses, phone numbers, money, toys and itineraries. The taxi ride was very quiet. Mike and I were so connected that we had a total conversation through eye glances alone. (I wonder where we will end up? This is surreal.) It felt like we were riding through the black of night, waiting to arrive at the palace, where the wizard of OZ would help us, and, in no time, we would return to Kansas. Evan was sound asleep, while Mike and I held each other's hand, with Evan between us.

The Statue of St. Jude Thaddeus that greeted us with hope in 1984.

Mike was the first to spot the hospital, immediately nudged my arm, and pointed to it. There, on the very top of an eight-story building (the only building of more than two stories in the vicinity) were enormous letters, lighting the sky: St. Jude Children's Research Hospital. The signage was perched high above, in a most fitting way. We were on a high. We arrived. The night watchman had been waiting for us and ushered us into a waiting room. He instructed us to wait there until the nurse from the seventh floor could come down to get us.

The entrance to St. Jude Hospital, 1984.

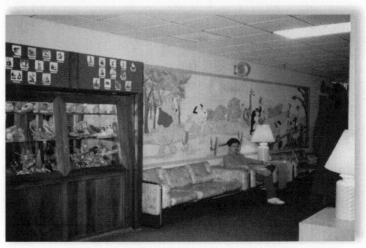

St. Jude Hospital waiting room, 1984.

Evan was now wide awake and had his second wind. Mike carried him from mural to mural, mostly Winnie-the-Pooh, all painted in very friendly, warm colors. The couches and chairs were all brightly colored, as well. In one corner was a very large enclosed

glass case filled with exquisite bird figurines. In another corner
was a huge fish tank. Another whole side was an inside mini-
playground, where younger children could ride on rocking horses
and color and read and run around and play house. A large por-
trait of Danny Thomas, his wife, Rose Marie, and famous daughter, Marlo, hung on the wall and, having looked around briefly,
Evan turned to us with his often-repeated, famous quote:

"You know, I think this is going to be the perfect hospital for me."

Evan, too, had arrived here with great hope.

A very friendly nurse appeared and said that we should come with
her. As if she were the leader of the scout troop, we followed her
down the hall and into the elevator in line. Like an experienced
tour guide, she explained that we were going up to the seventh
floor, that only the sixth and seventh floors housed in-patients,
whereas floors two through five were totally devoted to research.
"The research accomplished on the lower floors, was applied to
those children on the upper floors." Mike carried Evan, and I
brought up the rear with the bag and "extras." It was now past
1:00 a.m., and we were given a list of instructions that had to do
with being admitted to the seventh floor:

1) The floor plan resembled the spokes of a wheel with two con-
centric circles. The inner circle of rooms was germ-free to the
greatest extent possible. These were children's rooms, and they
could only be accessed through the inner area, or hub of the
wheel. There was an outside perimeter "wheel" that contained
parent cubicles. Each parent room had a large glass window,
making it possible for parent and child to see one another, and
an intercom system for communication. However, there was no
physical access between the child's room and the parent's room
without walking around the perimeter walkway and trespassing
through the double doors into the inner area.

2) Once inside the inner area, one could proceed to a large sink
outside each child's room. Before entering, we were given in-

structions on hand washing, using the non-scented, large white bottle of generic, antibacterial soap and accessing the water turn-on valve with the knee. We were to dry our hands with a special anti-bacteria towel and place the used towel in a special receptacle that could only be opened by the foot.

3) Sterile gowns and slippers were located on the shelf above the sink and were to be used each time one entered the patient's room and discarded in a separate receptacle each time one exited.

4) Using our elbow, we were instructed to push the 8-inch silver button that said PRESS and the door would automatically swing open.

5) The air was ventilated in the patient's room in a specially-engineered way. Parents were asked to be in the room for only one-half hour intervals at a time. (Perhaps having no chairs in the room was on purpose.)

The sink outside Evan's room where the extensive washing and gowning procedures were done to limit germ exposure.

6) The bathroom adjacent to Evan's room was to be used only by him.

After we reviewed the rules and, despite the time, (*this is crazy!*) they gave us an examining gown for Evan to wear and told us that the doctor would be there shortly. (*Are you kidding me? It is almost 2:00 a.m., and Evan cannot stay awake! He needs his rest. He is exhausted! What kind of a place is this?*) "Of course, we will help him get into the gown, no problem!" Our serious-looking young resident-physician apologized to us for the late hour, but, he explained, at St. Jude it doesn't really matter what time of the day or night it is. He went on: "I suppose the answer is simple. Millions of cells are reproducing every 24 hours, and the task of the doctors is to wipe out every single cancer cell, so no one wastes any time here." (*I agree with that!*)

Another nurse came in and asked me to go with her, so that she could show me where they kept bread, peanut butter, ice cream and most anything else children might want. "Just take what you want, whenever Evan asks for something to eat between meals." As we walked down the inner area to the kitchen, I couldn't help but look (Nana would disapprove of my poor etiquette here) into each room, as I walked by. I began to feel quite sick. I mean sick, as in faint and weak. None of the children had any hair and all appeared to be very, very sick. (*Oh My God! My child did not look like he belonged HERE; I didn't WANT him to belong here! Please, Lord, be with these children and their parents and please, Lord, keep Evan safe!*) I was anxious to complete Evan's work-up, receive our medicine, and then leave this frightening place. I had so much hope that these doctors could save Evan, but the children on this floor were a terrifying reminder that we were not dealing with measles.

The adjacent parent cubicle to Evan's room was unoccupied, but unfortunately, there was only one chair for one parent (the rule). Since it was the wee hours of the morning, the nurse offered to find another empty cubicle down the perimeter hall for Mike, but that tomorrow, he would have to check into a hotel, because the rule was only one parent per patient was allowed to spend the night.

A nutritionist walked into the room, as if it were two o'clock in the afternoon instead of two a.m. She had a list of questions that she wanted to ask me concerning Evan's history. Together, we filled out the questionnaire regarding Evan's eating habits and his health history, all the way back to my pregnancy. I was so tired that I wondered if I were answering the questions correctly. (*Why would this be necessary in the middle of the night? Why is the nutritionist not at home asleep? Does she live here? No one will believe this back in Charlotte!*) Evan was now beside himself with exhaustion, as were Mike and I, and I kept wondering why this couldn't have been done the following morning. The doctor spent about an hour with Evan and ordered some tests that were to be completed in the morning (the regular morning). Finally, around 3:00 a.m., Evan fell sound asleep. I put our only suitcase on the floor of my little cubicle and "crawled in" to my half reclined chair.

The next morning, bright and early, we met Dr. Sharon Murphy. She was a tall woman with a big smile, dark eyes and straight hair. This was an era when there were almost no female physicians, and it looked odd to see the combination of a long, white physician coat with high heels. I would characterize her as a "no frills" lady. She carried herself in a manner of someone who was used to, and commanded, respect. She was extremely articulate and, combined with her mid-western common sense and dry humor, she was forcefully persuasive.

Becoming a physician was not a childhood dream for her. She was more or less recruited to medicine by friends of her family who were nurses. Growing up prior to the Women's Movement in suburban Chicago, she graduated first in her high school class and first at The University of Wisconsin. When she was accepted at Harvard Medical School, her college advisors insisted that she go. She once quipped that the transportation system of Boston helped her decision as to which clinical specialty she would choose. There, on the subway, she pictured a future practice of obesity-induced diabetes and atherosclerosis, cigarette smokers, and alcoholics, and decided to invest her efforts in the younger spectrum of life, where she could make a larger impact. She was always "to the point" and didn't waste time mincing words. She was widely known as "Murphy."

She introduced herself to Mike and me and to Evan. The first words out of her mouth were directed to Evan: "Evan, do you know why you are here?" "Because I have a back 'ploblem' Evan said bravely, describing his illness in terms we had used the last seven weeks. Dr. Murphy quickly corrected him and said, "Evan, you have cancer, and it is a disease that will take a very, very long time to make better. You and I are going to work together to get rid of this cancer."

"Murphy" knew enough to be honest with kids. She would later say: "Any kid beyond a certain age understands the words cancer and leukemia, and most of them figure out what they have anyway. There's no way that you can ever keep the seriousness of this disease a secret from them. If you don't tell them the truth, they will never trust you, and they won't carry through on the whole program." I, myself, was rather appalled when she came out so bluntly with the word "cancer" in front of Evan because the word carried such a stigma, and I was sure that Evan was frightened, as well. She was a little scary to Evan, but at the same time, he was reassured that this person, who had such presence, would surely be able to help him. We told Evan that other children came from all over the world to see her for Evan's exact problem, and if anyone knew what to do for his back, she would.

Murphy's wisdom is worth quoting here: "When I was first in training in the early seventies, I was taught that you didn't actually tell a child that he had leukemia. This was considered cruel. Yet they all really knew. Over the years, it's been obvious to me that honesty with families and children is the only policy that you can conceivably adopt, although you don't ever have to take away their hope. Even with a child you know you're going to lose, you look him in the eye and say, 'You are really sick, honey, and you could die.' Because if you don't admit to them that you know they could die, and they feel like they're dying, they think you're so stupid that you'll never be able to help them. Then I always follow with: 'I'm going to take care of you no matter what.' I can almost see the relief in the child. I don't even ask the parents anymore if they want me to tell their kid that he has leukemia, because in many cases they haven't dealt with this as much, and they don't know what to say. I always tell the child, with the parent present, so they know what I've said, and it seems to relieve everyone. It's like it allows the family to be closer because they can talk about it. Then they no longer have that secret."

She explained to Evan that the first thing she was going to do was a bone marrow procedure and a spinal tap. Evan did not need to hear the words twice, for he quickly remembered that was exactly what he underwent with Dr. Golembe back in Charlotte, and he immediately was very tense. As Dr. Murphy later proved to do the entire time Evan was under treatment, she started to explain to him exactly what she would do. First, there would be a "popgun," and it would numb the area of his back, so that the bone marrow procedure would not be so painful. Though Evan had had the "numbing medicine" before, the word "popgun" was unfamiliar and scary. He asked if he could skip that part. In a very matter-of-fact way, Dr. Murphy said, "Look, there is nothing to it. Dad, stick out your hand." And with that, Dad got the popgun demonstrated right into the top of his hand. Evan laughed the entire rest of the day about his daddy's numb hand, that Mike over-dramatized, a small price to pay for a little laughter.

Unfortunately, the experiment did not make the popgun hurt any less and, even more unfortunately, the numbing did not help the pain of the spinal tap and bone marrow very much, because Evan had such extensive involvement of the spinal cord. Dr. Murphy told us that the afternoon would be spent in the x-ray department, and that she would be back to talk with us in the evening of the next day. Evan traveled by wheelchair down the five levels to x-ray.

The whole hospital was now bustling with children. Unlike Mike, I was not used to the hospital landscape. Children, who were in

wheelchairs, had big, ugly bags of medicine hanging from the attached poles. Some had tubes in their noses, their arms, and their
legs. Some had no legs or no arms, and all had no hair. Some
had a "Cushing-oid look" that, I was later to learn, came from
steroids. It was like the sun had come up, and we had been delivered to a different planet. To me and to Evan, the sight of these
children was grim, serious and sickening. One could not help but
wonder how soon Evan would look like "one of them" and again
I silently hoped that we could get our information, our medicine,
and leave for home. I wanted to shield Evan from the sight of
these children. The incredible part about this was that they all
seemed comfortable with each other and often played with only
one arm (the other out-of-order arm taped down for an IV drip).
Those who could run, did so, and chased and teased and cried,
like any other group of children. Many kids being wheeled around
in wheelchairs were holding on to their emesis basins. These children were on high-dose medications that made them sick, but, at
the same time, they had learned to live with their plight. When it
was time to vomit, they would take a quick time-out, throw up,
and then go back to playing again, without missing a beat. It was
the strangest thing. I had been taught as a child "never to stare at
people who were different," but there was nowhere else to look,
because everyone looked different.

The St. Jude plan was not only to gather data, study and research
cancer, treat children, but also to treat the family. So it was no
surprise when Mike and I landed on the interview list of a social worker/therapist. She was soft spoken, gentle, and somehow
encouraged conversation from two exhausted parents who really
didn't feel like talking. It was frightening to hear her numbers.
Of parents who lose a child, (*I am NOT READY to hear this*) over
95% of parents split up. This is mainly because losing a child is
the highest stress that anyone can experience. People grieve in
different ways and at different rates. One parent may need to
talk about his feelings; while another parent may need to remain
silent. For those couples who were spared the death of their child,
there was another group of couples who split due to the stress

of a child undergoing chemotherapy and the constant worry of whether their child will die. It certainly gave us pause to think about our marriage. Fortunately, Mike and I had a strong marriage. We were a team at home and a team at the office. We were a team through this nightmarish trauma. We looked at each other with relief. Given the stress and sadness that we had already faced, and not knowing what would lie ahead, we vowed that we would always have each other, and we were grateful for that.

In addition to the sight of these sweet, little munchkin patients, a most noticeable spectacle was the appearance of plaques EV-ERYWHERE. Each plaque represented a $1,000 donation with an inscription that either began: "In honor of," or "In memory of." There were far too many plaques "in memory of" for me. There was a plaque on every door, on every room, on every piece of furniture,

Plaques, plaques and more plaques!

on every television, every piece of equipment. Even the bathroom stalls were labeled as a donation in honor of a child. The hallways were lined with them floor to ceiling. We passed thousands of plaques just on our way from the seventh floor to x-ray. This was my first-day-introduction, as I became familiar with our new hospital. I felt so nauseated the entire day, that I ate absolutely nothing.

On the way down to x-ray, we "wheeled" past a new sub-lobby. The focal point of this room was a long, substantial table that carried the largest doll house I had ever seen. The glass enclosed doll house was at least six feet wide and five feet tall. The plaque on the table gave credit to a fourth-grade class in a school in Tennessee that devoted a year to its creation. Each room (there must have been twenty plus rooms counting the attic) was decorated with miniature furniture, window treatments and accessories. The house was completely electrified, with interesting miniature light fixtures in each room. There were color coordinated rugs and carpets. Miniature family members were "living" in different rooms. The attention to every detail was astounding, and it was fun just to stand there, taking it all in.

There was a split personality component inside me. Strangely, half of me kept saying prayers of thanks that St. Jude Hospital had been built, and that it had experienced "cures" for leukemia. I was thankful that we had found our way here, and that they could help Evan. I continued to be thankful for our leukemia diagnosis. The other half of me was nauseated, because I didn't want Evan to belong to this very elite group of children. I hated it. I wanted to go home. I wanted to get Evan's medicine and get out of there. I didn't want to see any more bald children; I didn't want to see any more dying children; I didn't want to see any more children without limbs. I hated IV bottles and needles and white coats and spinal tap trays. I hated plaques and the very smell of the place. Most of all, I hated feeling so guilty about feeling this way. I felt so ashamed and embarrassed, that I absolutely could not acknowledge this until writing this book.

The staff seemed to be totally acclimated to the sights and sounds and smells. They were able to look past the bald heads and the IV poles and could look into these children's hearts and reach out to them. The nurses, the technicians, secretaries, the doctors -- everyone who worked there made a point to know these children by name, their histories, their families, their siblings and their diagnoses. They kidded with the children, laughed with them, brought them gifts, encouraged them, and I knew that they were better people than I.

After Evan's x-rays were taken, we were told to wait in the hall to be sure the pictures came out well. (*Where had I heard that before?*) Dr. Murphy happened by in the hall and took a detour to look at the films herself. She came back out with a more serious look on her face that plunged me down further with anxiety. (*Is this déjà vu?*) She invited Mike to step inside to view and compare the x-rays just taken with the ones that Mike had brought from Charlotte. (A pat on the back to Mike for realizing that, wherever we ended up, the doctors would want to compare the very first x-rays taken -- in our case, 3 months ago in Charlotte -- with the present-day ones, and so he checked them out of the hospital before leaving town.) Mike came out looking white as a ghost. His face was drawn. It reminded me so clearly of our hallway meeting at Montreat, because when I asked him what was the matter, he said nonchalantly, "Nothing, really nothing," and I knew that I was not to ask any more questions until we were alone. (*Oh God! Not another agonizing discovery by film! Please God, keep Evan safe. Please don't punish me for my ugly thoughts!*)

We returned to the seventh floor and got Evan to bed, wearing the same pajamas that he had on the night before -- preferring his home pajamas to hospital gowns. (Why had I only brought one pair?) Mike asked me if I wanted to go down to the cafeteria to take my turn to eat, but I declined. Food was the very last thing I could think about. As soon as Evan fell asleep, the two of us exited the inside area and met up in our one-parent cubicle. Prepared for the worst news, I asked him what had happened in the x-ray department, and then he told me a very upsetting story.

The x-rays ordered by our pediatrician on one of our very first visits had been misread by the Charlotte Radiologist. A tumor, clearly outlined on this first x-ray, had been read as normal. Mike was livid to the point of being uncontrollable. He felt that the tumor was so obvious that, whoever "read" the x-ray, must not have even looked at it! Yet, he remembered the friend of ours who read it and went out of his way to tell Mike that he had seen "his son's x-ray and that it was normal." Mike remembered thanking him. "Something had to be done about this atrocity! This is pure negligence, malpractice! How could he have been so careless?

This person should not be allowed to look at another x-ray ever again!" One did not need to be a psychiatrist to figure out that this was misplaced anger. I had a second job on my hands now. One was to care for Evan, and the other to contain Mike's fury, keep him focused on the problem at hand, convincing him that he could deal with this when we returned to Charlotte, not now. Never one to listen to me, he went to a pay phone, after Evan fell asleep, called the head of the radiology department and exposed this gross negligence. Threatening and angry, Mike demanded to be heard for the sake of all future patients. He proposed that each x-ray be re-read by a second and different radiologist, even though insurance companies would only pay for one reading. I couldn't help but ask Dr. Murphy if this error might have changed the diagnosis or made any difference in our treatment plan. Dr. Murphy replied, "No, the diagnosis would still have been the same, but that billions of cells had multiplied during this lost time." Evan was a whole lot sicker than a month ago, and we had put Evan and ourselves through months of anguish. She added that she worried that some of the cancer cells had already become resistant to treatment.

Mike returned to Evan's bedside for his one-half hour, one-parent-at-a-time visit, while I stood at the window of the outside perimeter hallway on the seventh floor and gazed out over the scenery. A guard was standing at the corner, and I pointed to a large bridge in the near distance and asked him what river that was. He looked at me quizzically, as if perhaps I were one of the parents from a far-off country. He replied very loudly (as if I were deaf) and slowly (as if English were a second language for me), "It's the M-i-s-s-i-s-s-i-p-p-i River." (*How is that possible? I am in Memphis, Tennessee and doesn't Tennessee abut North Carolina? How could North Carolina be on the coast and Tennessee be bordered by the Mississippi River, the halfway dividing point of the United States? How could only two states cover half of the country?*) I rethink my stupidity and then marvel to myself at the toll that anxiety and exhaustion can take on one's mind. Next to the guard, in the corner, was a pay phone, to which I would become well acquainted over the next 24 hours.

I needed a friend, and I needed a cry. I didn't feel that I should call Nana, because I feared that, if I called her and let down, it would only pull her down as well, and I needed her to remain strong and "up" for Jenny. I needed a "Pat-fix." She was happy to hear my "hello," but then my quivering voice returned, the tears began to run and I was unable to talk (*Why am I falling apart now, when I had been so ecstatic just a short day and a half ago? Was I not thrilled that Evan was accepted as a patient here, at St. Jude? Was I not relieved that we were finally at the end of our journey? Why am I falling apart? Why can't I talk?*) Pat understood and remained patient and quiet. I began describing the thousands of memory plaques. I began venting about the sick children everywhere. "I don't want to be here, Pat. I hate this place. I don't want Evan ever to fit in here, because I am so afraid of losing him. (There's the real feeling!) What is ahead for us? Will we be just another plaque? How long will it be until Evan looks like all these other children?" Pat is a good listener, and at the end, she can only assure me that if anyone could go through this, she is sure I can. Her last bit of encouragement: "Now pull yourself together, because Evan needs that!" and then we hung up. It was my turn to visit Evan. I will remember the drill: Put on the sterile gown and the sterile shoe covers, turn on the water with my knee and wash my hands with anti-b soap, dry my hands with the anti-b towel, throw it into the receptacle using my foot, press the large silver button next to the door and enter. Mike's half hour was up. He had gotten a room at the closest hotel, and because it was late, said good-bye and reminded me to get as much rest as possible.

After my half hour visit, I returned to my cubicle and picked up the microphone to tell Evan that I thought it would be a good idea to turn off the T.V. and get some sleep. I would be back in five minutes after I changed into my nightgown and washed my face, and that he should finish his program and then shut his eyes, because tomorrow would be a long day. I walked down the hall to the bathroom, and I was thinking about how long it had been since I had had a shower. I felt so grimy that I likened it to hell-week in college. Using one end of my towel as a wash cloth, I tried to take a sponge bath from the little sink in the bathroom. The water was only lukewarm for some reason. My hair was extra oily and looked terrible. My face hadn't seen lipstick in over a month, and I was surprised, when I took a few minutes to examine my face in the mirror. So, who cares? I was looking forward to my chair and, half clean, I slipped into my nightgown and robe, and brushed my teeth.

Back in the cubicle, I picked up the microphone to say a final goodnight to Evan, but he replied that he needed me and would I please come. "Of course, sweetie." I put on my slippers and robe, walked down the long hall on the parents' side, opened the double-doors to the inner area, passed the large nurses' station, stopped at the special sink, put on my sterile gown and sterile shoe covers, washed my hands with the anti-b soap, dried them with the anti-b towel, and threw away the towel in the special receptacle and entered Evan's room by pressing the large silver button with my elbow. "What can I do for you, sweetie?" "I just need you, will you hold my hand?" There was no chair, but I stood next to his bed, bent at the waist, resting my head on his pillow. (I was too tired to stand erect.) When he seemed to be dozing off, I gently put his hand down from around my neck and tiptoed from the room. I took off the sterile gown and disposed of it and the shoe covers in the special receptacle and walked swiftly past the nurses' station, through the double doors, around to the long parents' corridor and back to my cubicle. (If only I could lie down and go to sleep. I was so exhausted.) I took off my slippers and sat back on the chair only to hear Evan groan. Perhaps he would just go back to sleep.

"Mommy, Mommy," he cried. "Yes, Evan, I'm right here. Look. You can see me through the glass. What can I do for you? What is the matter?" "Mommy, I need you, please come, I'm scared." "I'll be right there, sweetie." I found my slippers and robe, quickly walked down the outside hall again, through the double doors, past the nurses' station. I stopped at the sink, washed my hands with the anti-b soap, dried them with the anti-b towel, threw it in the special receptacle and reached for a brand new sterile gown and shoe covers, pressed the large silver button to enter the room. "Mommy, it hurts to turn over, can you help me turn over? Do you mind helping me? I'm sorry to call you out of your room." (*God, this child is so dear!*) This would always characterize his personality: sensitive and thoughtful. After he was "comfortable" (using the word loosely), I explained that tomorrow was going to be a very long day and that he needed to go to sleep. I, too, needed to get some rest, so that we could learn more about the hospital tomorrow and have time to play. I repeated what was "on tap" for tomorrow. Evan nodded that he understood, and I walked out again, took off the gown and shoe covers, disposing of them in the designated receptacle, passed the nurses' station, through the double doors, around to the long parent corridor, down to my room, shut the door, took off my slippers and robe and got into my chair once again.

"Mommy, are you there?" "Yes, Evan, you can see me, I am right here only a few inches from the glass, and I am going to sleep, but I will be able to hear you all through the night, and if you need me, I will come." "But Mommy, I need you now. Could you come now? I'm sorry to ask you to get up, but I'm afraid to go to sleep and I need to talk to you." I was too tired to find my slippers or robe. I shuffled barefoot down the hall, through the double doors, past the nurses' station to the familiar sink, with the familiar soap and towel, and forgetting the gown and shoe covers, (should I call them foot covers now? Am I really joking here?) I shuffled in to see my dear sweet boy. "Mommy, what will happen to me tomorrow? I explained that Mommy and Daddy were meeting another new doctor, and that we would learn tomorrow about the medicine that would help his back. I wasn't sure what else would happen, but I promised that I would be right next to him every bit of the day and that nothing would happen without my first explaining it to him. "You can count on it!" In a more or less pleading voice, I told Evan that we needed to get our rest and that mommy was very tired and that mommy couldn't stay in his room, but that I would be right on the other side of the glass, and he could see me and call me on the microphone, and we could talk, if he needed me. I leaned over to kiss him and made sure that there was nothing more I could do for him. I shuffled out of the room, almost unable to pick up my feet. I shuffled past the nurses' station, through the double doors, around the corridor, and down the long hall to my room and my chair.

3:15 a.m., Trip #4 "Mommy, are you there? I need a kiss good-night."

4:05 a.m., Trip #5 "Mommy, the pain is bad. I'm sorry to wake you. I need you."

On the final trip, at 5 a.m., after I heard Evan calling out for me, I was pushed over the edge. I felt that I was sleep-walking. (This just isn't working.) I felt so sorry for myself. When I reached his bedside, I helped him turn over and gently kissed his forehead. "Thank you Mommy," and he went back to sleep. FORGET THE RULES! FORGET THE PROCEDURES! I am too tired to leave his room. I eyed an 8 inch ledge on the window that faced the nurses' station. The ledge accommodated my one hip and one bent leg. I used my knee for a pillow. When Mike arrived one hour later, he put his arm around my shoulder and woke me quietly. He suggested that I go to the cubicle, and that he would take over. Gratefully I followed his instructions.

I slept through Mike's initial games with Evan. I slept through the chatter of the television programs. But all of a sudden in a groggy state, I heard Murphy's voice, and I bolted out of my chair, angry that I wasn't in the room to hear every detail of what she had to say. I hurriedly dressed, ran down the hall, through the double doors, past the nurses' station, cut short the drill, and entered Evan's room, just in time to hear the very end of her conversation. All that I could ascertain was that Evan was "appropriate" to enter into the study (called Total XI) and that in an hour we would be meeting with her and Dr. Gaston Rivera who was the primary author of the protocol.

As an explanation, I learned that a "protocol" was like a recipe for a making a cake. The best and brightest of the research team convenes to discuss the success of the previous protocol. Sometimes with only intuition, they reviewed the variables: what drugs were effective, whether the dosage of the drug should be changed, whether the drugs should be taken in combination and over what length of time. They discussed irradiation and should the number of "rads" be increased or decreased. How often should a bone marrow or spinal tap be scheduled? In general, they conclude that, to make the cake, they list all the ingredients available. Given those ingredients, they juggle the order that they are mixed together. Is the cake better with two eggs? Should you bake at 350 or 375? Then, in hopes of getting a better result, they review details: are you using two pans or one? Will a specific oven-type affect the baking time? When each cake comes out of the oven, there needs to be a re-evaluation of the result: the flavor, the texture etc. Simply stated, the researchers keep rearranging the variables in an effort to establish cause and effect. It turns out to be a guessing game under the name of "experimental therapy."

Like all new protocols, Total X, the protocol before Evan's, reflected past experience, theoretical consideration and intuition. One idea for Total X patients was that the probability of drug-resistant cancer cells could be reduced by giving very intensive induction (the first massive doses of chemotherapy). The first eleven patients were slammed with high doses of drugs at the beginning of induction. When two died and six had severe, life-threatening infections, an immediate change had to be made. Dr. Murphy's exact words were: "... pulling one child back from the grave." Because of this intense toxicity to the body, one child had to undergo a splenectomy. Trying to treat the total body infection that had developed, the child was administered another toxic drug, that unfortunately, left him deaf. Despite all of this, Brandon was the first patient to go off the medicine of Total X for leukemia and was presumed cured.

When we arrived in October of 1984, we learned that Total XI was only conceived in January, 1984. Dr. Rivera and Dr. Murphy were

reluctant to quote figures and statistics and gave repeated remind-
ers that Evan was being treated with a new protocol that was not
yet 10 months old. The past record could not be used as a yardstick
with which to meaningfully predict Evan's outcome. All we could
do was hope for the best and take each day at a time (a hard thing
to do for two compulsive, type-A parents).

Mike explained once again to Evan that Mommy and Daddy
needed to go out in the hall for a minute to talk, while he watched
his program. We would be right back. Outside the room, Mike put
his arm around my shoulder and then around my waist, as if to
hold me up. I spoke first. I told him about the night before and
the number of trips I had made back and forth. I began to cry. I
was so exhausted that I was sure if I slept all day and all night for
a month, I would still feel tired. I felt so sick; I had a headache;
I felt queasy. My legs were numb. I needed a hot shower and a
night's rest. I could read Mike like a book. I knew the low tolerance he had for complaints. I wondered if being a physician and
hearing people every hour talking about what hurts and what is
wrong had "hardened him." The bottom line: there's no pity party
here! I must keep it to myself and, above all, not complain. I knew
what he was thinking: How could I think about how tired I was
feeling, when Evan was hurting so much? (*Shut up, Helen. Buck
up! Quit whining!*) I stopped in my tracks. "But, I'm entirely OK
now. Please outline the conversation with Murphy that I missed.
Don't leave out a detail!"

Soon, we would hear the results of the bone marrow and spinal
tap. We told Evan, in an encouraging way, that soon Mommy and
Daddy would learn more about his problem and finally hear all
about the medicine that would fix it. We reminded him that he
had a "buzzer" next to him, if he needed a nurse, and that the
nurse was right outside his room and would come in a flash.
Luckily, a favorite program was on TV, and with him clutching
his blanky for comfort, we felt OK about leaving for the meeting
just down the hall. (I needed a blankey, too.)

Mike and I were both anxious to sit down and talk to Murphy and Dr. Rivera because we were thirsting for some tangible news from the experts. We were now on the cusp of treatment, and the adrenalin was pumping. What was Evan's disease like? Were there different degrees of leukemia? Did they think that Evan's particular disease would respond to treatment? What were his chances now? How long would we be here? Or more importantly, when was it time to return to Charlotte? What was the protocol? What were the medicines? What were the side effects? We had so many questions.

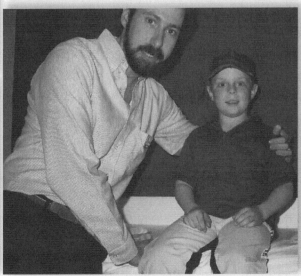

Three of Evan's many wonderful doctors:

Left: Dr. Murphy
Lower left: Dr. Rivera
Lower right: Dr. Golembe with Evan.

When it came time to meet with them, we did all the listening. We were told that Evan's leukemia was widespread. (*God! I don't like the sound of that!*) and that they were hopeful that with the initial induction of treatment, he would go into remission. The results of the bone marrow and spinal tap (*God! Do you hear me? Please give us some good news here.*) placed Evan in the high risk group (code for: the worse prognosis group). The reason for the high-risk designation was that Evan had "chromosomal trans-locations" and involvement of the central nervous system. Mike dug further, and Murphy did not want to go there, but finally she gave us the grim reality: her opinion was that Evan had about a 20% chance to live. This was based on the analysis of Protocol X (the protocol concluded right before Evan's group). The fact was that two-thirds of Total X leukemia victims with translocations relapsed after their therapy was concluded.

"There are two different therapy groups. (I am trembling. I look down at my foot. It is shaking double-time). The high risk group will be given higher strength drugs. (*Helen! Pay attention here!*) Our hope is that he will attain remission within the 8-week in-duction period. (*Oh God, we are going to lose him. Please don't let this happen! Did you just say eight weeks?*) Remission is of-ficially attained when the patient no longer has any cancer cells. (*Why can't this be me instead? I would gladly take this cancer from Evan.*) We would like to start treatment immediately. This was a commitment on our part, as parents, to follow "the plan" to the best of our ability ... even knowing that we would be giving Evan toxic drugs." (*Torture me more. It can't get worse!*)

Somehow, the signing of the informed consent was worrisome. I would have far preferred assurances rather than best chances. We were warned about the many side effects that were totally unpredictable. Of course, that made us uneasy, as it would any parent. But what choice do we have? Essentially, we had already made the decision that the experts here were our only (and best) chance. We were hopeful, but desperate. We realized that Evan's treatment plan was built on prior experience; each an improve-ment over the last. Anything they asked us to do, we would auto-matically do anyway. I felt as if we were signing his life away, but, actually, we were signing to get it back. We were anxious to start the treatment, and so were they.

Quoting from the actual consent form: "Acute Lymphocytic Leukemia (ALL) is the most common type of cancer in children. Leukemia is a malignant disease originating in the bone marrow that affects the blood forming cells. Through studies conducted at this center and elsewhere over the past 20 years, a plan of therapy for children with leukemia has been developed. Briefly, the plan consists of the use of chemicals referred to as 'chemotherapy' that destroy leukemic cells in the bone marrow, while allowing normal cells to recover in number and function. When this objective is obtained, usually in 8 weeks, children feel well, and no leukemic cells can be detected in blood and marrow examination. This state is called a remission from leukemia. Thereafter, efforts are made to maintain the remission. At the same time, infiltration of leukemic cells in the central nervous system has to be prevented with medications. The classifications of risk factors are as follows: 1) children who have white counts above 25,000 2) children who have sites of leukemia outside the bone marrow and blood, usually the central nervous system, lung or abdominal organs 3) children who are less than 1 or older than 10 4) children who had immune "markers" on the surface of their leukemic cells, indicating malignant cells, were more developmentally mature 5) children who demonstrated chromosomal abnormalities called 'translocations.'"

Whenever we talked with Dr. Murphy or Dr. Rivera, I made it a habit of keeping quiet. I trusted that Mike would know what questions to ask and that his questions were more sophisticated, based on his medical knowledge, and that he would be able to gather far more valuable information than I. He would impress upon me that a physician's time was precious, and, afterwards, he and I would have all the time necessary to rehash information in layman's terms. Retrospectively, this was a mistake. This was not a benefit of being a doctor's wife; this was an emotional unfairness to me, relegating me to the status of a "politely concerned babysitter." As a parent, I had a right to ask questions.

However, this time, when we started to discuss treatment, I couldn't help but speak up: "When would we be taking the medicine back to Charlotte or, more to the point, how long would we be in Memphis?" Murphy, not one to spend time on mundane details, simply answered "you will be given a print-out sheet that will describe each day's medicine. It's all in there." She looked at her watch and asked if there were any questions adding that she had to run, because she had a parent-teacher conference to attend for her son ... and that we would see her "around." (*God! A parent-teacher conference! The phrase stunned me. I guess the world is still functioning outside this hospital. For us, time had stopped, and even the world had stopped. When I looked out the window of the seventh floor, I wondered where the fast-moving cars were headed. Were people out there living normal lives? Was this a weekday? Were other kids in school? Was our doctor involved in a life outside these walls?*) Before she left the room, she rifled through her folder of papers and found our protocol that she handed to me and said, "Here, this is the schedule you will be on for the next eight weeks." (*Surely she meant eight days.*) I looked at the menu. She meant eight weeks. I became frozen in my seat. I quickly scanned the information. Literally, this is what I read:

Total XI-Treatment Plan
Early therapy for #9291, Kaufman, Evan Joel
Started 24/10/84

Week one:

Day one - 24 October 1984 - prednisone, VNC, PK and VCR.

Day two - 25 October 1984 - prednisone, ASP.

Day three - 26 October 1984 - prednisone, ASP.

Day four - 27 October 1984 - prednisone, VM26, ARA-C, I.T.

Day five - 28 October 1984 - prednisone ... and so on ...

What did all this mean? What are these abbreviations? How are these drugs given? Evan will want to know if there are needles. Will he get sick? Are these IV drips? Could we get these in pill form? It doesn't say whether these are taken at night, during the day? Surely she didn't mean that the eight weeks would be spent here? When I looked up, I discovered that I was the only one sitting there. The doctors had left due to other demands on their schedules. Mike had already rushed back to Evan, in case he was becoming uneasy that we were away so long. (*Wait a minute!! Please!!*)

A particularly friendly and sensitive nurse approached me and asked if she could be of some help. Tears running down my face, and a voice that had given out once more, I asked her if she could please tell me what all these abbreviations meant. She summarized: VCR was another name for Vincristine, a needle inserted into a vein of the hand and then the medicine is "pushed in." It wasn't bad. The ASP stood for Asparaginase, a shot in the thigh that would make Evan tired but not "vomity." VM26 -- all day nausea -- it would be given through an IV line. ARA-C, a particularly potent drug ... after being administered, you can set your watch by the vomiting that would start and end in exactly 6 hours time. I.T. stood for LP or spinal tap -- this hurts, but not as bad as a BMA (bone marrow), the most dreaded procedure of all. Like every parent who is handed these sheets of the future treatments, I can't help but turn to the last day: December 11, 1984! On that date, we would find out if Evan had achieved a remission. I'm not sure what that means. I mean, I know that we are hoping for no more cancer cells on that date, but I wondered if it would be our first opportunity to go home and be completely through with medicines and this nightmare. (*Eight weeks! That's two months! I needed to call home and talk to my Jenny-girl! I needed to break the news to Nana and Pop. I came prepared for a weekend! What is happening at the office? Is it time to wake up yet?*) My mind is swimming with details. Of all things, my Mother's favorite poem pops into my mind:

> *Be Strong!*
> *We are not here to play, to dream, to drift,*
> *We have hard work to do and loads to lift,*
> *Shun not the struggle,*
> *Face it! 'Tis God's gift,*

Say not "The days are evil. Who's to blame?"
And fold the hands and acquiesce-Oh Shame!
Stand Up! Speak Out! And bravely in God's name,

Be Strong!
It matters not how deep entrenched the wrong,
How hard the battle goes, the day how long,
Faint not, fight on! Tomorrow comes the song.

(Maltbie D. Babcock)

This was going to be a long, rough road.

When I found my way back to Evan's room (a victory considering my directional-disability, combined with my shocked system), there was a note that a parent of Kaufman, Evan, #9291 needed to go down to the admissions office and speak with one of the administrators. This fell under my job description as the "keeper of important papers," insurance details, itineraries, plane tickets, and now, our new Protocol XI. I left, happy for some solitude. It was a major job to fight back tears, and I noticed that I seemed to be crying at any new information. I also became aware that I was shaky, perspiring, and feeling a little lightheaded. I thought back and realized that I hadn't eaten since arriving. I better go to the cafeteria after meeting with the administrator. I needed some food right away. I noticed that I was too weak to think straight.

When I got off the elevator, I lingered through the long hallway to the main part of the hospital. More plaques. This time I can't help but read inscriptions on plaque after plaque after plaque. There were many dating back to the 1970s and from all over the country: Ohio, Virginia, Florida, Pennsylvania, Washington, California, West Virginia, and Maine. Each plaque deeply affected me. It was clear that they were written from the hearts of grieving, sad, humbled people, who had lost their children. Danny Thomas would later be quoted: "This is something that no parent should have to do." I could look at the plaques now, with love in my heart, and appreciation for all the children who died and, with their lives, helped physicians learn how to treat this disease, but who were not fortunate enough to live in a time when doctors knew what to do for it. Each of these children made Evan's therapy possible, through experimentation and research, but mostly trial and error. Those errors cost so many people such heartache! Each plaque represented money that the hospital needed, in order to make any strides in learning to treat this disease. But to a parent, such as I, who was losing my child, the plaques represented grim reality. My knees became weak, and I stood there sobbing. (*This is it, the moment that I am officially falling apart.*) I have no strength left.

Another mom, a total stranger, saw me, put her arm around me and said, "Let me help you." The only thing I was able to say was that I couldn't find my way to the administration office, but she knew. She and I walked together down another long corridor, her arm around my shoulder, until we came to the office. We walked silently. Without a word, she pointed to the door, then left. I walked in, and a very nice person motioned me to come into her inner office. When I sat down on the couch, it all spilled out, and I cried uncontrollably. Here, it was safe to let down. I wanted to explain to her that, in fact, I am normally a very stable person, that I manage an office, that I take care of two children, run a household, and I am very organized. And, by the way, I am not the least bit hysterical. She probably never would have believed me anyway.

After a minute or two she said, "Mrs. Kaufman, thank you for coming down here. Before we start, is there anything I can do for you? I am still amazed at what came out of my mouth: I told her that I was extremely upset, because I just learned that we would be here for eight weeks, and I had only packed one pair of pajamas for my son. I had no clean pajamas for him! She knew that I wasn't crying about the pajamas. Calmly, she assured me that the hospital had all kinds of clean pajamas and hospital gowns and that the reason she had sent for me was to acquaint me with the fact that St. Jude Hospital was in the business of caring for the kids totally. She explained that, whatever need Evan had, it would be met. Many children come to the hospital on the spur of the moment and from distances much farther away than Charlotte. The hospital staff was used to this. No matter what the problem, I should come to her, and together we would solve it. For example, if Evan wanted a special sort of food, like Pizza Hut pizza, not to worry. There would always be some employee who would be happy to run out at any hour and bring it to him. Clean clothes, entertainment, food? Whatever he needed, we should just let her know. There was a K-Mart a few blocks from her house, and she offered to stop there on her way home from work to buy Evan pajamas! What size was he anyway?

She assured me that soon I would become acclimated to the hospital and how it ran. She told me that all parents feel overwhelmed when they arrive, and that I was in good company! "Soon, you will be meeting key people who will be able to help you through anything from the medicine room to hotel accommodations." She went on, "there are certain hotels in the area that have a special arrangement with St. Jude and these hotels keep a certain number of rooms available for St. Jude families. When you need a hotel, stop by my office and get a green card." The card will list the hotel to which you are assigned. She told me that I would meet Ollie. He walked through the waiting room on an hourly basis calling, "Hotel, Hotel," and that meant that he was leaving for his round of hotel stops. We could get in his van, always parked at the statue, and we would have free transportation from the hospital to our specific hotel. She cautioned that we should be mindful of the fact that the hospital was located in downtown Memphis, and so were the hotels, and that it was not a good idea to go outside one's hotel room at night, alone. This was so much information to take in, nor was I sure why she was even TELLING me all of this. After all, we "resided" on the seventh floor, where I was beginning to appreciate my little cubicle, Evan's sterile room, and a tray of healthy food that appeared on demand. I was relieved that all of this "hotel talk" did not apply to us.

She asked me for my insurance card, that I compulsively kept filed underneath my driver's license in my wallet. I told her that I could not remember what our plan benefits were, but that I could make a phone call and find out and get back to her (the insurance procedure at our office back in Charlotte). I told her that we would pay any amount for Evan's treatment (*Did I even KNOW what THAT would be?*). She just looked at me with a smile on her face and explained that that was the least of my worries. The hospital would file for insurance, but no family ever received a bill beyond what their insurance paid. (*I had not heard correctly. After all, I managed a medical office and realized the financial demands of medicine.*) "You mean this is not costing anything?" "Oh! To the contrary," she said "it costs millions of dollars every single day just to run the hospital but that the hospital had been set up by Danny Thomas, the Memphis businessmen, and a group called ALSAC. They pledged not to charge any patient for any treatment here. (*I had heard correctly. How could this be?*). I would later learn that the cost of treatment for one child over three years was so exorbitant that no family, no matter how financially well off, would be able to afford to come here. Danny Thomas and his support team had to find another way to support this hospital financially. How incredible it was: any desperate family could come to this hospital if they had a child with cancer!

As she drew up papers for me to sign, directing insurance payments to be made directly to St. Jude Hospital, I began to daydream about the day I would be able to do volunteer work here and somehow help St. Jude Children's Research Hospital. Would I be able to do a major fundraising activity in Charlotte and make a contribution so that one more child like Evan could receive treatment? I hoped so. (*Thank you, God, that this hospital is here.*) She then showed me the mail room and box #9291. With a hug, she assured me that we were in good hands. She hoped that I would feel better, and that Evan would soon feel like walking and playing.

I wandered out of her office feeling like a lost child, not sure which direction to turn. Could I possibly face food? More plaques. More children going by on stretchers and in wheelchairs. More bald heads. Parents were talking with one another. Kids were playing. I began to look at this place in a different way. However, I still wished we could get our medicine and leave. Totally by chance, I saw an arrow to the cafeteria and decided that, if I am going to have enough strength for Evan, I better eat. The cafeteria was only half full, and there was no line, so I took a tray and some silverware and went through the entire line, with nothing on my tray. (*Come on, Helen, you've got to find something. Go back through the line again and choose SOMETHING. Surely you can eat a sandwich, a salad, or just an apple.*) Filling my tray, I looked for a quiet place to sit. I passed table after table of people talking and laughing. A common sight was a family with a child in a wheelchair, an IV pole and emesis basin in tow. They seemed to sit at the lunch table as if they were at home enjoying any meal, exchanging stories of their day. Periodically, the child would lean over to grab the emesis basin, vomit with little "to-do" or alarm, and then the conversation would resume. It was commonplace! I can't quite comprehend the general milieu. I found the perfect table. It was in the corner, and I faced the wall. With one elbow on the table to prop up my head, I started to eat my salad. After eating a third of it, I realized that I had forgotten to put the dressing on. My cold diet cola was refreshing. I opened my backpack and rummaged for the notebook that described the next eight weeks. I needed to get organized, if we were going to be here for such an extended time. I needed to make a list of things that Nana and Pop could send us from home. I should make a list of things I needed to tell the office staff to do and what to send.

When Mike called the office, he learned that the neurology community, usually a hotbed of competitors, was pulling together in an act of compassion. Specifically, Dr. Mike Nesbit called the office and offered to help out with hospital consults, as did Dr. Ron Follmer. Others offered to see office patients who were "piling up with problems and side effects," without the physician support needed to handle the load. I thought about poor Jim Pugh, Mike's new partner, who joined our practice shortly after our trip to Williamsburg. He had been going it alone for a month now! He must be exhausted! I finished my salad with a prayer. (*Dear Lord, I am totally and completely at your mercy. I feel there is nothing left in me to fight. I am exhausted and weary. There is so much to face. I have already put my son in your hands. Please fill me with Your strength, not for tomorrow or next week, but I pray for just enough strength to make it through today, Amen.*)

I got up from the table and noticed that eating lunch helped my jitters. I wondered if any of the food would appeal to Evan. Maybe I should take something back to him. Discussing this with one of the cafeteria workers, I was directed to the side room, especially catering to the children. Acquainting myself with even more procedures, I walked into the adjacent room and saw a lady handing out what looked to be McDonald's Happy Meals. They were brightly colored boxes, folded to look like a house. They contained snack food, appealing to the universal children population. (*They really think of everything here!*) I must return to the room now to see Evan, and to send Mike down to the cafeteria for his turn. (*Wipe your eyes, Helen. Put a smile on your face. Be strong! Your mother would be strong. I will give Evan the mantra: 'You can do it,' 'You WILL do it'.*) I walked past the plaques, but I refrained from stopping. (*There is a little boy upstairs who needs me, not some weak crybaby … but a mother who can say, "we will go through this together and it WILL turn out OK!"*)

Mike has obtained (from somewhere) the directions associated with our itinerary over the next eight weeks. When I finished, I felt overwhelmed again. Induction therapy will include 6 drugs and after reading about the drugs and how they were administered, I started down the list of side effects: high blood pressure, irritability, constipation, leg and abdominal cramps, hair loss, anemia, seizures, burns if the drug leaks out of the vein, chills, fever, rash, swelling of the face, irritation of the pancreas, abnormalities of coagulation factors, stroke, increased blood sugar, mouth ulcers, drop in blood counts … Despite such a complete and descriptive list, we would learn that excellent advice was almost always obtained from the other moms we talked to during induction. Everyone had his own story. Parents of patients who had relapsed once, and more than once, had so much to share and had such accumulated wisdom. They served as a great resource to "newcomers" like us. Many times they were our "handbook for survival," both in practical matters and for spiritual strengthening.

October 24, 1984:
Day #1 of Total XI

Was this a preview of the next eight weeks? Sitting in the cubicle, I heard Mike getting frustrated with Evan. I tossed our new notebook aside, "Mike, please, wait for me to come." I could hear Evan crying. With little patience, Mike was "teaching" Evan how to swallow a pill and it wasn't working. Evan was trying his hardest, but kept gagging and spitting out half-dissolved, bitter tablets. Thinking the problem was with the liquid, Mike continued to order every liquid he could think of: milk, then apple juice, then grape juice and finally cola. Evan was motivated and ready to do whatever it took! His back still hurt and it was still painful to move. But now we were saying that this was the medicine that was going to make his back stop hurting, and so Evan was eager to cooperate. Swallowing a pill was daunting for a six-year-old. I have no idea where this idea came from but Evan was willing to try. I told Evan to choose one of the drinks that were lined up on his hospital tray. The trick here was to imagine our being at the beach. "We are standing on the water's edge and watching as each wave comes crashing to shore. Picture yourself wading in to the water, up to your knees. Now imagine the waves are splashing us in the face. Now, with this in mind, I want you take the pill and put it as far back on your tongue as you can but not so far back that it is uncomfortable. Now, swallow a big, big gulp of juice and picture that huge wave of juice crashing into the pill and taking it 'down the hatch' just like the wave of water sometimes knocks you down." Voila! Just that simple, Evan has swallowed his first pill.

With some age-appropriate visualization, Evan learned to swallow pills.

No sooner had Evan attained his first pill-success than a stranger appeared on the other side of the glass inside my parent cubicle. He picked up the microphone and introduced himself as Dr. Daughdrill. He explained that he was a personal friend of Randy Taylor (the minister of our church in Charlotte), and a resident of Memphis. Worried about us, Randy asked his friend to stop by and meet us. Mike barely looked up and had nothing to say to him. His exact words were: "Thank you very much, but we don't need any help, and if you will excuse us, we have some things we need to do here." I knew that Mike was exhausted from the pill-taking episode and distraught over the idea that each medicine could exact this much energy, as we convinced a six-year-old to comply with the "itinerary." I asked Dr. Daughdrill if he would stay there, while I made my way through the inside corridor where he was. I politely shook his hand and thanked him so much for coming, the very least I could say to a friend of our minister.

Dr. Daughdrill was not a medical doctor, rather, the academic kind. He was quite sophisticated and handsome and, within the first few minutes I could add descriptors of compassionate and sensitive. We had a heart-to-heart talk about all that had happened. It was embarrassing to admit that, in not so long a time, I was crying again on still one more shoulder about how grateful I was that we had finally received some help; and on the other hand, how difficult it was to be hospitalized in a city, where we had no support system in place (as compared to Charlotte). I was scared for Evan and worried about my other child back in Charlotte. At this point, he probably wished he had not asked, "How are you?" After a little while, I tried to express my thanks to this kind man who had gone out of his way for a complete stranger.

Before he left, he told me that he was leaving town for the next three weeks and insisted that we use his car during the time he was away. He asked me which hotel Mike was staying in and then told me that tomorrow morning a blue Cavalier would be sitting in the parking lot, with the keys under the mat. He handed me his business card and told me to call his secretary, after three weeks had passed, and she would arrange for a car pick-up. After he left, I looked at the card. He was the president of Rhodes College. (I will add his name to my list of angels, whom I had the good fortune to meet.) His kindness touched me deeply!

During each interval of time that Mike and I spent with Evan, we routinely ran through the repertoire of games to play, for a patient on his back. "I am going to Grandma's and I am going to take a toothbrush and a light bulb and a loaf of bread." "I am thinking of an animal that begins with P," and on and on and on. When Evan's supper arrived, it was not appetizing to him. I told him about the secret little kitchenette that had peanut butter and jelly and that I could go and make him a special sandwich, if he wished. That seemed to please him, and I felt good about the smile on his face. But after I brought it back, he could eat only a few bites.

I offered to stay with Evan, in order for Mike to go downstairs to eat supper. But Mike decided he was exhausted and that he was going to leave the hospital, go back to the hotel, take a hot shower and get a good night's rest, because tomorrow would be a particularly long day, with more new medicines. He took Evan's hand and looked him straight in the eye and said, "Evan, you are going to be okay. I know you are. Please get a good night's rest and know that I love you dearly." This moment remains in my mind. I explained to Evan that I would be walking Daddy to the elevator and that I would be back in five minutes. In a very supportive way Mike put his arm around my shoulders. He told me that I looked tired and that he was worried about me. He advised me to turn in, as early as possible, and try to get a good night's rest. Tomorrow would be a big day. With a quick hug and a wink, he told me he loved me.

When I returned to Evan's room, Evan needed some preparation. "Are there any shots? I'm really scared." I explained that tomorrow there would be another pill day, another shot in the thigh (1 quick needle), two new drugs called VM26 and ARA-C that would drip into his vein through an IV. (Evan could not comprehend the idea of a needle stuck in his arm all day. His entire needle repertoire to date included only quick stabs.) I promised that Mommy and Daddy would be right there with him and that these are the medicines that would make him better. It was now past 11:00 p.m., and Evan finally fell asleep. I tip toed back to my cubicle, but, for some reason, I found it difficult to do the same. My thoughts were now turning to home and Jenny and when were we ever going to be able to return to Charlotte? Would the procedure tomorrow be terrible? What was happening at the office? I was so worn out, but too tired to fall asleep.

The head nurse appeared early in the morning. She was explaining to Mike and me that Evan was stable, and that it was time for him to become an outpatient. (*Oh! My God! NO!*) I heard not another word of the conversation, for my mind was racing ahead. (*How was that possible? I thought we were going to be in the hospital for eight weeks! How would he eat? Here in the hospital we just filled out the order for supper, lunch and breakfast, and it just arrived. We would be unable to take Evan to a restaurant, he was unable to move! Mike had to carry him everywhere. Didn't she understand that?*) I wondered if Mike could tell her: "If it is okay with the hospital, we will just go ahead and stay put, thank you very much."

Mike reasoned that, while it was true that Evan continued in pain, it really didn't matter where his bed was. Evan was not immunosuppressed, anemic or feverish, and he did not need intensive monitoring. He could understand why it was time to become an outpatient. (*Whose side are you on, anyway?*) In a very persuasive way, he convinced me that being an outpatient was really not a bad idea. Think of it this way: 1) We would stay at a hotel, where I could sleep in a bed, rather than in a chair, and where Evan would feel more comfortable in a more home-like environment, rather than the sterile environment of the hospital. 2) He reminded me that there would be a hot shower there! 3) We would "set up camp" in the hotel room, buy some toys for Evan, and make it cozy. We could drive to the hospital in the mornings for his treatment, and on a good day, if it was a quick-treatment-day, and Evan felt like it, we could sight-see in Memphis and then return to our little home. (*Dear God, help me with this change! Is this why the woman was describing the hotel rules? Is this why you sent Dr. Daughdrill for a visit?*) It began to sound like a good idea, and I was thinking positively.

Then Mike turned to me and dropped the bomb, "Besides, I need for you to get used to the routine and learn how to drive back and forth to the hospital because I have called back to the office and talked to Jim. "Helen, I must get back to the office soon." BAM! The sledge hammer slammed into my stomach. "You what? You are going to leave me here? I am going to drive to the hotel by myself? I don't know where it is? I don't know the way! I can't carry Evan! I can't leave Evan in the hotel room alone while I go out and get food for us! I don't know the procedures of the hospital. I can't do it by myself. I need you. What if he reacts to the drugs? Please don't leave." I was sobbing. (*Helen, no complaining! This is getting you nowhere!*) A quick hug and nonchalant assurance that I would be fine ended the conversation. No further discussion.

I told Mike to go back to Evan, while I stayed for a few minutes to regain my composure. (*Dear Lord, I am really trying to function. Each time I think I am stable, a new sledge hammer hits me.*

Thank you for this hospital, for Evan's diagnosis, and that we are starting the therapy that hopefully will save his life. Please hold my hand and make me strong enough to face anything. I happily go through this if you will just keep Evan safe.) When I opened my eyes, I immediately focused on the pay phone on the wall. Thank goodness Pat was home. When she said "Hello," I started to cry again. "Helen, is that you?"she asked. Hysterically, I explained that Evan was about to be discharged as an outpatient. I had not slept in two days. I had not showered since we arrived. I was shaky, nervous, and weak. It was now time to live out of a hotel. Yet, I was told that the area is not safe enough to go out at night alone. Mike just told me that he was leaving for Charlotte in three days. I have no idea where the hotel is, in relationship to the hospital. I have a car but no directions. Evan can't walk. I can't carry him "the right way." We are starting on new medicines, and I won't know what to do, if I am alone with him in the hotel and he has a bad reaction. I am falling apart. If only I could just get our medicines and go home with Mike! I would give anything. I feel inept. I feel helpless. I feel so alone. I feel so sick to my stomach. I am so tired. I don't think I can DO this, Pat. "Helen, any mom would feel this way. Talk to other moms in the waiting room. That will be more helpful than anything I can say. But I can think of a few suggestions: before leaving the hospital each day be sure you have a telephone number in your pocket, if you need someone at St. Jude, should Evan have a bad reaction. Take food from the hospital with you when you leave, so that you don't have to worry about ordering food. You are going to do a good job, because you always do."

Pat was comforting and supportive. But she was firm. She even offered to come to Memphis. I love her! I fantasized for a moment about the comfort she would offer me and Evan, but with three children of her own, I knew that it was impossible. By the end of our conversation, I was somewhat pieced back together. I couldn't go in to see Evan like this, so I walked back to the bathroom to splash cold water on my face. My eyes told the whole story. (*Dear Lord, I am at the bottom again. I am weary and*

have no strength. How can I manage one more day? I put my
complete trust and soul in your hands. Help Evan face this treat-
ment, and give him strength.)

(*Quit worrying about yourself, Helen. You WILL do this! You*
can do ANYTHING it takes! Evan needs you. Your Mother would
be strong. Grit your teeth! Count your blessing!) I can hear Pop's
voice. (*Helen, the sun will come up tomorrow. Everything will*
turn out OK. You'll see!) So, again, I faced a new day.

I arrived back in Evan's room in time for him to be wheeled down
to the medicine room for his first treatment of VM26 and ARA-C.
The medicine room was the size of the school cafeteria. There were
beds lined up around the perimeter of the room and about 20 large
blue leather reclining chairs in the center. One rather small TV was
mounted on the wall and turned on, with no volume. Each bed and
chair was equipped with an IV pole.

When we arrived, we had the good fortune of meeting Betty. She
was middle-aged, with a grin from ear to ear. She had short blond
hair and carried herself like she was in charge. She casually asked
Evan to pick a chair or a bed. To instill just a little confidence, she
informed Evan that she had been with St. Jude, since it opened
in the '60s, that she had started millions of IVs on thousands of
children, and that she would do her very best with him. (What she
was saying, without scaring Evan, was that usually she was able
to put the needle in the vein on the first try, and that she would
try her best to do that with Evan.) I immediately liked her. Her
conversation was totally directed toward Evan, which made him
comfortable. She explained to him that she would always let him
know ahead of time what she was going to do (my kind of woman)
and Evan took an immediate liking to her, as well. Evan chose his
bed. When it was time for the needle, I covered his eyes but, at the
same time, he seemed to want to peek. Betty got the IV started
with ease. We each checked to be sure that Evan was getting the
medicine prescribed for him: "Kaufman, Evan #9291" appeared
on the medicine bags, and then she hung them. I watched each
drip for the next hour.

The mother next to us asked me if Evan would like a blanket. I told her "yes, good idea." I waited for the nurse to return to ask for the blanket, but our mom-neighbor returned first. She pointed to a far-away closet and said it contained just about anything we would need. She also explained that she was the veteran mother of the group. "No need to bother the nurses. I can answer for anything you need." Her teenage daughter was asleep next to her, and she took the opportunity to tell her story.

She had been coming to St. Jude for 7-1/2 years! I thought I had heard wrong. She recounted that when her daughter was first diagnosed, she endured three long years of daily treatment. She attained remission but after she finished the medicine on her protocol, only one month passed before she relapsed. I tried to imagine starting a new three-year treatment again. The second round, she was on a different protocol, same drugs, but dispensed in a different combination. This mother was hopeful that, at the end of that three-year period, her daughter would finally be totally off drugs. Unfortunately, after a few months on the second protocol, the cancer was back. Now they were on Evan's Total XI (her third protocol) that added a new drug, VM-26. Mom was in good spirits and had a good and positive attitude. She said that, all of their hope was riding on VM26, the new wonder drug. She just KNEW that at the end of the next three years, she would finally come off therapy altogether. She also reminded me that, if nothing else, even if she were on therapy, had no hair, and was sick most of the time, even if they had to commute back and forth from their home to Memphis, they were buying research time. There was always hope that the newspaper headlines would describe "the break-through cure" in time for her daughter. She lived in a very small town some 35 miles away, and for the 7-1/2 years minus two months, she had made the round trip once a week. This conversation was very timely for me. Was I not crying a few hours prior to this, because I was worried about doing this alone? Was I not worried about Evan being an outpatient? This mother had been doing it by herself, and her story was certainly far graver than mine! It was time to rally! Time to be strong! The lesson was not lost on me: "No matter how bad your situation is, it is far more fruitful to spend your effort and energy improving your lot, than complaining about it! There is no time for self-pity now or ever." (Sadly, my new friend's daughter did not make it.)

St. Jude must have had an organizational-wizard plan the lay-out and the synchronized medical-procedures schedule. The place runs with high efficiency and with the goal that each child should be treated with as little discomfort as possible. For example, after an IV is started, blood can easily be taken out through the IV by "pulling back the needle." So on IV days, Evan is spared the finger prick to get a blood sample. Instead, after the IV is started, the "blood room lady" comes to him to obtain the sample. In most hospitals, blood would be obtained in one department and then another needle stick to start the IV in another department. The idea here: put the child through as few sticks as possible. The child comes first! St. Jude Hospital is all about sensitive and caring human beings who have great understanding and compassion for children.

On our first medicine-room-day, I couldn't help but notice that there were some children receiving their IVs through a contraption hanging from their chests. I wondered if they had a disease unlike Evan's, or if this could be a contraption that Evan would need to have. My new neighbor-friend-mom explained to me, in front of Evan, that those were called "Port-A-Caths" and they were surgically implanted into a vein in the chest. The purpose of them was to give permanent access to the vein, eliminating the need to search for a good vein every time an IV was needed. What we didn't realize at the time was that, while Evan's veins were good, after a while, the veins often collapse from constant use. Additionally, not all nurses were like Betty, and some IVs would need to be started several times, due to a nurse's shaking hand or inexperience. (Evan would come to identify Betty as his best friend.) Some IVs would need to be started in the foot or the hand, to obtain a fresh vein. Port-A-Caths eliminated all those problems, that is, if you didn't mind having the surgery and subsequent permanent tube hanging outside the body. Evan immediately informed us that this was something he did not want to have, if he could possibly avoid it.

Evan's first day of medicine got off to a good start. When Betty made the rounds, she explained that the first bag was anti-nausea medicine, in hopes that it might help a queasy stomach, in light of today's medicines. Next, it would be time for the VM26, the drug that kids could sometimes tolerate. After the VM-26 dripped in over a period of four to five hours, he would then get ARA-C. Because it was our first time, Betty alerted us that ARA-C was the

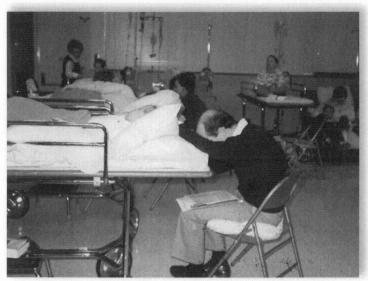

Medicine room treatements were long and exhausting.

one drug that caused all children to become very nauseated, that is, if VM-26 hadn't done the trick already. At the 10-minute mark from the very first drop that entered the vein, the children would begin to get sick and throw up every ten minutes for the next four hours. You could set your watch by it.

Betty took the time to go over my eight-week schedule with me. She marked which days would be rough. She marked the days that would take twelve hours and the ones that would take one hour. She reviewed, once more, which medicines were by mouth, which were by shot in the thigh or arm, which medicines were by "IV-push" in the top of the hand, and which were by IV drip all day long. She shared with me which physicians were noted to be excellent with kids, which hotels the children liked the best, which staff members Evan would enjoy knowing. She was knowledgeable and capable. She was honest. She was wonderfully helpful and supportive. Evan liked her immediately and later would boast that "Betty was a person who could start an IV with her eyes shut." I always said a quick prayer before entering the medicine room that Betty would be there. (Toward the end of Evan's treatment, Betty, herself, was diagnosed with cancer. She continued her devoted work with dying children until she could no longer work in the face of her own cancer.)

Evan intuitively recognized the importance of keeping his hand totally still, while the IV needle was inserted. He wanted to take no chance that it could be bumped in such a way that the needle could slip out, (we tried to convince him that it would be impossible), and then he would need to be restuck all over again. Therefore, when the needle went in, and the tape was applied, he would prop his arm on a pillow and freeze his arm there for the entire six hours. No one dared to get near the arm, bump it, or even breathe on it.

My heart went out to the mother, two beds down, whose active 2-year-old daughter had the same pole and bags and IV line hookup as Evan. The difference, of course, was that the little 2-year-old did not understand the importance of not jerking the arm, nor did the child understand why she couldn't jump out of the bed and run and play. The mom had her hands full and worked feverishly at reading book after book and using toy after toy to keep her child's attention diverted from that IV line (that the child occasionally pulled out.) She had no husband there to help her. (*God! why was I such a disgusting wimp?*)

Our first VM26/ARA-C day turned out to be as rigorous and tire-some and stressful as Betty had predicted. By the time the last drop had found its way through the tubing and into Evan's vein, Evan was retching every ten minutes, so much so that his little body would quiver all over, while Mike and I held his head. He was exhausted. At the conclusion of this long day, we would be going to a hotel room to rest, rather than back up to the seventh floor, and that would be a new experience. Mike was right; the hotel room was a welcome relief from the sterile hospital arrange-ment, and the required drill for entry. When we arrived at the ho-tel, we sat with Evan on the bed with a wet washcloth and emesis basin, until Evan finally stopped throwing up for the night. When he fell asleep, I took my first long, hot shower. It was a wonderful relief and I fell asleep feeling like I could do this. Evan could do this. We're going for the cure.

Evan woke up very early the next morning. He wanted to have or-ange juice and a toasted cheese sandwich of all things. (I learned that the body craves that which is depleted. Evan, who normally hated orange juice, would always crave it after the VM-26/ARA-C day, probably needing to replace the potassium lost by hours of vomiting). He could barely wait until Mike got dressed and ran out to scavenge for the required menu items. The orange juice was obtained easily at the local McDonald's up the road, but the toast-ed cheese sandwich was impossible to find at 6 a.m. When Mike returned with only the orange juice, Evan literally gulped it down and asked for another. By this time, I had Evan dressed for the day, and we jumped into the car, headed for the hospital for our next treatment, stopping on the way for more OJ. This day's treat-ment would be easier. The cafeteria ladies just smiled and pro-vided the cheese sandwiches, specially made for Evan. "Toasted cheese sandwiches" did not appear on their breakfast menu.

The entire rest of the day, Evan consumed one toasted cheese sandwich after another. (We would later learn that the Predni-sone, a steroid, would play havoc with his appetite.) The follow-ing morning, Evan again awoke with an intense craving. I volunteered this time to go out and find a place serving the toasted cheese sandwiches. Mike agreed that it would be a good idea, and smiled at me with a knowing smile, that some way and somehow, I would return with the bounty. So typical of our personalities: Mike would go to a restaurant and ask if they had toasted cheese sandwiches, and when the answer came back no, he would thank them very much and leave; whereas; when given the "no" answer, I would kindly ask to speak to the manager to plead our case. Usually, folks in the Memphis area held great compassion and empathy for the St. Jude families, and, usually, everyone wanted to help, if at all possible. This particular time, it was just a little more difficult, due to the 6 a.m. hour. After three unsuccessful stops, it dawned on me how to achieve my goal. I stopped at a 24-hour grocery store, bought some cheese and a loaf of bread and took it to the restaurant attached to our La Quinta Hotel. I made up the sandwich in the booth and tipped the man at the counter to run my sandwich under the broiler. So proud was I to be able to put a smile on Evan's face.

It became apparent why St. Jude sent so many families to this particular hotel. La Quinta was one of the popular hotels. (Moms in the medicine room told me that they would always be happy, if their "green card" assigned them to La Quinta.) The folks there were well-versed to the special needs of the kids, especially those with "steroid appetites," and they were always very accommodating. Evan gulped his sandwich down in a matter of minutes and said, "I really need another one." Mike and I looked at each other. We couldn't believe our ears! (This was the same child who needed dietary therapy for no appetite.) We gladly got out the bread and cheese, ran it down to the kitchen and produced his entrée within minutes. Always thinking about efficiency, I started to make two and three sandwiches at a time. In fact, I created an assembly line: Mike would slice the entire brick of cheese. I would lay out the slices of bread, brushing each with a scant of mayonnaise. Finally, when the restaurant got busy, I was invited to walk in to the back kitchen and help myself to the industrial oven with broiler. (Can you imagine the liability here?) On certain days,

Evan would easily consume a loaf of bread and a pound of cheese, for lunch alone. Welcome to the world of Prednisone.

I noted that my spirits were up, my energy level was up, and I was beginning to feel better. Could this have anything to do with hot showers? I was sure this was because I was active, as opposed to sitting by in such a passive way (not that this was any great contribution). I believe that, when one is relegated to a chair, nothing to do but wait, and left in a passive position, one begins to feel helpless and hopeless. Now I felt like a problem solver and felt like I was helping Evan.

Also, it was good for me to get into the car and find my way around. I quickly became familiar with Poplar and North Lauderdale Streets. I knew my way to the hospital, the grocery store, the drug store (and the hotel). What more would anyone need? I remember distinctly: I was standing in line at the grocery store one night and thought about how all of the people in line with me were living normal lives. Could I remember what that was like? They must be wondering what to have for dinner. They might be thinking about their weekend plans. Life goes on.

We propped Evan up in bed in order to watch television. He also seemed to have a better attitude in these new surroundings and with a new appetite. I think he reflected my new and improved attitude, which after all, was the only significant gift I could provide for him now. I even found a laundromat. The lady there would take all our dirty clothes and wash, dry and fold everything on the same day.

Every day we traveled to St. Jude for our daily cocktail. Mike would carry Evan, and I would drive, in order to practice the route. We were learning the outpatient drill: check in at the front desk, go to weight & measure, walk over to the blood room, take a seat in the waiting room and wait for our name to be called. Today was a shot in the thigh. Evan tolerated Asparaginase well. It was a sunny, crisp fall day, and we suggested that, after Evan had this quick shot, we could drive around (Mike could hold Evan on his lap, so Evan's back would not be jarred by any bumps) and perhaps cross the bridge over the Mississippi River. Evan liked the idea, but by the time he had his shot and a few toasted cheese sandwiches at the cafeteria, he was too exhausted to do anything but return home (to the hotel) and collapse. Pain is tiring.

We drove back to the motel room, carefully placing Evan in his "propped-up" position. Our dinner choices were: Wendy's, Arby's, the Two Sisters Chicken, IHOP, and, last but not least, McDonald's. We were beginning to function on schedule. While Mike went out to "bring home the bacon," my job was to fill a pan with hot water and give Evan a sponge bath in the bed, and get out his special toothbrush from St. Jude (a long stick with a square sponge-like tip, that we were instructed to use to prevent possible gum bleeds.) We were also given a special salve to put on sores that might appear in his mouth, due to the medicine.

My job description also consisted of monitoring the daily pills from our special one-week pill-dispenser box (a perfect job for an obsessive-compulsive person such as I) that was filled by the pharmacy at St. Jude. I certainly took the responsibility seriously, to be sure that each pill was given according to the schedule in my notebook. (In three years, Evan never missed a pill!)

I carried with me a stack of reading material for the waiting room, so that I could educate myself about leukemia, its treatment, each drug's side effects, and coping skills of family members. I was also interested in reading about how each of the drugs was discovered. I remember turning to the chapter on VM26, the so-called wonder drug. This drug was considered by the FDA to be experimental (that is, it wasn't approved yet) and, therefore, had to be administered at the institution that was given the limited permission to dispense it. Much to my surprise, I learned that it was not manufactured in a pharmaceutical laboratory and developed by a host of Ph.D. scientists. Rather it was a drug whose source was a common plant called the May Apple Plant, and found in the woods of the eastern half of the United States. This is a plant that had been used by the Indians and early settlers as a medicine plant. (*Are there other miracle plants growing under our very noses that might be the cure for this disease?*) The first year that children received this drug experimentally was in 1975, a scant three years before Evan was born. They were children whose diseases were terminal, whose diseases had not responded to any other drug or any conventional treatment. So these high-risk children were guinea pigs for the first study of this drug. (*Thank you, Lord, for all those who have gone this road before us. Thank you that Evan has something treatable. Keep him safe.*)

After our dinner and the sponge bath, we began to read about tomorrow's new drug, high-dose Methotrexate. It would be administered by IV, but instead of an eight-hour day, the drip would only take two hours. Because of the shortened medicine room time, we would have an appointment with Dr. Murphy first. I checked to see what time Betty would be leaving this day, in hopes that she would still be there, when we arrived in the medicine room. I read about Methotrexate: "highly active cells such as leukemia cells would be severely affected and destroyed quickly by this drug. However, the new growing normal cells needed to be protected at the same time. Normal cells would not be destroyed as quickly, so at the eleventh hour (the time when the leukemia cells were gone and normal cells would reproduce), the patient would be given a "rescue substance" called Leucovorin. This drug would stop the "find and destroy" mission and "rescue" the normal cells. Leucovorin was to be administered twelve, twenty-four and again at thirty-six hours post Methotrexate. We were allowed to leave the hospital after the drip and loaded with three plus doses of Leucovorin. (The extra doses were given to us, "in case" anything happened during the administration.) We thought it might be difficult to keep Evan up until 11:00 p.m. but an even greater hurdle awaited us: convincing him to swallow this nasty-smelling, brownish-purple creamy liquid substance.

We tried everything! First, we supplied him with cranberry juice, to chase the medicine down, but after tasting cranberry juice, he determined that it wasn't the right taste. He thought he could swallow, if it were apple juice, so we all got in to the car and found the apple juice at our favorite all-night grocery store. When that didn't work, Evan thought maybe an Arby's milk shake would take the taste away. We realized that we were approaching the deadline, and we pictured those normal cells that "needed rescue." Borrowing from the company that makes Dimetapp (the purple liquid we all have used for ear infections of young kids), we decided to disguise the medicine by mixing it in with the grape juice. It was a disaster. "Therapeutic" was important, but rescuing those cells took precedence. I, unhappily, admit that we tried the frontal assault, where I held Evan's arms down and his mouth squeezed open, while Mike squirted the medicine into his mouth. Mike and I both became polka-dotted with coughed-up purple medicine, after it came roaring back up the esophagus. We had long since left the hotel room and were in an all-night fast food place. The last attempt involved coca-cola, but instead of having just our clothes splattered, the purple puke now decorated the entire booth.

It was now 2:00 a.m. and we were panicked, not only because his good cells were not receiving the Leucovorin, but because he had become dehydrated. As much as we hated to disturb Murphy, it was time to get help. She instructed us to drive over to the clinic, as soon as possible. Murphy called ahead, so that a nurse would be waiting for us. The poor nurse on call must have become nervous for some reason, because when she tried to start the IV, her hand started to shake, as she inserted the needle. She missed the vein, and she pulled out and started again. After two misses, she excused herself and disappeared for five minutes. Mike and I discussed whether Mike should pick up the needle and try, in her absence. My vote was not to risk a repeat of the trouble we had gotten into back in Charlotte, when we took matters into our own hands and devised our own treatment plan. However, I agreed that she only had one more chance, before we would insist on another nurse. She returned looking a little calmer and we had good luck on the third try (*Betty, where are you?*). The Leucovorin was finally dripping into the vein. We slept, sitting up in the chairs next to Evan's bed between 3:00 a.m. and 7:00 a.m. By morning, Dr. Murphy stopped by to be sure we were all right. She mentioned that, for the next high-dose Methotrexate/Leucovorin day, be sure to ask for it in the form of a pill. Mike and I just looked at each other with a sigh. Learn by trial and error. We were already in place to receive the next day's appetizer.

The next evening, we gladly returned to the hotel, but I couldn't sleep. Had I been up on my reading, or had I thought to ask as we left the hospital, I would have discovered that Leucovorin came in liquid and pill form! (*There is no room for mistakes here! Helen, this is the last time I will allow myself ANY room for error.*) My reading was interrupted by a phone call from my Mother. Sweet Pat had worried about my going it alone with Evan and called Nana to suggest that she was needed in Memphis more than Charlotte once Mike returned home. If we could work out care for Jenny, maybe Nana and Pop could fly to Memphis? Many plans were discussed such as: Pop would stay in Charlotte, while Nana traveled to Memphis, or vice versa. But in the end, Mike's Mother agreed to fly from New Jersey to keep the Charlotte home fires burning, while my parents would fly to Memphis to help with Evan. As I verbalized: "No, I can't ask that of you," I was rejoicing inside at the thought. We could move from our single room to adjoining rooms. Nana was famous for entertaining Evan with our well-rehearsed mind games and reading to him. Pop would crown himself "the driver," familiarizing himself with the location of everything. His smiley disposition and his "get-up-on-top-of-the-mountain" philosophy would become an instant pick-up. (He would become somewhat well-known at St. Jude, as he struck up conversation with doctors and janitors alike.) Nana and Pop, Evan and I would all be together and support each other. (*Oh God! Thank you for my wonderful parents.*) Nana then went on to say that I should make a list of the clothes Evan and I would need, plus a list of toys that she could bring on the plane. Perhaps I should call the office to ascertain if Nana and Pop needed to bring anything from there. Nana mentioned that someone from the office called to say that their paychecks were overdue, Whoops! I guess she needed to bring the office check book, hmmm. Mike would return to Charlotte in a few days and be able to spend a little time with Jenny and relieve his partner from the load he was carrying. This had become a group effort.

Countdown: three days until Mike has to leave ...

Our life had settled down to a manageable pace/schedule. (*Did I just say that: manageable?*) We had three precious days left until Mike would change position with Nana and Pop. We were in a routine. We arose early, drove over to the hospital, signed in at the front desk, headed straight to the cafeteria, where Evan ordered to his heart's content. Mike and I would get a wake-up coffee. Then the drill: weight and measure room (always a piece of cake) and on to the blood room, which Evan hated, but it was just a quick finger stick (unless it was an IV day, and they could obtain the blood from the IV drip). One quick prick and we could leave for the waiting room. Usually there was something fun going on there: other kids playing, a game room off to the side, where Evan could play Pac-man until his back needed a rest, or simply sitting on the big leather brightly covered couches, where either Mike or I were good for a couple rounds of "I'm going to grandma's house," or "I'm thinking of a person who lives in Charlotte." Evan was fully aware/prepared as to whether it was going to be a bad day or a good day. Bad days were defined by a long, laborious treatment in the medicine room and lots of vomiting. Good days were a quick shot in the thigh, perhaps a few pills and maybe a quick 2-hour IV drip. A VERY bad day would include a spinal tap or bone marrow. I always talked to Evan the night before about the next day's treatment, and we could always predict his anxiety level the next morning accordingly.

This particular night, we were driving back to our home (as in La Quinta). Evan was clutching on to his emesis basin. I was driving very slowly, partly because I was a bit unsure of the way in the dark, and partly because one bump would cause Evan to wince. The inside of the car was quiet. Evan just did not feel like conversing. When he felt nauseated, he preferred being quiet and peaceful. This particular night we took a circuitous route, because I turned when I should not have. We peered from the car window. I looked up and there stood Baptist Memorial Hospital, one of the largest hospitals in the country at the time. Similar to the signage of St. Jude, letters were perched at the top. The bright, lit up letters atop the building were: "B. M. H." But the light was out for the H and therefore the sign read: "B. M." What would possess me to make the following comment, I do not know. But we needed a break in our solemn demeanors and glum faces. So, I looked up and pointed to the sign. "Look Evan, they actually have BM all lit up on the top of that building!" (This is a kindergarten child who is not reading yet, exactly.) I started to giggle just like a two-year-old who was going through toilet training and who is intrigued by "bathroom talk" (as Nana would call it). Evan immediately howled over this and we were all (this includes two adults) giggly about these "lit up" letters. (*Have I reduced myself to THIS? Normally, I would have gingerly reprimanded Evan for "such juvenile talk," but here I was, promoting such a thing! I think this qualifies as a "10" on the desperation scale.*) I have now set the stage for a recurring joke every day we pass the hospital. Nana will NOT be impressed.

Countdown: Two days until Mike has to leave ...

Mike got to experience, first hand, "Friday at St. Jude." (Actually, we had been there the three previous Fridays, but were probably hiding out in radiology or up on the seventh floor.) This Friday was our first experience sitting in the waiting room, when a large cart broke through the double doors, and the children all gathered around, at least the ones who were able to walk. We learned that companies throughout the United States donated toys to the children of St. Jude at Christmas time. In fact, the donations were so plentiful that a system needed to be in place to handle the volume and to make distributions weekly, throughout the year, instead of just in December. Some toys were suited more for boys, like cars and trucks, while others were girl toys, mostly dolls. Many toys were for either sex, like books and stuffed animals, so that the situation never occurred that a child was left out. The cart made the rounds through the waiting room and through the clinics. The two floors above (where the children were very sick) could not be included because of the germs. The medicine room which needed some pepping up was also off-limits because the children there were mostly asleep or vomiting, and they could not be bothered with mundane toys. Most of the kids could be bought off with these gifts, raising the excitement a few levels higher than usual.

On this particular day, Evan enjoyed a double-whammy good day. When I checked our #9291 post office box, I received a notice that a package was waiting for Evan. In some instances, just receiving mail was excitement in itself. Perhaps, the excitement of receiving a box was a hold-over from camp days. Today, the box was a most loving gesture from another mom in my Sunday school class. Betsy Buter had three sons of her own, and the fall months were the time when all of Santa's helpers (Moms) were out scouring stores for the hottest toys out that year. The manufacturers of Cabbage Patch Dolls and Transformers were clever to send only small shipments, an appetizing promise that another shipment would come, but the store would not know when. The non-stop promotion of toys on TV assured the manufacturer that these would be the have-to-have toys under the Christmas tree. This, of course, had the intended effect on the consumer, that is, that people would rush to Toys "R" Us, stand in line, and grab these hot toys off the shelves, but only one per customer. In fifteen minutes, the shelves were bare. Betsy pictured our inability to obtain one of these treasures and also pictured Evan at the hospital, unable to move very well. She realized that the Transformer toy was the perfect gift for an immobile patient. She dipped in to her own Christmas loot, presents saved up for her own boys and sent Evan this very toy that he coveted. (How do you ever thank a person with such a generous spirit and beautiful heart? Note to self: Add Betsy to my angel list.)

Little James offered his services to Evan. He watched from a few couches over as Evan opened this prized possession and immediately ran over to Evan and offered to show Evan how this super hero could be twisted around to turn into, or "transform," into a bat mobile. It turned out that James had only seen the same TV advertisement and wasn't any more familiar with the correct turns than Evan but they both got at least an hour of giggles and fun, trying to accomplish the goal, as seen on the cardboard plaque to which it was mounted. Carol, James' mother, was thrilled with this interlude, and we were fortunate to have an opportunity to meet her. Carol was articulate and friendly and immediately shared with us that she and James were planning to attend a Halloween party being held at the United Methodist Church on Poplar Avenue which was close to the hospital. Mike and I could not imagine that Evan had enough energy for this, but Halloween carried with it an immediate excitement that Evan did not want to miss, particularly with his new friend, James. He also would have his human wheel chair with him (Mike). Imagine my gratefulness to the organizers of this church who issued a blanket invitation to any child at St. Jude, of any religion, who wanted to experience a Halloween party. Welcome to the outstretched arms of Memphis citizens.

James was from the Midwest. Carol was a successful bank vice-president and her husband, Steve, (who was not there) was a business executive. During the party, Carol recounted his story. James got very sick very quickly. His abdomen swelled with enlargement to his liver and spleen. He became acutely anemic. Burkitts lymphoma was diagnosed within days. (I decided to read about Burkitts lymphoma out of my interest in James.) It was very rare and somehow related to the Epstein Barr virus found in Africa. Treatment was urgent because patients who have this diagnosis go downhill quickly and were often dead within a week of diagnosis. Using her skills as a bank executive, Carol swung in to action, arranging a conference call between her, Steve, the oncologist at Ohio State and Dr. Murphy. She and Steve were willing to go anywhere for treatment. Her assertiveness in securing the best for James was so sincere that when she called Dr. Murphy again, but this time at home late at night, Dr. Murphy could only admire her determination. After James' initial chemotherapy and remission, it was Carol whose intuition suspected James' relapse. He began having headaches, which he had never experienced before, and that were not a typical symptom of relapse. It was Carol who reported her intuition to Dr. Murphy, who subsequently agreed with her. Having done all that St. Jude had to offer, Carol organized a trip to France within 36 hours of the relapse. Carol was told that James needed an autologous bone marrow transplant (instead of using another person as a donor, the actual bone marrow is removed from the patient, "cleaned up" and returned to the same patient.) As a precaution that the bone marrow transplant might fail, Carol was madly researching where they would go for the next step. Carol was fighting the fight right up until the day James died.

Countdown: One day until Mike has to leave ...

The day after our late-night-Halloween-party, we were scheduled for a bad chemo day. With any luck, Betty would be in the medicine room upon our arrival and would start Evan's IV on the first try. We all checked and rechecked the bag: "Kaufman, Evan #9291." Evan's IV needle was taped down to his arm that rested on the pillow and remained immobile during the next six hours. Evan's emesis basin was stationed nearby. Self-designated "the keeper of Evan's psyche," and again I cannot imagine why this idea popped in to my brain, I told Evan that on this day, at this time, I wanted to try "something new" with him. With total faith in my pronouncements, Evan looked at me and, without speaking, inquired as to what I had in mind. I explained that I understood how hard it was to lie there, uncomfortable and immobile. It dawned on me that we really didn't need to stay in the medicine room and that I wanted to take him somewhere fun! Hmmm. All you have to do is shut your eyes and imagine ...and we could take a trip. And so, Evan and I were off to the beach. We packed our suitcases remembering to bring the important things: the flippers and the goggles for the pool, the inner tube, his blankey, the transformers and some suntan lotion. We spent a lot of time on the landscape: the hot sun, the hot sand and how our feet burned until we reached the ocean's edge, the sea gulls and how they swooped down to get their dinner. The sun screen felt oily. Can you feel it all over your legs?

We could hear the children laughing and one mother shouting to the kids to come in for lunch. We wanted to collect shells but we could only find a precious few. What we DID find was a jelly fish that had been washed up to shore and had an assortment of flies on it. There were a number of beach chairs, some filled with people reading, and some empty, whose occupants had gone for a beach walk. Let's count how many there were. A family, just like ours, had pitched a net and was slapping the ball back and forth. Can you hear that? What time of day was it? Well, let's see here, the tide is starting to come in, and a lot of people have gone in for dinner. Would you say 5-6:00 p.m.? By the way, what are we having for dinner tonight? Can you smell the grill that Dad turned on? Once the burgers hit the grill, the aroma announced the menu to everyone. After we decided to go back up to the house, we loaded ourselves down with all the paraphernalia that we excitedly dragged down in the morning. Let's see if we can name all the things that we have to lug back: 2 yellow buckets, 3 red digging shovels, 2 empty diet Coke cans, a half used tube of sun screen, 2 soggy towels and a beach chair. Can you feel the sweat running down your cheek as you try to drag this array of stuff up to the house? It is sooo heavy and the sun is still so hot. Can you feel it beating down?

With his eyes shut, we imagined countless destinations. We traveled to Disney World, back to Charlotte Latin School, returned to all the familiarities of home. One of the destinations was Heaven (painful for me), but it was definitely a good vehicle to discuss a difficult subject. The sky was the limit and part of Evan's preparation included what trip we would take in the medicine room. This "by-chance-idea" spread in the medicine room and other children were passing the time in their own time-travel-capsule. (*The next time I will be in this medicine room, Mike won't be here. Could I handle this? It is wonderful that Nana and Pop will be here. But they will look to me for the answers. I was getting scared. You can DO this, Helen! Lord, please guide me and help me and, above all, keep Evan safe!*)

Evan was now on a schedule of morning treatments each day. I was able to check the notebook and explain the next day's course. He was now on a complete and steady diet of toasted cheese sandwiches. The people in the kitchen adjacent to the hotel remained welcoming to me day and night. Making the sandwiches in the room, Mike and I took turns running to the kitchen for the "melt-down." We were pleased that Evan was eating, and neither Mike nor I gave any thought to the problems of this very limited diet.

The night before leaving, Mike explained to Evan why he had to return to Charlotte and how difficult it would be for him to leave. Mike wrote out a list of instructions for me that I carefully and seriously reviewed often.

√ Watch for any sores that appear in Evan's mouth.
√ Don't forget to check the pillbox frequently for fear of missing a dose.
√ Check the time for each pill.
√ Every day, when his blood is taken, write down the differentials so that it is available when you check in with me.
√ If anyone in the waiting room has a cough or more than one sneeze, cover up his face and leave as soon as possible.
√ Check Betty's schedule in the medicine room, so that you can time Evan's treatments with her being there to start the IV
√ Be sure to check the IV bags for Evan's name.
√ Don't leave the hospital for at least an hour after the last drip to be sure he has no reaction.
√ Carry St. Jude phone numbers or Dr. Murphy's home number in your pocket at all times should you need her (or somebody) in the middle of the night, or at any point during the day.

√ Keep feeling Evan for any fever and go immediately to the hospital, if he begins to feel warm.

√ Don't let him eat from anything but a paper plate or drink from anything but a paper cup.

√ Wash your hands thoroughly before touching his food.

√ Don't let anyone in the kitchen touch his food, only the plate, and ask them to please be careful with this.

√ Be sure the motel changes his bed linens every day and, especially we need a clean pillowcase.

√ Don't let his face touch the blanket on the bed.

√ Keep Evan's hands as clean as possible.

√ On Leukovorin days, be sure to ask for it in the pill form.

√ DO NOT catch a cold yourself, and so the list went on.

Then I realized ... I was in charge.

CHAPTER IV

CHANGING OF THE GUARD

I had carefully planned the "switch day." The most important factor was, of course, Evan's chemo for the day. Clearly, the Vincristine day would be ideal. We would arrive at the hospital on time, move through weight and measure, the blood room, and back to the medicine room for the quick shot, and of course, our daily Prednisone pill. I planned that we would have time for a quick nap, while Mike did last minute packing. Mike's flight took off just one hour before Nana and Pop were to arrive. I would envision their two planes passing each other miles above Tennessee. In addition, I purposely planned the switch to coincide with the return of Dr. Daughdrill's car. I felt it was such a help to have our own transportation, that I reserved a car through Avis. With Nana and Pop in the rental car and Evan and I in Dr. Daughdrill's car, we drove caravan style directly to Rhodes College where we dropped off the car. The four of us would arrive together at our little abode. The hotel staff had transferred our few belongings from our single room to two adjacent rooms with a connecting door. Funny how a sparse two rooms in an ordinary hotel could bring such a sense of marvel that we had such a spacious and wonderful suite. Evan watched with a smile, as Nana unpacked some beloved toys that he had not played with since leaving Charlotte. She sacrificed precious space in her suitcase that could have been used for extra clothes, but instead, the space was sacrificed for Legos. Evan responded to the two smiling faces favorably, anxiously telling them about his new hospital, and how he would be able to brief them about our daily routine.

There was only one intervening day before Evan was due to receive his VM-26. It was an eye-opener for them to actually see the hospital and how it differed from the pictures they had imagined through phone descriptions. Pop's new job as chauffeur came naturally to him, and he gladly dropped Nana, Evan, and me off at the statue in the front of the building so we had only a short distance to walk. Mike and I had passed the statue so many times in a hurry. It was Pop and Nana who now took the few extra minutes to read the inscription and inquire about the meaning.

The statue was of St. Jude Thaddeus, patron saint of hopeless causes. It was to St. Jude that Danny Thomas prayed one rainy night more than 70 years ago. He was a struggling young entertainer who wandered into a Detroit church and was so moved during the Mass, that he placed his last $7 in the collection box. The next day, he was offered a small acting part that would pay 10 times the amount he had given to the church. He believed that his break was due to his prayer that night: "Help me find my way in life, and I will build you a shrine." Thomas would always say that he prayed to St. Jude, because he looked upon himself as a hopeless cause.

Eventually, his career took off, and soon he moved his family to Chicago to pursue career offers in film and television, and he became an internationally known entertainer. As he climbed the ladder of a successful career, he always remembered his pledge to build a shrine to St. Jude. In the early 1950s, he began to think of how that would take shape; probably, in his new home of Hollywood. Fortunately, the pastor who confirmed Thomas as a young boy in Toledo, was now living in Chicago. The pastor was Cardinal Samuel Stritch, Thomas' lifelong spiritual mentor/guide. Cardinal Stritch advised: "Don't build a shrine; build something useful. Build something for children." Stritch started as a parish priest in Memphis and was well aware of how poor the population was in Memphis and their need for improved medical facilities. He encouraged Thomas to choose Memphis. By serendipity, Danny also met with Mr. Abe Plough (founder of Plough Industries, maker of St. Joseph's aspirin and later to become Schering-Plough) who immediately supported the idea of a children's hospital.

In 1955, Danny Thomas and a group of Memphis businessmen, who had agreed to help support his dream, seized on the idea of creating a unique research hospital devoted to catastrophic diseases in children. That it would be more than a treatment facility and rather, emphasize research, was a novel idea. Thomas convinced Donald Pinkel to move to Memphis and become the founding director of the hospital as well as convincing Dr. Lemuel Diggs, a hematologist, to come to St. Jude. (Dr. Diggs is credited with creating the first blood bank in the south.) Millions of dollars would need to be raised, and Thomas began to do benefit shows that brought scores of major entertainment stars to Memphis. Raising the money to build the hospital was just the beginning. Thomas was faced with the daunting task of funding the operation. He turned to his friends in the entertainment world, many of whom were sons of emigrants, as he was. He formed an organization called ALSAC (American Lebanese Syrian Associated Charities) whose sole purpose was raising funds for the support of St. Jude Children's Research Hospital. Unbelievably, since that time, ALSAC has assumed full responsibility for all the hospital's fundraising efforts, raising hundreds of millions annually.

A self-made man himself, Pop loved the story. And so it was that he became a St. Jude volunteer in his own small way, becoming a St. Jude supporter in Charlotte and spreading enthusiasm to family back in Akron. In the waiting room, Pop became friends with numbers of parents and would pass the time meeting and conversing with hospital employees. He wanted to learn as much as possible about the various families there and would compare, and be moved by, each parent's story. He would often round up friends for Evan and encourage Evan to interact more. However, Evan would most often use the waiting room time to quietly gather his thoughts and feelings. I felt at the time that Evan was psychologically preparing himself for whatever treatment he was dreading for that day. In addition, he seemed to distance himself somewhat, as if remaining aloof might keep him from joining the ranks of cancer patients. In the beginning, he did not look like most of the children there, and he wanted it to stay that way.

Pop loved meeting Ricky, better known as "button man." This young man looked more like a football player than a nurse. He most often wore Mickey Mouse ears and always wore his jacket that had so many buttons that there simply wasn't space for one more. Each button had been a gift of one of the patients at St. Jude, and the purpose of each button was to bring a smile. Pop found out that one of Ricky's jobs was to transport patients from one part of the hospital to another. But en route, he would take it upon himself to lighten up the day of his little patient, tell a joke or, at least, lend some bit of wisdom to give courage to each child. He always learned the name and thereafter could wave a personal hello to his new friend. Ricky is the kind of person that Pop admired. Ricky was always thinking about the kids, not about himself. He made everyone around him smile. (*Thank you, God, for people like Ricky and like Pop. They bring so much sunshine to people.*)

Back at La Quinta, we settled in to our space and routine. Pop took dinner orders, I continued with Evan's sponge baths, while Nana prepared to read the story of choice or play a game or simply cuddle with Evan for one last TV program. The adjoining rooms were particularly convenient, because Evan could go to sleep at a set bedtime, with the lights off, while I could work in Nana and Pop's room. There was always reading to do, regarding leukemia, and now, additional work included making out salary checks for the staff at the office, paying bills and quarterly tax returns. In the first package came some 75 office patient insurance forms that had been stacking up for me to complete over the last month. No one wanted to bother me with the office clerical work, but no one had the authority to hand it out either.

A big surprise came when Nana unpacked the carrying case with the "box" inside that played the movies. She brought the three necessary cords. I initially worried that they would not work on a hotel TV. But in no time, Annie was bad mouthing Ms. Hannigan. The next day, Pop got directions to a movie store from someone at the clinic, a store where we could rent movies to play back at the hotel (an astounding concept). The next two movies that

Evan would memorize, with no volume, were Karate Kid and Ferris Bueller's Day Off. Perhaps I should resist "reading a message" into everything, but certainly the karate kid had to beat all odds to win the championship round, and Ferris was a likeable negotiator, whom Evan admired and wanted to emulate.

On this particular night, Evan awoke abruptly, screaming from a bad nightmare. I ran to him and asked him to recount the dream. He had already forgotten it, but he was shaky and teary, and I held him to comfort him. "Thank you Mommy for coming. Did I interrupt you? Are you OK? What do you think heaven is like?" (*Oh God, am I now preparing Evan to die? Please give me the right words.*) "Honestly, Evan, no one knows. But I believe it is going to be a good place, a happy place, and we will be there together." With only a shadow of light streaming in from the other bedroom, I noticed something on Evan's pillow, as I spoke. Worried about keeping the pillow case completely clean, I helped Evan move out of the way, in order for me to examine this more closely. Oh God! I found clumps of Evan's hair, not a few strands, but clumps large enough to pick up in my hand. As I cleaned the case off, Evan sat stroking his fingers through his scalp. More clumps were falling. I wrapped my arms around his sweet body and held him close. "I'm sorry, Evan. We will get through this together. It will grow back, once you are off the medicine, I promise. I love you. Good night sweetie."

The next day, after our daily-double dose, two things happened out of the ordinary. First, Evan felt like browsing through the St. Jude gift shop, a very large "store" with toys, clothing, and toiletries. It resembled an army commissary more than a hospital gift shop. Evan was looking for the perfect hat. This hospital carried the widest selection, with sizes for everyone (Ugh!). Evan chose an army-camouflage motif that, in the end, would be worn to threads, with only a safety pin to hold it together. The second milestone of note was that Evan was able to walk ever so slowly, but independently, out to the car. It was the same excitement that new parents feel when their one-year-old takes a first step. Could this mean that the medicine was helping? Did this mean that Evan was beating cancer? Did this mean that Evan would be experiencing less pain? Dr. Murphy smiled. "Keep a 'goin!"

Nana and Pop learned the St. Jude routine fast but were unable to stomach the medicine room. I could well understand this. The kids there were so subdued, unlike the kids in the waiting room. Evan became so sick so fast that it seemed that he would never recover. At the same time, my parents would not leave the hospital -- always focused on the reason for coming to Memphis to begin with. Pop spent those long afternoons getting to know patients and chatting with parents, while Nana would devour all reading material related to children with cancer.

Midway through the induction period, Evan was scheduled to have another bone marrow. The procedure was scheduled for a "Vincristine-push" day. Evan was so nervous all the way to the hospital that nothing Pop could say would elicit a response. In the waiting room, Evan was perspiring, and I worried that maybe he was running a fever. Mike felt bad that he was in Charlotte while Evan and I had to go it alone this time. Dr. Murphy sensed immediately how nervous Evan was so she wasted no time in preparation. She believed in explanations, and Evan knew it. He used this knowledge wisely. He was more than willing to play dumb, listening and questioning each detail, a good stall tactic for time. Although his questions were asked in highly anxious tones, they were received with a calm, motherly compassion (and also humorously).

"Wait a minute, wait a minute, what are you going to do first?" (the bone marrow or spinal tap).

"I think we can do either one first, Evan. Which would you like to do first?"

"Do the one you think we should do first. I'm trying to get ready. I know I can do it, I know I can do it."

"O.K. Evan" Dr Murphy took charge, "I think I'll get the bone marrow out of the way first."

"But why are you going to do the bone marrow first? Is it going to hurt more? Don't you think we should talk about this some?"

"Maybe it is going to hurt, honey, but I'm going to do it first, 'cause I can't figure out a way to do both of them last."

Evan stalled and negotiated for as long as possible. It was finally time. After this particularly long appointment, Dr. Murphy referred to Evan as "Dr. Kissinger" (the negotiator from the Nixon days), and the name stuck. From then on, she would address him as Dr. Kissinger, and Evan grew to like the reference.

Another example of the animated and affectionate way that Dr. Murphy related to Evan was during the exam. She would run a humorous dialogue, as she ran through the body's systems. For example, before looking in Evan's ear with the otoscope, she would say, "Well honey, is there any cauliflower in this ear?" I can still see the excitement on Evan's face (and the surprise on Murphy's face) the day that Evan asked me to buy real cauliflower, and tearing off a small piece, planted it in his ear. Taking after his grandfather, Evan was always up for a joke, even under dire circumstances. Pop loved it.

With our treatment plan settled in, I decided one night to write home to Evan's homeroom class back at Charlotte Latin School. Thinking ahead, I decided that it was a good idea to keep Evan's classmates informed about Evan's health, and also to keep the children reminded that Evan was still a classmate. God willing, if Evan ever got to return to kindergarten, it was important that kids remembered him and would welcome his return. I decided to write the letter "from Evan" (almost dictated by him.) Due to Diane's sense that this might be a treasured document someday, she kept the letter:

Dear everyone in my class,

Have you all wondered why I haven't been to class in so long? I'm in Memphis, Tennessee at a special hospital getting a special kind of medicine. I have to stay here 'til Christmas, and then I hope I can come home. I'm sort of used to the clinic and the hotel now. They even know me at the hotel, and the waitress at IHOP knows me too. Before, I was too sick to eat out, and my parents would bring me bowls of cereal to eat in the room, but now I feel a little better, and I like to eat eggs and pancakes in the morning.

Every day, we go to the clinic. The first stop is the weight and measure room. That's nothing. No needles there. They just take my temperature, my blood pressure, my height and weight. I gained 6 pounds over the weekend! Mom and Dad said it's because of this medicine that has made my stomach so fat, but as soon as I stop taking this one kind, my tummy will be the same again. Then we go to the blood room. That's not too bad. Stella is my favorite "blood lady." She's very good and doesn't hurt. She has a "pop gun" that sticks my finger, and you don't even know it.
Next, we sign in at the desk with Leonard. He's real nice, and he tells my doctor that I'm ready. Then we go back to the waiting room, where there are millions of kids and parents. Mom always goes to check the mail, and she al ways comes back with stuff to open. Whenever there's something from a friend, I always sit and talk about the friend, and sometimes I shut my eyes and picture the friend in my mind, just like I'm back in Charlotte. I get very nervous waiting for the doctor and usually send mom at least twice to the cafeteria to get something to snack on. I can't go to the cafeteria myself, in case they call my name and we'd miss it. Dad and I sit in the waiting room and play games, while we wait. Finally, they call my name and we see the doctor: Dr. Pui, Dr. Murphy, or Dr. Ochs. "Murphy" is my regular doctor. After this, I go to the medicine room.

This is where you get sticks and pricks and IVs. I have a friend there named Betty. She's my favorite "poker." She knows just how to do it. She always counts to three, so I know exactly when the stick is. Today is a free day which means all I have are some pills to take. I might ask Mom and Dad to wheel me around the mall, so that I can visit some toy stores. We can't go on the weekends, because it is too crowded, and I can't be around sick people.

I bet you wonder what I have that I am too sick to come to school. Well it's called leukemia. Inside my body, the good soldiers have been fighting trying to kill off the bad soldiers. The medicine I am taking kills off the bad soldiers. Guess what? The medicine also killed off the soldiers who grow hair. In fact, my hair is falling out, and it looks funny. I bought this cool army hat that I will probably wear to school, if Mrs. Totherow says it's OK to wear a hat in school. My hair will grow back in. I guess it's worth it, in order to feel better. You don't have to worry about getting this disease from me, because it isn't "catching." I still have a little trouble walking, but it's not as bad as it use to be. Mom says there's a chance that I will get to come back to school close to Christmas break. I hope so.

Well, that's all for now. I am sending you a picture of my hospital and my hotel.

I sure do miss all of you. See you soon, I hope.

Your friend,

Evan

November meant that Thanksgiving was approaching. Dr. Murphy informed us that she was going to be gone for almost two weeks, combining an international oncology meeting with a well-deserved vacation. Dr. Pui would take over for her. The news was met with a little anxiety by Evan, who did not like change. Everything was going smoothly, and Evan wanted it to stay that way.

On this particular appointment, Dr. Murphy seemed unrushed, so I asked her again about the December 11th deadline (the date that we would learn if Evan made it into remission.) I wanted to be assured that we would be returning to Charlotte then. She answered that, if the eleventh fell on a weekend, "we would see if you could have a weekend off!" I could not imagine to what she was referring. "Were we not through with the chemotherapy on the 11th?" I asked. As if I were a little slow, she stopped and looked at me and carefully explained further: December 11th marked the end of induction therapy, meaning the initial push to kill off all the leukemia cells. If the bone marrow showed no more cancer cells, we would start on "maintenance therapy." "How long is maintenance therapy?" I inquired. "Two and a half years" was the answer. (*Oh My God!*)

I could not wait to call Mike from the phone booth outside the La Quinta. Did he realize that there was maintenance therapy after induction? Yes. Did he know it lasted two and a half years? Yes. Were we going to be in Memphis two and a half years? I don't think so. Would we be on medicine each day for two and half years? Yes. (*God, where have I been?*) So much for Mike's communicating the "medical lingo" for me.

After Evan fell asleep, I once again fell apart. This time Nana and Pop were there to hear an endless stream of fears and frustration. It came to mind that, just as I felt overwhelmed with this news, Evan would feel the same way, and I needed to think about the best way to break this new, little turn of events. I wanted to present this in a positive way. I needed more information. I needed to know what the regime would be like, what medicines he would be taking, whether we would be able to take the medicine to Charlotte. I guess I was jumping the gun ... after all, we still needed a good outcome on December 11th.

During our next day's treatment, a two-hour drip, I asked Nana and Pop if they wouldn't mind standing in for me in the medicine room for about 15 minutes. I had left a message in Dr. Murphy's office to please leave our maintenance schedule (or "print out" as it was called) with the clinic nurse. So, when Evan fell asleep, I quickly walked over to the clinic. The nurse had prepared it. Fresh off the printer, this 1-inch thick document, with punched out holes on the side, would spell out our fate (if we were lucky enough to get there) starting with:

Total XI
Maintenance Therapy
1984, 12 December
#9291 Kaufman, Evan Joel

(*God, there isn't as much as a day in between!*) I am overwhelmed. At first glance, the menu looked to have some of the same drugs, but in different order, and now in neat pairs: Pair #1: Vincristine and Prednisone. Pair #2: 6-Mercaptopurine (6MP) and Methotrexate, Pair #3: VP-16 and Cyclophosphamide, and Pair #4 VM-26 and ARA-C. Following the list, a description of the side effects followed. Several of the drugs were new to me. I, then, honed in on the following sentences: "When the tolerance of the patient is well adjusted, most of the maintenance therapy can be administered by a home oncologist. Visits to St. Jude Hospital will be necessary only when VP-16 and VM-26 therapy is scheduled. Spinal injections with chemotherapy, as described above, will be given every eight weeks during the first year of therapy. After the one-year remission mark, patients in Group #2 (the worst risk group) will be administered 1800 rads of radiation to the skull. Immediate side effects of radiation include nausea, vomiting, hair loss, decreased appetite, drop in blood counts. Up to four to six weeks after irradiation, children may be noted to tire easily."

As every parent tends to do when first perusing this 100-page-document, I turned to the last page. There I read the last date of the last chemo treatment:

25 March, 1987

This date will always be famous within our family. Every "25th" of the month, Mike and I would celebrate; every September 25th, we held a "6-month party," and every March 25th, it was time to rejoice. The date was something to live for. Little did we realize at the time, but March 25 would hold a second, momentous meaning for the entire family.

I asked for an appointment with Dr. Pui. I explained that Evan and our family would give anything to be together at Thanksgiving, if at all possible. Would there be any way that we could go home, even if it were just for a day. In looking ahead, I had figured out that the Thursday of Thanksgiving was only a prednisone pill and the Vincristine shot. The shot could be given by Dr. Golembe in Charlotte. I bet he would be willing to call Dr. Pui, giving assurance that he would be responsible for this one injection. Dr. Pui answered that he would agree to the above idea, but that the major problem was not the administration of the medicine. He lamented that Evan would be unable to travel by plane. With his current white cell count, it would be too dangerous to fly in an airplane, exposed to germs in the circulated air. He questioned that Charlotte was too far to drive. He tried to make me feel better by describing the wonderful "spread" available in the St. Jude cafeteria on Thanksgiving Day. This was going to be a challenge.

Meanwhile, a trip to the mailbox yielded a very interesting (and timely) letter from a Charlotte Latin friend. She included a newspaper article about Robert Vinroot, husband of Pat, the guidance counselor at Charlotte Latin School, already a special family friend. The article was about Robert's quitting his job as a commercial airline pilot to form a new non-profit organization, "Mission Air." His calling was to transport patients who needed emergency medical treatment and for whom time was precious. Obviously, being home for Thanksgiving did not qualify as an emergency run, but just in case, I called Pat to inquire about this new service. Pat was happy to hear from me and assured me that she would pass on all the information to Robert. "Just in case," I called Dr. Golembe, our Charlotte oncologist, with the possibility that we could be home for just a day and could he give Evan the Vincristine, if all the stars aligned for a visit. The St. Jude pharmacy filled the prescription and would keep it on hold, in case we needed to take it with us. I refrained from telling Jenny or Evan of the possibility, since there was no need to disappoint them if it didn't work out.

As luck would have it, Robert called the Monday of Thanksgiving week saying that he had a trip past the Mississippi and would refuel in Memphis. Since he would be flying home with no passengers, he would be glad to pick us up. So, in a few days time, I needed to pack up our little "home" at LaQuinta (St. Jude was happy to store our things). I needed officially to clear our plans with Dr. Pui, give Barry Golembe a heads up, and lastly, ask my dear friend Paula if she could pick us up at a tiny, local airport in Monroe, a small town south of Charlotte. Pop was petrified to crawl into this small plane, where Nana, Pop, and I each had a seat, and Evan had to sit on my lap. This was better than any amusement park ride for Evan, who could watch the pilot's instruments, only an arm's distance away. A strong friendship between Robert and my Dad began, as did Dad's support of Mission Air ... and a mission it was.

Pop would later say that, stepping back to earth from that "feather plane" was one of the happiest moments of his life. Paula was almost able to pull her Chevrolet station wagon onto the tarmac, and we were zipping up Independence Boulevard, close to home, in a matter of minutes.

Two kindergarten moms, Melissa and Camilla, had heard through the grapevine that we were on our way home, and they thoughtfully placed a large sign in our front yard, welcoming our little boy home. It made Evan feel so good, so important, and added to the celebration mood that we all were feeling. Mike's Mother had left the day before, and so there was no opportunity to thank her for her part in holding down the fort. Jenny and Mike had been waiting at the back door, and screams were heard when we pulled up.

Oddly, the neighborhood looked different, the house looked different. Everything looked different, except for my sweet Jenny-girl.

Once inside the house, Evan slowly walked from room to room just to be sure that everything was where he left it. Mike read my mind. When we left a month ago, Evan couldn't walk; actually he couldn't even move without great pain. Though bald and pale, dare we think that he is returning to good health? Jenny was thrilled to see us all, but I could tell immediately that she was conflicted. Following her up to her room and, after a big hug that lasted for some time, I learned that the very first middle school dance was being held that very night. She had decided that it was more important to be at home with the family, but there was another part of her that made the sacrifice grudgingly. I put my foot down. She could be with the family all day tomorrow. Tonight, it was imperative that she attend. She was happy with my insistence and relieved that the decision was not hers. Did she have "the perfect thing to wear?" No answer. 'Cmon, we're running out to the store." Mike could not believe that, at this special time, I would be interested in shopping. He was right. I was not the least bit interested in shopping. I longed to sit, relax and enjoy my family in my own home. But at this moment, Jenny deserved to come first.

We returned from Marshalls with a smile on her face, packages in hand. Jenny had clearly moved into another stage of youth. No longer interested in matching hair bows, she was going to debut, with large, baggy pants that were meticulously rolled up from the ankle to mid-calf. To make the roll even larger, the pants were worn so low on the hip that I worried as to how they would stay on. (The crotch is now somewhere mid-thigh). The matching sweat-shirt-jacket was trimmed in yellow and hung somewhere around the knee. We carefully chose a yellow/white stripped blouse that hung out over the pants. She explained that she wouldn't dare buy a new pair of tennis shoes because then it would look like she purchased the entire outfit for the dance, and it was way cooler to wear clothes with a few holes. Long earrings dangled to the shoulder. (*Is it time to retire the petite pearls that go with everything?*)

It was a far cry from the sweet Easter dress with the cinched waist that she wore last year. But I was operating on the parent mantra "Pick your battles," and this wasn't the battle, and this wasn't the time. Deborah Dee's mom arrived on time for pick-up and my sweet Jenny-girl was out the door. Times were changing.

From the moment I realized that my Thanksgiving trip fantasy might come true, I began dreaming up Norman Rockwell Thanksgiving scenes. Our wonderful family would be together in an idyllic setting, home. In my dream, one could smell the turkey in the oven, with Pop's chestnut dressing to the side. Sometime after getting Evan to bed, I consulted with Nana and Pop about tomorrow's Thanksgiving meal. They were one step ahead (as usual). We were having Harris Teeter roasted chicken, pre-packaged green beans, baked potato, already prepared jello salad. The only homemade contribution was pecan pie (Pop was FAMOUS for his crust).

Early the next morning, we took a quick trip over to the Nalle Clinic to meet Dr. Golembe for Evan's Vincristine shot. Not a soul was there (Dr. Golembe, himself, unlocked the clinic door), and it was mortifyingly apparent that I had thoughtlessly asked him this favor at the expense of his own family's time. (*What was I thinking?*) The paperwork and bureaucracy of trying to accomplish this at the hospital would have taken all day. He politely asked about our experiences at St. Jude Hospital, but I cut short the conversation so that he could return home, as soon as possible. Pop made an extra pie that I took to Dr. Golembe as a thank you. It was hardly enough to express our gratitude, but he knew how much we appreciated this.

Our Thanksgiving Day was exactly that, a day that we gave thanks over and over again. Our family tradition was always to go around the table and each family member took a turn describing the one thing for which he/she was most grateful. The responses were all running along the same theme, until it came to Evan. Perhaps the tears and serious answers were too much for this six-year-old. Evan said he was most grateful for his new, army camouflaged hat.

For as restful and rejuvenating as Thanksgiving Day was, Mike was quite unhappy with my willingness to return to Memphis on Piedmont Airlines. (We didn't have a choice.) To help assuage my own conscience, I purposely booked the flight the Friday morning after Thanksgiving, thinking that few people would be traveling that day. Also, I chose the 6:40 a.m. flight. (*How many people would fly then?*) I also carried a breathing mask for Evan to wear during the flight. It was on this early return trip that Evan discovered, by accident, the airport game room. With a stool to stand on and a quarter in hand, he could play a few minutes of Pac-Man. Evan never wanted to go from game to game; he only played Pac-Man and became quite the expert. In truth, we suffered no repercussions from the decision to come home for Thanksgiving (that is, to fly back commercially), but I worried so much about the germs, and Evan's comprised immunity, that Mike and I made a pledge to one another that we would NEVER take a chance (even a tiny one) again. Ever.

Mike cancelled all of his patients for the first half of December. It was impossible for him not to be at the hospital for our December 11th conference day. The day before would be awful: a bone marrow, a spinal tap, and an all-day drip (and of course, a night of vomiting). But on the 11th, we would hear the hopeful results: that the bone marrow and spinal fluid were clean (showing no more cancer cells) and that Evan attained REMISSION. I was already prepared to embark on the next phase, maintenance therapy, that would entail daily chemo for the next two and one-half years. If Evan does not attain remission, we will start with induction all over again, perhaps, with the same drugs but in a different order. I can't go there.

The day after Thanksgiving, we were sitting in the St. Jude waiting room by 9:00 a.m. (central time), listening for our name to be called over the loud speaker. Thank you Piedmont Airlines for your efficiency. How strange it was to feel that we were back in our usual routine, our usual schedule: first, weight and measure, second, the blood room and so forth. Mike loaded up the rental car with our stored clothes and toys and our "box" that played movies, so that we would be ready to leave after Evan's treatment. We got lucky. Our green card was sending us back to LaQuinta. Strange how there was comfort in going back to the familiar, the familiar motel, and even the familiar route to get there.

The day was sunny and warm, and I thanked God that we were alive to enjoy such a beautiful "mother-nature" day. Evan had an easy shot, several pills, and a quick visit to the clinic. After dumping off our stuff, we made our way to Mud Island River Park. As the name implies, the park is located on an island in the middle of the very wide Mississippi River. In a scaled down version, the park recreated the path of this mighty river, from the headwaters to its outlet at The Gulf of Mexico. Visitors can walk along this model and then end up at the adjacent museum that showcases the importance of the river from the early days, during the Civil War, up to the era of modern barge transportation. Nana, who always stressed the importance of educational trips, would have approved. Mud Island was interesting, and the weather was beautiful, but the whole excursion was too much for Evan. Halfway through, he needed to be carried, and when we finally returned to the motel, he slept the rest of the afternoon and night, right through the dinner hour. The lesson we learned was that the ideal excursion had to be high interest, in the fresh air (for low levels of germs), few people in attendance (cutting down on sneezing and coughing), a wheel chair for transportation (of course wiped down with anti-bacterial wipes), and finally, within close proximity so we could get home to the motel when Evan got too tired. This should be easy to find, right?

Mike and I kept a mental count-down of days until December 11th. As I pondered about life, about happiness, and our two little treasures, I concluded that humans like routine and thrive on knowing what to expect. The routine, itself, hardly mattered. So, here we were in a most low-quality life. But the structure felt good. We knew exactly how Evan would react to his menu of drugs. We knew when he would be deathly nauseated and what to do for it and how long it would last. We knew where our meals were coming from (the St. Jude cafeteria). We knew that each day we would be watching either The Karate Kid or Annie. After Evan fell asleep, Mike would spend the rest of the evening reading Immunology Journals, hoping to learn every detail he could about leukemia, and I would spend the evening on the office work that arrived daily, via our St. Jude mailbox. On any one day, we could spout off the number of days until December 11th, and while I was thirsty for good news, part of me was OK with this interim time. I didn't want to risk a back slide. I didn't want to start over. I didn't want any more bad news. I had been hit too many times in the gut, and the very thought of another terrifying proclamation made me sick.

With one week to go until December 11th, a phone call to our little "LaQ" hotel room shattered the idea that we were on the home stretch and living a calm existence. Evan's blood work had returned, and his hemoglobin was borderline low. Dr. Murphy wanted us to return to the hospital, in order for Evan to receive a blood transfusion. It shouldn't be surprising that two hyper parents, such as Mike and me, would have long since anticipated this moment and tried to make arrangements for this eventuality. Neither Jenny nor I were blood matches for Evan. Mike was a match, but he had been exposed to Hepatitis by a dirty needle during his internship year and would never be able to be a blood donor. To make matters worse, this was an era when The Red Cross refused to take "directed donors," fearing that donors would no longer give blood to anonymous recipients, thus creating a blood shortage. This was also during a time that the news media was full of stories about people receiving tainted blood. Back in Charlotte, a neighbor, Jane Faircloth, stepped forward and said she was a blood type match and volunteered to be Evan's donor. We went behind the scenes and got a verbal agreement that the hematology department at one of the hospitals would agree to take Jane's blood and directly infuse Evan in the next chair. However, we were in Memphis, not Charlotte. We were desperate again. We drove to the clinic and begged to delay the transfusion, until we could talk to our doctor. Dr. Murphy was working in a different part of the hospital, and a mid-day conference was not on her schedule. We waited hours for her. (*Was God getting tired of my same prayer?*) Finally she arrived and agreed that, because Evan's count was borderline, she was willing to cancel the transfusion and wait and see. Score one for our side. (Evan never did have a blood transfusion, but we came mighty close.)

December meant Christmas: all of the street decorations and all of the TV commercials reminded me that this fun holiday was around the corner, but I had not purchased one gift, nor would there be a chance to shop. Evan wanted very much to "roam around" the mall (even in a wheelchair), but it was out of the question because of the crowds, even on a weekday. He would have loved to peruse Toys "R" Us, but it was even MORE off limits. Then, Nana suggested the old-fashioned way to shop: catalogues! Soon, our mailbox could not fit all the Christmas flyers we requested, and then flyers appeared from random stores that bought customer mailing lists. We had flyers selling everything from pool supplies to burp-up babies. Evan was entertained for hours, circling in red all of the items that looked good. Is this the same child that got tired of opening gifts back in Charlotte?

There is a milestone worth noting. Mike and I were beginning to discuss two presents for each of the kids. This is important because it suggested that the two of us were planning ahead, albeit for only three weeks. Until now, we dared not plan for even one day ahead. This was a huge step. We thought we would see Christmas, and we thought it would be a wonderful holiday. This is how real people live. Maybe we were turning into real people again. Maybe ...

Christmas for Jenny was a no-brainer. Pop had become friends with the Charlotte Toys "R" Us manager. The manager was so invested in our story that he began to hold back hard-to-come-by toys. He reserved a coveted Cabbage Patch doll for Jenny, and a new transformer for Evan. Aunt Pat and her daughter, Sara, who was one year older than Jenny, and one year "cooler," went on a shopping trip to choose a perfect outfit for Jenny. (This is called one foot in childhood and one foot in adolescent youth.) But the most amazing gift of all was the manager's choice. He listened, as Pop described Evan's passion for the Pac-Man game at the airport game room. He held back a personal Pac-Man game that was bright blue and the size of a loaf of bread. Two "C" batteries made the on-switch come alive, with a jingle that continues to live in my head. Had I known the importance of this toy and the joy it brought Evan, I would have gladly bought two. Though Pop would personally not know one toy from another, this was one more example that he would always arrive on top of every situation because of his personality and the friends he made everywhere, a trait that Evan would inherit in spades.

The second Christmas discussion was full of emotion. Evan sat on the lap of the St. Jude Santa (the Santa that used anti-bacteria soap after each child) and explained that, even though he had difficulty walking, the ONLY present he wanted was a BMX two-wheeler with training wheels. It needed to be black with racing checks on it. Santa told him he would try, but that it might not fit down the chimney. Not one to give up easily, Evan went into a long and detailed description of different places at our house, where the bike could be left. Santa looked at us, and then at Evan, and promised that it would be there. Let's see. Out of which catalogue did Evan see a bicycle with racing checks? Pop was on the case, as well as the manager at Toys "R" Us. A host of friends were searching back in Charlotte. Who would have believed that we would be looking for a BIKE?

December 9, Sunday: We had an easy clinic day today. One of our new mom-friends told us to visit "The Peabody" and the ducks. We were a little unclear about her reference to the ducks when she went on to describe the small café there, known for their chocolate desserts. This appealed to Evan, so off we went on another excursion. The Peabody Hotel remains a downtown landmark in Memphis. Still claiming the opulent charm of the 20's, the lobby is decorated by a mammoth black marble fountain. Sometime in 1933, the hotel owner, who had returned from an unsuccessful hunting trip, decided to put his three decoy ducks in the middle of the fountain. It caused quite a stir, even making the front page of the newspaper. He immediately seized the momentum for a marketing strategy and replaced the decoys with three North American mallards. He also created a position on his staff called "Duckmaster." This person was hired away from the Memphis Zoo, and it was his job to train the ducks to parade from the elevator (the duck pen was on the roof) in the foyer to the marble fountain. After swimming for a short while, the ducks were trained to parade back. This unique, even crazy idea, did exactly what it was meant to do, bring visitors from everywhere to visit the hotel. To this very day, Presidents, Hollywood stars, and even celebrating patients, visit The Peabody and the ducks. There is still a "Duckmaster" on staff today.

December 10, Monday: We sat in the waiting room in silence. Evan was mentally preparing for what he faced. Soon, they would call his name. We would walk down the clinic hall and wait in the room for Dr. Murphy. The nurse would come in for the prep. He knew the drill. Lie down in a fetal position, facing the wall. I would always take the stool next to his head and hold out my hand for the gripping and clutching part. Dr. Murphy would get to the bone marrow and spinal tap as soon as possible. This never became any easier, nor did preparation help. It was painful and agonizing. It never got easier to watch either. After the two procedures, Murphy reminded us that tomorrow was our conference, when we would "take a look at where we are and what lies ahead"... (code for finding out if Evan attained remission) ... as if we needed a reminder.

In the medicine room, Betty was there to start the IV, and she found the vein on the first try. Was this a sign that tomorrow would go easily as well? (The magic-game was always available to me when I found myself in out-of-control moments.) Mike checked the bag for the correct name before it was hung. Evan fell off to a deep sleep, from the exhaustion of the morning. There were so many questions in my mind: If we make it into remission, would maintenance therapy include bone marrows and spinal taps? Could some of our treatments be given in Charlotte? If so, how often would we need to return to Memphis? What will be our new regime? If we don't make it to maintenance, maybe we should consider selling our house and moving to Memphis. Surely, some medical group in Memphis could use a neurologist. We were prepared to do anything it took. Surely the medicine had worked somewhat because Evan could now walk short distances. Aside from slight personality changes and unusual food cravings due to the steroids, aside from his little bald head, Evan had not been plagued by side effects. He had not missed one treatment, not one pill. We followed our directions to the letter. As the last medicine dripped into his vein, he started vomiting and continued, during our ride home and in to the night. December 11th was upon us.

December 11, Tuesday: We left LaQuinta early. It was another beautiful day, perfect for good news. As we had done every day for the last two months, we checked in and took a seat. (*Lord, you have taken us this far. Thank you for your mercy. Please, just let us attain remission. It is all that I ask.*) Dr. Rivera was called out on an emergency, and so our conference consisted only of Murphy, two anxious parents, and one frightened little boy. Murphy was shuffling through papers, but she had a smile on her face. I remember hearing the initial words "clear marrow." So far, so good, but I remained silent. Mike began grilling her about topics he had been reading about. Not wanting to spend our precious time on esoteric research questions, I looked for an opening in the conversation, to bring the topic back to Evan, and relevant details like when we begin our next protocol, and will we be living at home or in Memphis?

"I gave you the maintenance schedule, right?" Looking down at her chart, "We have already been in touch with Dr. Barry Golembe (they are efficient here), and he is on board with administering the chemotherapy at his clinic. Of course, you will need to return every three weeks for your VM-26, but, otherwise, we will be supervising from a distance."

Innocently I asked, "When does maintenance therapy begin?"

"Tomorrow."

"So when do we get our first treatment from Dr. Golembe?"

"How about tomorrow?"

"How will he get the medicine for TOMORROW?"

"Well, Memphis IS the headquarters for Fed-Ex. He'll have the medicine tomorrow, if not today! Stop by admissions and pickup your flight tickets." And then, injecting a little humor, she added, "that is, unless you would prefer to stay here." She looked at her watch; she was in a hurry to leave ... Hardly enough time to sing her praises or profusely thank her.

"Wait, Dr. Murphy, does this mean that Evan is in remission? (I needed to hear it.)

"Yes, Helen, Evan is cancer-free. And we need to keep it that way." And just that fast, the meeting was over.

To the degree that I was traumatized when we were admitted, and forced to absorb the verdict that we would be living in Memphis for the next eight weeks, to that same degree I experienced the shock of learning that it was time to leave. My obsessive, list-making personality immediately engaged. We needed to call home, pick up our tickets, pack up our things, check out of the hotel, return the car, and on and on. But for once, I let go of efficiency and savored the moment, the warm sun and the last of the colored leaves. It was time to go home and start Day #1 of our new protocol ... time to start a new life.

CHAPTER V

THE LONG HAUL

Arriving home during the Christmas holiday was fitting for our mood of celebration and enormous appreciation for our "good life." We were starting a new regime with Evan's medicine, and we slid into the pattern effortlessly. Week #1 would be called the "hungry week," because it was impossible to satiate his appetite. Welcome to the world of steroids! Unexplainably, a random food would strike his fancy on the first day, and that would set the menu for the entire week. For example, he might have a Kentucky Fried Chicken week, or a pizza week, or toasted-cheese-sandwich week, and demand only that one food all week long. In addition, he would undergo a personality change that included screaming, demanding, high frustration, and temper tantrums. The schedule for week #2: one pill per day, concluding the week with an all-day IV drip at The Nalle Clinic. Week #3 was the easy week: a pill per day and, at the conclusion of the week, a quick shot in the thigh. The two medicines of Week #4 necessitated a return trip to Memphis, because these medicines were experimental, and the Food and Drug Administration would only allow St. Jude Hospital to administer these last two drugs on-site.

Christmas 1984 was the best Christmas yet. Every single room in the house looked wonderful and new and different. For the first time, we put up the Christmas tree in the library, a small, paneled room with many bookshelves. The reason that I wanted to put the tree there was because of a cozy working fireplace where the family could cozy up together, with the fire going and the tree lit. It turned out to be a fortuitous decision, because the day before Christmas, we had a first-ever snowstorm in Charlotte, North

Carolina! It was the first snowy, white Christmas that I could remember, but it also meant that we were without electricity.

On Christmas Eve, per usual, we attended the 5:30 p.m. children's service at church. It was always a candlelight service and
one that was meaningful to the children, as well as the parents.
Evan put on his gray, dress pants and his navy blue blazer, his
white button-down collar shirt with his red tie. He also added his
camouflage army hat that covered his little bald head. Mike and
I looked at each other when he came down the steps and were
both thinking the same thing: that the camouflage baseball hat
looked rather unusual with a sport coat and tie, but neither of
us said a word. We were so pleased that he felt well enough to
go to church, and that he could walk into the service without being carried, that we really did not care what he had on his head.
The service and music were wonderful. As we filed out of the

Christmas Eve, 1984.

church, a well-meaning older woman, who sat behind us, tapped me on the shoulder and said, "You should know that little boys who wear baseball hats a lot end up with hair that doesn't grow right. It will be very thin." That was code for: "Baseball hats should not be worn in the sanctuary!" Always protective of Evan and worried that he was in earshot, I simply said "well, thank you very much and Merry Christmas." We turned around quickly to stop further comments and continued to file out to the main aisle. In less than a minute, I noticed that Jenny had fallen behind, and that she was still in the pew and speaking to the older woman. Jenny, too, understood the hidden message that this "well-meaning" older woman was trying to convey but could not let it pass: "thank you very much for your concern for my brother's hair, but you should know that my brother has cancer, and he has no hair, and he wears this baseball cap because it's hard for him, but we appreciate your concern, and I want you to know that, when his hair finally grows back, we will surely have him discard the cap." I couldn't believe my ears. She was never afraid to stand up for her brother. She was offended that anyone would criticize us for allowing Evan to be at church with a baseball cap. Thus began her "protection-cop" role. Three cheers for my spunky Jenny!

On Christmas morning, Evan ran downstairs and there, near the tree, was the bike with black and white check racing stripes, and he screamed with joy. Mike and I were joyously screaming inside, as well. Imagine thinking that we would never see him able to walk again, and now he was jumping on the seat of this bike, inside the house from room to room (it was still snowing outside). It was rather miraculous. He was thrilled to death (life), and so were we.

Jenny seemed particularly content, because we were all home together. It had been very difficult for her in the last two months to be in the house without her brother or her parents. Even though her grandparents were there to make sure that she got to her piano lessons and scout meetings, that her homework was done, and that there was a homemade dinner on the table, she had a difficult time feeling comfortable. One day she was part of a normal family unit, and the next she was the only one left behind.

Because of the snowstorm, the electricity flickered and then went out, and the four of us kept warm, huddled around the fire on Christmas Day. We had the doors shut to keep the heat in, while the rest of the house was freezing. Although I immediately worried that Evan might catch a cold, I focused on the joy that we felt. We played Monopoly most of the day (Evan's favorite game), and by the time we had to quit, "lucky" Evan was a hotel landowner, charging high rent to anyone landing on his Park Place and Boardwalk, Illinois-Indiana-Kentucky Avenues, Connecticut-Vermont and Oriental. He owned everything!

The joy of Evan receiving the perfect gift, but the greater gift was watching him be well enough to ride it.

With New Year's Eve around the corner, Mike and I began thinking about a New Year's resolution. While most people were gearing up for hopes of higher salaries, better vacations, successful kids, we were more than satisfied with status quo. It seemed like a good trade-off: we won't ask for more or better; just don't make us face less or worse. In thinking about a toast, I began to examine the word: "rut." I think the word has gotten bad press. A rut implies nothing new ... nothing exciting ... nothing wonderful on the horizon ... but it also connotes: nothing tragic, nothing that changes lives, nothing that starts a tsunami of fear and anxiety. In reality, "rut" isn't so bad. I am fine with being in a rut ... honestly!

Together, we arrived at the perfect toast: "Here's to the wonderful rut we're in!" and we repeated it every New Year's Eve thereafter.

At the Charlotte clinic, Evan began to ingratiate himself to the staff, nurses, and secretaries. Always worried about Evan being around sick children, the staff suggested that when he arrived, he should walk right through the waiting room and straight into the treatment room. Evan interpreted this as "the important man at the Clinic" and seemed to adopt a demeanor of "owning the place." Pop also wanted to express his appreciation to the staff with regular deliveries of Rice Krispy treats, his homemade brownies with caramel centers, and his cherry and peach pies that he would deliver on Evan's treatment days. We all tried to show appreciation especially to Dr. Golembe who made getting our treatment in Charlotte possible.

Dr. Golembe was a pediatric oncologist who, in his own right, was well trained and exceptionally skilled. At the beginning, I felt awkward that we had sought treatment at St. Jude, instead of staying in Charlotte under his care and direction. Dr. Golembe now was asked to simply carry out St. Jude's instructions. But Dr. Golembe realized that our hope of survival hinged on getting this new drug, VM-26, and he made me feel that we had done the right thing. He was more than happy to do anything he could do to participate in Evan's recovery. He was jovial with Evan and usually had a joke, and always a grin. He gave me strict instructions to call him without hesitation, home or office, if I sensed that Evan was getting into trouble. I'm sure that St. Jude required a mountain of paperwork to be completed every time he saw Evan in the clinic but he never complained about it, nor did he let us feel like it was an imposition. He was upbeat and hopeful that, somehow, Evan would beat the odds.

Evan was determined that he would return to his kindergarten class at Charlotte Latin School. I felt that it was taking a chance for him to be around other children who might be coughing or sneezing due to the unseasonably cold weather, and I was ready to home-school for the remainder of the year. But he wanted to go back so much. I had to comply with his request. After the holidays, we were off to his kindergarten class. I actually accompanied Evan on the first day, in case he should get too tired and need to return home, or if the visit didn't go exactly as Evan had pictured it. I decided that my letters back to the school were apparently a good idea because the children certainly had kept up with Evan's health- progress and were happy to see him. As we walked in, the children were engaged in a free play period. Feeling shy, he walked up to the table and began to pick up some toys. Fellow classmate, Sara Farmer, looked up at him and said, "Evan, I'm so glad you're back in school." I could have picked her up and given her a hug. When she graduated from Latin, I told her that I still remembered what a kind child she had been and how much that one comment had meant to Evan. Evan might have gotten tired that day, but his enthusiasm far outweighed his exhaustion. He wanted to feel like he was a normal kid. And even though he was still on medicine, there was nothing so wonderful as being at home and waking up in his own bed and putting on different clothes every day, and going to school, and coming back home after school. This was what normal kids do, and this was the gift that Evan wanted more than anything else.

Evan explained to his friends that on certain Fridays, he was going to be flying back to Memphis, in order to get some more of the medicine that was helping him feel better. Piedmont Airlines had a 6:05 a.m. flight to Memphis every Friday morning, making one stop in Nashville. With the time change and a waiting rental car, we would be able to arrive at the clinic by 9:00 a.m. We figured that we would be through with our appointment with Dr. Murphy by 10:30, and into the medicine room by 11 to receive our medicine IV drip. With any luck, we would walk out by 6 p.m. giving us enough time to return to the airport and leave for Charlotte on the last flight home. That was our plan for our first trip back. We were about to learn a lesson that changed all future trips.

Pop arrived at our house ever so faithfully a little before 5 a.m. He ran this transportation service for us every trip back without fail.

The first important rule was to travel light. On this initial trip, we had no need for luggage, because we were not spending the night. All we needed was Evan's Pac-Man game, one or two transformers, and Mike's notebook of questions for Dr. Murphy. We knew the way from the Memphis airport to the hospital, and it began to feel like this was going to be easy.

It was very cold in Memphis, and we were surprised that there was snow on the ground. (*Maybe Memphis was not in the same weather band as Charlotte?*) We parked our car and entered the hospital as if it were a second home. The routine hadn't changed: first was weight and measure, then blood work, back to the waiting room, an appointment with Murphy, and then on to the medicine room for the VM-26. In the medicine room, as luck would have it, Betty was there to start his IV, and Evan propped up his arm on a pillow just like he always did, with clear instructions that no one should get near his arm because he did not want the needle to fall out or become dislodged somehow. As predicted, toward the end, Evan began to get sick. When 6:00 p.m. came, and the last drop had gone into the vein, the IV was disconnected. I could tell that Evan far preferred the status of visitor rather than resident.

When we left the hospital, we were in shock at the amount of snow that had fallen all day. We were told that the city of Memphis really knew how to keep the roads clear and that we had no worries. Evan continued to throw up every 20 minutes in the car, and we felt bad that we were pushing ahead with our return to Charlotte, instead of checking in to a hotel room. After returning the rental car and obtaining our tickets, we were off to the gate. My very large tote held a towel, emesis basin, drinking cup etc. for Evan, and we were hoping that he would soon be through with the vomiting. Surprisingly, people here were familiar with St. Jude and were used to seeing sick children streaming in and out on a daily basis, and were not shocked by the many bald children throwing up in the airport; Evan, one of them.

The storm outside became worse very quickly, and we were told that many flights were delayed and/or cancelled, but that ours was still scheduled to leave. When they made the announcement that any families with small children could board, I remarked that we were lucky once again. The three of us hurried down the jet way. I was first. As I lifted my right foot onto the plane, the jet way bridge gave way, and I could feel my left foot dropping down. By instinct, I quickly lunged into the plane. As the jet way fell further, it was snagged by the open door of the plane. Mike, too, could feel the floor underneath him fall, and by instinct, he took a huge jump back. The jet way bridge must have been very heavy, because it actually bent the door of the plane, as it lodged into a precarious position. End result: one stewardess and I were on the plane, and on the other side, stood a breathless dad, protecting his son. An emergency siren sounded. Mike and Evan were quickly ushered back into the gate area. I did everything I could to convince the stewardess that it would probably be safe for us to take a big jump over the crevice and return to the gate area inside. She was not won over, and it was apparent that we were not going anywhere, anytime soon. The airplane could not drive over to another gate, and so I wondered how I would ever get back inside the airport. Unfortunately, I was carrying the sick-child's tote, and on the other side, Mike was carrying the sick child.

An hour-and-a-half later, Piedmont Airlines maintenance crew pushed a ladder up to the emergency door in the back of the plane. An employee climbed up the ladder and motioned me to turn around and begin the descent. He put his arms around my waist to steady me and help me in the midst of this snowy down pour. After the employee went back up to get the stewardess, we were both ushered back into the terminal.

Inside the terminal, there was general chaos of stranded, desperate people and long lines to reissue tickets. I thought the logical place to start looking for them might be back at the gate. People were crowding and rushing through the hall, while the gate areas were deserted, all except for the two people at gate #1. As I approached, there they were. Mike, unflinching, held Evan in his lap, while Evan continued to vomit on Mike's shirt, jacket and pants. They were two pathetic souls, sitting alone and tranquil, amongst the pandemonium. I found an employee of the airlines and described our predicament. We were no longer concerned about flying out; we just wondered if we could go SOMEWHERE. There were no rental cars left and no way to return to the hospital. Another Piedmont Airlines employee was summoned, and she began to phone different hotels close-by. She found the last available room at the Holiday Inn next to the airport and asked a buddy to drive us there in a runway-emergency truck. She also called the St Jude night number and left a message for the transportation department to begin work on a return ticket for the next day. At the hotel check-in desk, we asked for an additional sheet and blanket, explaining that we needed to get Evan out of his soaking, smelly clothes, bathe him, and wrap him up for the night. No sooner had we arrived in our room, there was a knock at the door. The desk clerk was standing there with the sheet and blanket, as well as, several maids' uniforms for Mike and me. She held out a large, empty bag for our clothes, with the promise that they would be washed in the hotel laundry and returned in a few hours. Around midnight, Evan quit vomiting, as predicted, and fell asleep, swaddled in the sheet and blanket. Mike and I looked at each other and shook our heads. We were safe and warm. Dressed like the Holiday Inn cleaning crew, we smiled. Life was good. This is not the conclusion that many people would make. But for us, at this time, we were grateful for small miracles, and this was one. Of the thirty trips back to St. Jude, this was the only time we ever tried to make the trip in one day.

With Christmas behind us and the cold weather outside, I looked forward to the spring. I began to appreciate the rhythm of Evan's chemotherapy. I sought the help of a therapist to help me learn how to be an effective parent with a prednisone-belligerent son. During the steroid week, Evan was always out of sorts, demanding, and had a tremendous craving for food in large amounts. He often stood at the landing of the stairs and screamed, "get me a toasted cheese sandwich and make it NOW!" This behavior would not have been allowed in normal circumstances, but this was not Evan. I came up with the following response: "Evan, I would be happy to make your sandwich. I know that this is the prednisone speaking, instead of you, else I would not let you scream at me." So I attempted to (1) let him know that ordinarily his screaming at me would be unacceptable, (2) identify for him the reason why he was talking this way, and then (3) assure him that I would always get whatever he needed while he was sick. Other weeks were also predictable. Certain weeks Evan felt pretty good. I dared to think that maybe we would be able to take a small family vacation, if timed just right. Heretofore, this thought would have been absolutely out of the question.

The vacation idea was also somewhat frightening. First was the looming worry of what we would do without Dr. Golembe around the corner? Could we chance leaving our tenuous umbrella of safety? On the other hand, it would be so much fun to see Jenny and Evan enjoy a kid's dream of going to Disney World. We would definitely need travel insurance, in case we needed to cancel our plans at the last minute due to low white counts. Second, would I be able to reserve a wheel chair for Evan, since we were not quite sure of his stamina/energy level? Would we be able to stay right on the grounds of Disney World, so that it would be a quick trip back to our room for a nap? Would there be available food, so that we could keep Evan on a well-balanced diet? It turned out that Disney World was well-designed for kids, particularly special-needs kids. And so, our very first trip, during the spring of 1985, was to Orlando, Florida. For so long, we were hanging on to life by a thread, and now we dared to spend a day in a frivolous way. It was such a blessing to arrive at a point where life had become doable and enjoyable.

The spring marked the March 25th anniversary date of Evan's last chemo day, albeit, two years hence. This is the day that we will celebrate "no more chemo!" And of course, that very thought was enough to fill my whole, entire heart and soul with encouragement and hope and excitement. At the same time, oddly enough, the date also carried anxiety. The medicine kept the cancer at bay. Would it return once Evan was on his own?

Spring also posed a major worry. On our February trip to St. Jude, Murphy reminded me that spring was the time to be mindful of chicken pox. She explained that the virus responsible for chicken pox was particularly virulent, and if Evan (or anyone immuno-suppressed), were exposed to this virus, it would send his im-mune system into a tailspin. She suggested that I alert the school, particularly moms in Evan's grade, to call me, if their child came down with chicken pox. If Evan were exposed to the child within close-range, we would need to take Evan to the hospital to re-ceive an immunoglobulin vaccine that the Red Cross would sup-ply. This was nerve-racking. The window of dangerous exposure was the 24-hr period PRIOR to the spots appearing. Therefore, one could not be "careful," because one could not predict illness ahead of time. The only thing I knew to do during play time with other children was to encourage outside play, with the thought that fresh air would reduce his risk. In the entire time that Evan was undergoing chemotherapy, we only had one episode where a mother called to announce that her child had broken out with chicken pox, and in fact, by chance, Evan had been playing with her child at school the day before. We immediately contacted Dr. Golembe and met him at the hospital that afternoon.

I looked for ways to shave off travel time and make our month-ly trips back to Memphis as efficient as possible. We switched our clinic day to Friday mornings. That way, we could spend the night and fly back on Saturday, without Mike's missing any more work than necessary. Pop would always be at our house at 5:00 a.m. and drop us at the curb, eliminating the extra time to park in the airport deck. I always used the same "good luck" suitcase that was a perfect small size for the three of us. This bag could be carried on, as opposed to checked in. (In fact, years later, this suitcase remained permanently packed and stored under the bed, always ready for a moment's notice departure.) We always used

Avis Rent-a-car, and Evan made friends with the Charlotte clerk. After we were on a first-name-basis, she would wave us on and call out, "I'll have a car ready." She, then, called a co-worker in Memphis, who not only had the paperwork ready for signing, but, unbelievably, had the car parked at the curb! This shaved off another 45 minutes to ride the van to the rental car lot.

Is it possible that we brush shoulders every day with uniquely caring and compassionate people, but that we are too rushed to realize it? Does it take a sick little boy to introduce us to a sector of humanity that is kindhearted and benevolent? The folks at the Piedmont Airline desk surprised us that Christmas, by putting together a wrapped present, with Evan's name on it: a Piedmont Airlines hat, a deck of cards, a pen and pencil, and airline wings for his jacket. The combination of our airline friends, the Avis ladies, the hotel clerk, the long list of St. Jude caregivers and so many others, revised our attitude about people and those worthy of emulating.

The fall of 1985 marked the beginning of Evan's first grade. It was a time to sit down with the teachers and discuss Evan's difficulty in keeping up academically. I requested that no teacher call on Evan to read in front of the class. It was a necessary assurance so that Evan could protect himself from embarrassment, and have peace of mind during the school day. Often, he was tired at the end of the day. Latin was known for its fast pace, and Evan used a lot of emotional energy to cover up his weaknesses. Yet, we were extraordinarily fortunate with the compassion and understanding that everyone showed us. Both the teachers and school administrators relaxed a rule, allowing Evan to wear his hat in the classroom. We were touched when the parents, as a group, asked if his classmates could wear baseball hats, too. It was a vote of support from the other children and made Evan feel acceptance in this little cocoon world.

One day, Evan came home from school and asked if he could sign up for the soccer team. I was taken aback with the idea that Evan could participate in a rigorous activity. But again, Evan wanted to be normal, and this was what other little boys in his class were doing on Saturday morning. Evan wanted to try it, as well. I located the director of the Myers Park Little League and asked if he could participate. Evan was excited about learning to play soccer, being part of a team, wearing a uniform, including special shoes. It was somewhat difficult for Evan to play soccer because he had an unusual running style, due, in part, to the removal of part of his rib and a collapsed vertebra. Also, steroid-use had added pounds that slowed his running speed. He was usually at the very end of the group running in one direction and at the very end of the group running in the other direction. He seemed to be winded more quickly than the others and, in general, not in good physical shape. But, he did add something uniquely important to the team. This little boy with the army camouflage hat was neither the best player nor a talented player, but he was the #1 athlete who treated every single play as if that play would win the game. His heart and soul were on the field! Not only did Evan display this fierce drive for himself, but it motivated all the children that played around him.

On the week that we travelled to Memphis, Evan flew back to Charlotte with his soccer uniform on, and we drove straight from the airport to the field, where the game was already started. After a long trip home and throwing up until midnight, the night before, Evan would run onto the field, as if he were well rested and invigorated. He had an intense drive to participate with the other kids and pushed himself to do what the other kids were doing, no matter what the price. He was never a child to give up. This would later become Evan's hallmark signature: to work harder and longer than everyone else, surmounting roadblocks, and eventually getting to the finish line. I think he was born with this drive.

Another admirable quality was Evan's deep appreciation for life, itself. Early on, he began to think up ways to express his appreciation to St. Jude and to the doctors there. Evan kept a "St. Jude box of toys" in his room. Any toy that he could part with would be placed in the box. When filled, he would set the card table up at the curb on a Saturday morning, with a sign that read: "Help the children at St. Jude Hospital." At the end of the day, he would carefully count out the money he had made, and then I would send off a check to the business office at St. Jude Hospital. Our local news channel noticed this one Saturday and featured him on the local news. He could remember all too well what it was like to be in a lot of pain every day and unable to roll over in bed. Now he was playing soccer! This good fortune was never taken for granted, and often he would take a moment to express how grateful he was, just to be able to run. Question: Did Evan develop this deep sense of appreciation because he got sick? Or was he born with this sweet and sensitive nature that took nothing for granted?

Typical of his generous and responsible nature, Evan sold his toys to help the children at St. Jude.

During one snow mist, we got up early in the morning to see if Charlotte Latin had been called off for the day, due to icy roads. This particular day, the school was not called off, and Jenny was complaining bitterly. Evan immediately piped up: "you should be happy that you have a wonderful school to go to and that you are well enough to go." He always was thinking in terms of how lucky he was. This trait was inherited directly from Pop.

On the other hand, it must be said that Evan was also happy to accept any small offer of kindness by people in the community. On one particular occasion, Evan was contacted by a former athlete with connections to the Duke Basketball program. Both Mike and I were graduates of Duke, and even before their basketball program became so successful, we were fans from the early days. Surprise! Evan was invited to be the guest of honor at a Duke Basketball game! He was absolutely thrilled to death, and as a footnote, so were Mike and I.

Evan was the honored guest at a Duke basketball game in Cameron Indoor Stadium.

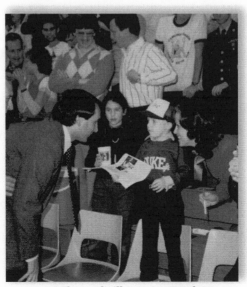

What a thrill to meet Coach K!

Evan needed some Duke paraphernalia for the game, so we visited the Duke store ahead of time. He wore a new Duke shirt and a Duke hat that unfortunately, did not come in the proper size, so the hat fell way down over his ears. We arrived at Cameron Indoor Stadium and couldn't believe that we had four seats directly behind the basketball players and Coach Krzyzewski. Before the game started, they announced this special guest in the auditorium, and then, each of the basketball players stopped by Evan's seat and signed his program. It is hard to describe the electric excitement from that day. In fact, it was documented by the Durham Herald newspaper. On Sunday morning, Evan's picture was featured on the sports page, above the write-up of the game, with his Duke hat down over his ears. What a marvelous gesture it was of our friend in Charlotte, and of "Coach K"!

We were beginning to feel quite comfortable when midway through treatment, we were facing a grim reality. The protocol for high-risk patients called for 1800 rads of cranial irradiation. Mike began researching cranial irradiation and its effects on children. He asked Murphy if we could put this off until, God forbid, Evan ever faced a relapse. As a neurologist, he reasoned that the radiation would do permanent damage to Evan's brain, similar to killing off brain cells from a stroke. He hoped, with any luck, we could avoid it altogether. Unfortunately, it was part of the protocol, and we thought we had no choice. For the rest of Evan's life, Mike would regret not standing his ground and fighting to stop the irradiation that he was convinced was a mistake.

The radiation treatments began with a "marking appointment." Evan thought it was funny that the doctor used magic marker on his face that we were not permitted to wash off. This was followed by two weeks of daily appointments, each lasting only 30 minutes. I explained to Evan that he would need to lie on the table and be perfectly still, to "freeze," even holding his breath for a few seconds. Could he do this in order to get well? Again, I was met with skepticism that a patient as young as Evan would be able to fully cooperate. The medicine to put him to sleep was on hand should they need it. Again, with enough preparation, Evan was totally cooperative. It was at this time that we met a radiology technician by the name of Jimmy Carter. He would take extra time with each child, in order to help his little patients feel comfortable, and perhaps avoid the anesthesia. He would also carry a wad of one dollar bills (his own money) in his white coat, and the children grew to expect to leave his department with a bill in pocket. Pop admired Jimmy so much that, at the end of radiation, Pop donated a "wad of ones," to help the cause. As usual, the psychologists at St Jude were already studying the side effects of cranial irradiation. Sadly, we were told that, after extensive educational testing, before and after the radiation, Evan indeed experienced the same problems as the other children. The resulting learning disability would challenge Evan for the rest of his life.

No hair ... but lots of hats.

Academically, Evan was falling behind. The school was bending over backwards to address his dyslexia and scheduled him to meet daily with Karen Marsh, who would try to supplement his reading time in the classroom with a blitz of phonics. His teachers were very supportive and even appreciated Evan's work ethic and high motivation.

During this first grade year, I received a phone call from the speech pathologist that the school brought in to do screenings of all first graders. She was calling to inform me that she had identified Evan as having "immature speech," specifically, he would need speech therapy in order to pronounce "r" and "s" sounds properly. (In all fairness, she was not aware of Evan's situation.) She informed me that this was serious. She asked me if I had noticed his poor pronunciations, and whether I was worried about it and considered it a problem. I suppose I was having a bad day, and I couldn't help myself with the answer. "Well, my first and foremost worry is that his life be saved, and that is the biggest problem. I am worried about his getting off chemotherapy, and whether he will relapse then, and that is a problem. Academically, I am worried that he is not reading yet, and that is a problem. I am worried about his self-esteem, especially when he hears that he will probably have to leave Latin and attend a special school for children with learning disabilities. And yes, somewhere down the list, I am aware of his pronunciation of /r/ and /s/, but I am not losing sleep over it. I am trying to prioritize his problems and will call you to schedule therapy, if everything else, higher up the list, resolves." When I hung up, I felt ashamed of myself. This pathologist was only trying to do her job... but a mama-bear can only hear so many short-comings about her cub.

CHAPTER VI

SUNSHINE RISES WITHOUT WARNING

With less than a year to go, another shocker was brewing. Our household was running on a timetable. The air around the house had settled in: on schedule and serious. All focus was beamed at Evan. Was he eating properly? Every time he got up to walk away, all sets of eyes were staring. Is he limping, even a little? Does he seem tired? Do we need to adjust bedtime? Have his sheets been changed daily? Is everyone washing his hands frequently? Are we offering some fruit and some vegetable daily? Is he drinking enough milk? Are we limiting friends to outdoor play and fresh air? Is he brushing his teeth with a soft-enough brush? Are we limiting his exposure to crowds, as much as possible? And, of course, my own pet project: How are his spirits? Does he need pepping up? Does he need something to look forward to? Does he have the WILL to keep a' goin'? Is he somewhat happy? Conversations begin and end here. Our routine cannot be altered. We are sticking to the agenda!

I am the maestro of this orchestra. The daily medicine course, the weekly blood counts, the monthly trips back to Memphis, the family activities, Mike's work schedule, the office demands, the yardman, home repairs and Jenny's school schedule were all parts of the complex harmony, and each part needed to blend with the next. Nana and Pop came over to the house every day to check in and offer help. We were running in such a synchronized way, there was simply no room for one of our members to step out of tempo.

When most middle school students were bonding with their best-friend group, and were shopping for 'hip clothes' and noticing

the 'cool boys' in the grade, Jenny was living in a world of serious adults. Every big challenge in the world of a pre-teen would
have seemed too minor to mention at home. Ever-sensitive Jenny would consider mountain-like school problems to be minis-
cule, considering. On one level, I realized that this exclusive focus
on Evan was severe and perhaps unhealthy. To what limit will a
mother go to save her child?

I began to feel tired, noticeably exhausted. It was not surprising.
I was working full time in the office and working full time when
at home. On many nights, it was necessary to do office work (paychecks, quarterly taxes and financial budgets, as well as to write
out home expense checks) from the time the kids went to bed
until wee hours in the morning. Huge demands came from every
direction: the office, running a household, parenting a pre-teen,
and caring for a child undergoing chemotherapy. Mike encouraged me to get a physical when I seemed to lack my usual energy.
Approaching my fortieth birthday, I reasoned that it was time to
establish base lines for cholesterol, bone density, blood pressure
etc. I realized that near-collapse is when one is relieved to have a
10 second rest at a red traffic light, or is grateful for a nap during
the sermon on Sunday.

Three days after my physical a phone call came in to our medical
office, and I answered the phone in a high-traffic, public area near
the check-out window.

"Mrs. Kaufman, please."

"This is she."

"This is Lisa at Dr. Rankin's office. I just wanted to call with the
good news. Your test is positive."

"Could you please excuse me? I need to change phones."

In the privacy of my office across the hall, and with the door closed, I switched the call from hold and asked to what test she was referring.

Realizing that this was not the ordinary response, Lisa immediately placed me on hold. I was puzzled, but at least she said that it was "good news." When she returned, she spoke with accuracy and detail. "The pregnancy test that was done on July 5th, yielded a positive result."

"Are you spelling my last name with a "K" or a "C"?

"K"

"Is the first name Helen?"

"Yes, ma'am. Were you here in the office on July 5th for the test?"

"Well, I was in the office but I was unaware that I had a pregnancy test."

And thus started the chain of miracles.

I hung up the phone, sat down and simply stared out the window. My magical thinking gripped my unsuspecting consciousness. Is this a replacement baby? Is God giving me this baby in preparation for losing Evan? (*Oh God, please NO!*)

I immediately called the doctor's office back. "I need to come in ... this afternoon even ... to see Dr. Rankin. I realize that it is late to be calling, but this is an emergency."

"I'm sorry, but Dr. Rankin is out of town for the holiday and will not be back in the office until Tuesday."

"Is there ANY doctor who is there? This is an emergency."

"Well, Dr. John Glover is here."

"Fine, when is his last appointment for the day? I will be in the waiting room and happy to wait for however long it takes."

This turned out to be another miracle. Dr. Glover was kind; he was calm. His first words of encouragement were "All of my older mommies return to me, to tell me that the baby is the best thing that ever happened." I explained that my situation was a lot more complex than just my age. We talked about Evan's medical issues. Could we tell if this baby might have chromosomal translocations like Evan and be predisposed to cancer? I described my "thoughts-of-terror," that is, that this baby would replace Evan. We also discussed my fear that my age would put the baby at risk for some deformity. Dr. Glover listened intensely to the stress in my life. We talked about the possibility of quitting my job because it sounded to him like I was already handling a much too heavy load. He understood me and I began to feel better. After verbalizing all the worries, I also began to feel a wave of joy for this third baby that we had wanted and planned for...that is, until Evan got so sick. The answer to my last question numbed my body and soul:

"Is there any way to tell when this baby is due?"

Dr. Glover popped out a round wheel-dial from the pocket of his white coat. "Well, this may be off, but right now, **I would say that this baby will be born on March 25th**."

"*Oh My God!*" This was the very date that appeared on the last sheet of Evan's chemo schedule. We have been celebrating the 25th of every month, since we started! This is NOT by chance! This is NOT a quirk of fate!

Driving home, I tried to make sense of all of this. For a year and a half, we had been struggling daily, always keeping in mind that our goal, our date of March 25, was looming like the prize at the end of the race. If we could only reach March 25, Evan would be off chemotherapy. Evan would start a new life of being normal. March 25 would mark the end of this extended nightmare. At this point, it looked like we would attain this.

On the darker side, were we about to lose Evan? What if he lived until March 25, but as soon as the chemotherapy stopped, the cancer returned and claimed Evan. It had been a long time since these thoughts occupied my head, and my anxiety took over. I could not ignore the two green traffic lights on the way home indicating that all is go...that we will all be O.K. For some reason, when I arrived at home, I kept my secret to myself. Even when Mike and I were finally alone, I was not ready to share my news. First, I needed to have some long talks with God. I was exhausted. I needed sleep, and I needed some strength to face tomorrow.

Three days passed and, in a quiet moment, I told Mike that we were pregnant. Always going for the humorous comeback, he replied, "Does this mean that we are back on the list for "extended day" at the church?" (Parents take turns babysitting during the church hour.) If he were shocked, he didn't show it. He was excited and positive and thought it was wonderful news. I shared with him my absolute worry of having a healthy baby, and wondered if there was some test that would tell us if our baby were somehow predisposed to having cancer too, or any of a number of genetic abnormalities found occasionally in babies of older women.

Mike took the next few days to research my questions and finally consulted Dr. Glover. There was a brand new technique called Chorionic Villus Biopsies (CVS). This test was being done by a doctor who had trained at Boston's Mass General and now was doing the test in Columbia, South Carolina. Unlike the amniocentesis test that gave the same information, the villous biopsy could be done within 3 weeks of conception (as opposed to 6 months). Within a day, we were on Route 77, driving from Charlotte to Columbia.

A full week went by, until the call came in ... again to the office. In a deja vu-like setting, I took the call in the privacy of my office. I was told about a list of possible genetic abnormalities, all of which were negative. I needed to hear it again. "You mean that our baby is absolutely healthy in every way that you are able to test?"

"Yes"

And then the caller asked me if I wanted to know the sex of the baby. SHOCK! I had not even realized that such a thing was possible. It was astonishing to think that a parent could know the sex of the baby even BEFORE the baby was born! Without much hesitation, I said "yes."

"It's a girl."

This time I ran down the hall to Mike's office. "It's a girl," I repeated. For me, this somehow meant that it had nothing to do with Evan's illness. It was nothing short of a miracle, a miracle from God. Evan was finishing treatment. Our third little sweetheart was on the way. We were going to be the family of five that we had always hoped for.

Mike and I decided, together, that it was too early to tell the children. What a challenge it was to consider all the changes that would be happening. The age difference between the baby and Jenny would be almost 14 years! How would that work? We did not have enough bedrooms...surely the baby and Jenny could not share a room. I mused for a moment, a room decorated with Madonna on one side and the Cookie Monster on the other? Should I quit my job? There was so much to do, so much to think about. It was time to prepare for our little family of five. It was time to leave the long, black, terrifying tunnel, and walk into the light of beautiful flowers, sunny days and a joyful life ... well, not quite.

Perhaps Jenny was first to pick up on some unspoken cues, to sense some hidden secret, so she conferred with her friend Paige, who agreed to help her gather information and piece together the clues to the puzzle. They spent one Saturday scouring the house. They came up with two facts: #1 There were two new dresses hanging in my closet. They looked weird, but nothing to base a conclusion upon. #2 There was a new bottle of vitamins in the cabinet in the kitchen. They were prescription vitamins, and they had my name on it. Jenny and Paige wrote down the name "John Glover, MD" with a plan to call his office during lunch time on Monday. Conveniently, his telephone number was listed on the bottle.

During lunch hour at school, the two girls roped off the area surrounding the pay phone outside the cafeteria and made the call.

"Is this the office of Dr. John Glover?"

"Yes, can I help you?"

"Well, yes. Actually, I was wondering if you could tell me what kind of a doctor Dr. Glover is?

"OB-GYN" came the response.

"Could you repeat that slowly?" (They needed to write that down.)

"Thank you."

Jenny and Paige were baffled. They had never heard of those letters and did not know what they stood for. Thinking of a way to get a quick, but accurate answer, the two girls went to the middle school counselor with the question:

"Mrs. Vinroot, could you please tell us, (reading from the paper), what an OBGYN doctor is?

This was an immediate alert, a red flag. Mrs. Vinroot explained the answer but immediately wanted to know why the girls were asking. Did one of them have a problem? Did one of them need to see this kind of a doctor? Was one of them in trouble? The inquisition lasted far too long, and finally the girls confessed to their Sherlock Holmes investigation. Mrs. Vinroot was convinced that no one was in trouble, and she kept their confidence, but it surely provided a good laugh in the end.

Finally, Mike and I decided that it was time to tell Jenny and Evan. After church, we always went out to lunch with the children. The original idea was to provide a family time, when we could discuss topics, perhaps even theology. Unfortunately, I don't remember that ever happening but we continued to share lunch together every Sunday afternoon. This particular Sunday, we chose to go to the "all-you-can-eat-brunch" at the Park Hotel near the South Park Mall. After piling high our plates, in a gluttonous way, Mike nodded at me to start the conversation.

"Well kids, we have something to tell you. We have enjoyed being parents so much that ..."

Jenny interrupts: "that you're going to have a baby!"

I couldn't believe my ears! How would she have known this? Evan couldn't believe his ears either: "Wait a minute" he protested. "We haven't taken a family vote yet ... I mean is this thing already started? I want to vote!" Our sweet intimate family lunch had veered off course. The whole family constellation, family air, family environment did a U-turn and flew down a totally different direction.

The thought of this new addition in our house gave everyone excitement, the kind you feel when everyone is anticipating something good on the horizon. The first round of decisions had to do with the nursery. We came up with a plan to reconfigure the second floor of our house. The plan would add a master bedroom and bath (previously we were sharing the bathroom with Jenny), would provide space for a nursery, and the new baby girl would share a bathroom with big sister. (Actually, big sister would be leaving for college, by the time the baby started kindergarten).

Because we knew that the baby was a girl, we forged ahead with the pink walls and white trim, the white rocking chair, and the pink bedding. Evan was excited, coming up with name suggestions, and everyone talked non-stop about what it would be like to have the baby here, and who would get to hold her. The atmosphere at our house switched overnight, like walking out of a funeral home to the last minute of a tied football game between Ohio State and Michigan.

There were still some details that did not seem to have a good solution. Evan's last treatment was scheduled for March 25. This could not be changed. The baby should be born around March 25, but we could play with the date since we were scheduling a C-section. I kept trying to figure out a way to attend Evan's last treatment. I finally acquiesced to giving up the very last trip to Memphis that Mike and Evan would have to do without me, and chose to have the baby born on MY birthday (also my grandfather's birthday), March 23.

As it turned out, the baby came early, March 18, which was only a "1-pill day" for Evan. He was pleased to be in Charlotte and could be part of this exciting family occasion. Jenny was excited because it was the first day of her spring break, and she envisioned spending the week playing mommy with the baby. I was hoping that, despite the C-section, I would be allowed to travel to Memphis for the last treatment but, in the end, I was unable to go. However, I did create a last-treatment party at home that included Evan's (now) two sisters, two grandparents and two parents. After the ceremonial cake, I gave Evan an inscribed gold pocket-knife that measured a scant one inch. Evan always wanted to carry a pocket knife in his pocket. I attached this special pocket knife to a gold pocket watch chain, so that it would have little chance of getting lost. The knife was inscribed with the date and the words "We Made It."

Evan and Mike made the trip back to Memphis on the 25th. Even though it was a significant occasion, the trip itself was uneventful. Mike said his thank yous, of course, to (Dr. Sharon) Murphy and Dr Pui, to Betty in the medicine room and her staff, to Ollie for the many rides to LaQuinta, to so many people too numerous to name. It was even an emotional good-bye to our friends at Avis and Piedmont Air Lines. How is it possible to say good-bye with the caveat that "I hope I never see you again." It seemed that our whole life revolved around this place. What will it be like now? Evan showed his new pocket knife to everyone. It was as momentous leaving, as it had been arriving.

Susan Staver Mary was the miracle gift to me, as I had always prayed for three children; she was a miracle gift to our marriage because she pumped fresh enthusiasm into two worn-out souls who were used to living in the trenches. We were two people who were going through the motions of breathing but not living. She was a miracle gift to a big sister who couldn't wait to dress her up, play with her, teach her to be a cheerleader, and who was grateful for making us a family again. She was a miracle gift to two grandparents, who seized still another opportunity to help out in a meaningful way. But most of all, Evan benefitted from the birth of his little sister, because the focus of attention was lifted from him every time our beautiful little girl giggled. Our hovering had become unhealthy for him, and this birth gave him the chance to see what normal was really like.

Beginning with Staver's birth, the days were brighter, the nights were livelier, the vacations were more fun, the future full of hope. The metaphor that always popped up into my vision was of a beautiful hand painted Limoge bowl that had dropped and that pieces with sharp edges were lying all over the floor. Staver came along and pieced the bowl back together again in the most beautiful way.

As for me, I was sure that Staver was God-sent. It was time for new breath in the family. It was time for some light-hearted smiles. No one will ever convince me that her intended birthdate of March 25th wasn't a direct message/sign. I will always believe that Dr. Glover was planted right where he should be, when I needed to talk my feelings out with the perfect doctor/counselor. No one will ever convince me that Staver wasn't born as a treasured gift to a broken family.

During the period of time that we thought Evan was going to need a bone marrow transplant, every family member was tested to see if we might be lucky enough to have a bone marrow donor in our midst. To be a donor, one needed to match 100 different markers (as opposed to a simple blood type match). Not one family member was a match. Thankfully, in the end, Evan didn't need the transplant. Then I learned ...

Baby Staver was a perfect match.

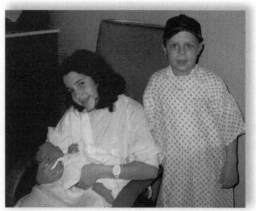

Jenny and Evan were excited to welcome our sweet baby Staver.

CHAPTER VII

"I JUST WANT TO BE NORMAL!"

On one of the last visits with Dr. Murphy, I could not help but ask the obvious: "If Evan were to relapse, what would it look like? How would it present?" She was prepared with the answer: "Usually it will present the same way it did before; in Evan's case, he will probably start limping again. Don't drive yourself crazy with this. Just enjoy this time." How does one do that?

I was convinced that our new baby would redirect anxiety about Evan's health and help me with a new perspective, appreciating our new family without daily chemo treatments. Had I forgotten how easily one becomes sleep deprived with a newborn and how difficult everything is when one is chronically tired? Was it possible to stay on top of Jenny's activities and school work and social life, research Evan's learning disability, and continue to do all the books for the office, in between night feedings for the baby? I couldn't help it. Every time Evan turned his back, I was focused on his gait; was he favoring one side or the other? Was there a small limp? Was his appetite diminished? Am I too tired to think straight?

Evan's reading difficulty would now take the front row seat. It was time to address this situation and explore every possible avenue of evaluating and then "fixing it." Finding the best learning disabilities specialist was really more difficult than finding St. Jude. Cancer hospitals publish their success rates and their research. The best place to go was quantifiable. It was far more difficult to ascertain where we could receive the best help in the educational world. We called everyone we knew who could give us a recommendation. Where do we go from here?

Dr. Mel Levine was a nationally known pediatric neurologist who was the head of the Center for Children with Learning Disabilities at Massachusetts General Hospital in Boston. We were on the waiting list for over six months when we received a call saying that Dr. Levine had given up his position at Mass General and was moving to another University Hospital. Did we still want to remain on the waiting list? We couldn't believe our good luck: Dr. Levine was starting a new center at The University of North Carolina at Chapel Hill. "Yes, we would like the first available appointment."

Evan called me into his room one night and told me he needed some hugs and love. This was usually the time that he would open up... or a time he liked to hear me reassure him. So I lay down and started the conversation with what would be happening next week. "Well, this coming Wednesday, we are going to go....." Evan interrupts, "to a new world-famous doctor about my reading 'ploblem.'" I couldn't believe my ears. "HOW did you know this?" and begged him to tell me. "Well, first I heard you talking to Dad about a new hospital. I figure that I am not sick, so it has to be about my reading. Then, I remembered Sherree Drezner told you about a world famous doctor who knows about reading problems. I figure if he is world famous, it must take a long time to see him, and he must work at a hospital, so, it's been a long time..." "Evan, why didn't you just ASK me?" Folding his arms behind his head like a business executive, he said "I usually have to wait until the right time, so I just wait for you to come to me and tell me. You always do."

I addressed his anxiety about the new encounter: "OK, Evan, let me tell you all about what will happen ..." Again, he interrupts: "Oh, I know: we will go there, fill out sheets of paper, and then some lady who smiles too much will take me into a room and will tell me that we are going to have a good time... some fun... playing games, and she is going to learn about my reading problem, so that she can help me read. I've done this before, you know. I mean, I don't mind, because I figure there won't be any needles, any shots, any medicine, or any blood work." When he realizes that the appointment would be in Chapel Hill, he adds, "All that I ask is that we can go to the 'underground restaurant.' " He remembered a restaurant called The Rathskeller on Franklin Street, from two years ago! "Evan, when you grow up, I know you are going to be successful, even if you never learn to read another word. You amaze me! Tearing up I whisper, I just want you to be happy."

From all the evaluations done at St. Jude, before and after the cranial irradiation, I silently suspected that Evan had a learning disability. Dr. Ray Mulhern, the psychologist at St. Jude, tested Evan and then sat down with Mike and me and reviewed the numbers with us. Being an educator myself, I reasoned that the younger the child is when tested, the less valid are the scores. Peppered with denial, I also rationalized that Evan had missed so much school that it was no wonder that he was behind.

By the time Evan entered third grade, his teacher, Sally Johnson, and the Lower School Head, Claudette Hall, felt that it was time for us to find another placement for Evan. The euphemism for getting kicked out of a private school is to "not have your needs met." According to Ms. Hall, Charlotte Latin had "failed Evan." This was an interesting concept, since Evan's major need, at this point, was not educational; but rather, to feel comfortable within his surroundings. His real need was to stay at Latin until his chemotherapy was finished. Our only blessing regarding this news was from Dr. Ned Fox, the headmaster, who had a special empathy for Evan. Despite the enormous time-demands of his position, he spent several periods observing Evan in the classroom and his unbiased opinion was that Evan needed special help that Latin could not provide. He sensed the pain that this pronouncement inflicted and followed it with a promise to Evan: "I will always hold a space for you back at Latin." Turning to me, he said, "You will not have to retest or reapply. All you will have to do is make a phone call and let me know that it is time to return, and you will be able to." Evan held on to this statement, this promise, and quoted it often as an assurance to himself.

After the appointment with Mel Levine and the work-up by his staff, we were told that Evan would definitely benefit by changing schools. Despite his comfort level with his friends at Latin, he needed an environment that would take the pressure off, and one where the teachers understood his limitations. Because this came from "the world expert," Evan was willing to accept his fate. He was hoping that he could finish out the school year. We countered, "Evan, the sooner we get started, the sooner we will finish." Then we asked Evan what he thought about making the switch now, instead of at the end of the school year. "Dad, Mom (slightly exasperated), that's for you to decide. This is not a kid decision!" (*God! Parents can learn a lot from their kids!*)

Leaving the restaurant, he said, "My true feeling is that I'd rather be at Charlotte Latin, but I may as well get this over with. I am scared that everyone will forget me and not remember me, when I go back." After a little bit of quiet time on the way home, Evan addressed this one last time: "I guess this is a good thing. I'm going to have to work really hard. When I'm older, I'll be used to working hard, and this is going to make me real successful ... I just want to be normal." I was astounded at his thinking ... and, at the same time, it made me sick.

Evan needed to tell his peers about going to the new school, and it was difficult for him. He feared that everyone would view this as a school for dummies. I tried to give him the words: "a school for regular kids who have a problem reading." I explained again and again that his teachers said that he had "superior intelligence but that his reading is far below how smart he is." My job was to engrain in him and assure him that he was a smart little boy! (This is hard to do when your child "feels dumb.") Finally, I came up with the right explanation for him: "just like St. Jude was the best place to make you walk again, Fletcher is the best place to teach you how to read." (*Well, I hoped so.*)

In January, 1987, we finally moved Evan to The Fletcher School. It was one of two private schools that served students with learning disabilities. We were lucky that they had an opening mid-year. Evan hated leaving his beloved Charlotte Latin, and he was unhappy switching to Fletcher* because "it wasn't normal." First, it was located in St. Mark's Lutheran Church, squeezed into six classrooms. There were four children per grade in grades two through eight. All of these kids had different kinds of deficits: some couldn't read, some couldn't do math, some couldn't write, some couldn't do any of the above. After visiting several times, we thought that Evan might be the worst reader there... and he was. The school had no playground (but it was located near a city park); it did not have any art classes or PE, and most importantly to Evan, it did not have a football team. On his last day at Latin, he summarized his feelings: "My life is in shambles," he said, "I can't read, I don't eat right. I can't run fast. I can't do anything right." BAM! ... a punch to my stomach. (*What do I say to that?*)

It was difficult to know just how to respond to his despair. Having met with so little success, Evan was beginning to protest vigorously whenever we read at home. It was hard to know whether to push him, or to accept his faltering drive to read. The answer was both. It was important to push Evan up to the highest level he could achieve, but then to be satisfied with whatever that level was. With enough encouragement, enough special education, and enough hard work, I had to believe that he would eventually read. Our job was to motivate Evan, by rewarding his effort to read and to convince him that hard work WAS beneficial.

Always looking for the silver lining, our good fortune in attending Fletcher was Evan's new teacher, Mrs. Howell. She and Evan enjoyed kidding with each other. In the morning, when Evan arrived she would say: "Good Morning Henry" (as in Henry Kissinger, because Evan was always negotiating how much work he

---

* Evan attended The Fletcher School in its infancy. Within the next several decades, the school grew to serve nearly 265 students per year in grades K-12. Students today enjoy a large campus, new buildings, and state-of-the-art technology. The school has gained national recognition but most importantly, it enjoys many success stories.

needed to do for her) and Evan would reply back "Good Morning Mrs. Hannigan" (who was the harsh and unattractive head of the orphanage from the movie Annie). A relationship was forged with her that began to make him feel positive.

I was not sure whether or not Fletcher was equipped to turn his reading disorder around. However, one thing became clear almost immediately. Since every student there had a "learning difference," Evan was relieved of the pressure to cover up his reading problem. He no longer had the strain or the anxiety of "what if someone finds out." It was OK to be dyslexic. Most everyone else was, too. This, alone, freed up a lot of emotional energy to be redirected to learning.

With only three other students in his class, the entire day was spent in an "individual setting," that offered a lot of immediate feedback and encouragement. Mrs. Howell and others would assign reasonable chunks of homework and although Evan complained about the school, he began to experience first-time success, and that felt good. (*Thank you, God for Fletcher!*)

Reading could hardly have been more of a struggle. Evan knew most of the rules (from years of phonics tutoring), but could not apply them. He would be stumped by a word in a sentence, sound it out, be told what the word was, and then miss it again in the very next sentence. He absolutely couldn't apply suffixes like es, s, ing, ed. It was necessary to sound out "sight words" each time (like: a, the, in, it) again and again, as if he had never seen the word before. I noted that, when he didn't know the word, he would often look away as if the answer were somewhere floating in space. (It was as if looking at the word, or trying to break it apart, would not help.) Often, he would decode a word such as "mom" and verbalize the word as "mother." He would read along and substitute words that weren't there because he thought he could guess what was coming next. When decoding a word with many syllables, such as "cafeteria," he would struggle with each syllable so long that, when he got to the end syllable, he totally forgot the beginning syllable. One specialist described his reading thus: "Picture a sentence of ten words. With every single word, it was necessary to take a dictionary and look up the meaning and the pronunciation. And with words that have several meanings, keep the alternatives in mind. Now go back to the beginning and try to read the sentence and know the meaning."

Evan was in constant movement during his homework. Even though Dr. Levine did not find that Evan had A.D.D. (Attention Deficit Disorder), Mike was convinced that a trial of Adderall would help him concentrate. Taking the situation into our own hands again (mistake), Mike tried Evan on an initial trial of the drug. Soon, Evan became adamant about NOT taking this medicine. It made him feel funny, and he simply refused to continue taking it. Smart Evan had the answer that had no retort: "If Dr. Levine had thought it would help, HE would have given it to me." Every homework session was a trial of patience. Evan was so miserable trying to read, that he wanted to change the subject every other sentence with stories of what had happened that day, or what a word reminded him of last year. During these stories, his hands were waving in the air in a slightly clumsy way, like very young children sometimes do. No sooner would he complete a few more reading sentences than he would interrupt: "Oh yes, let me tell you..." This was called "Evan's diversion strategy," and he perfected it with great acumen.

The educational specialist in Dr. Levine's group mentioned the advantages of Evan's learning to use a tape recorder. It could become his best friend as he could record classes or use it for oral reports. I could immediately picture his listening to a book on tape that would make him feel somewhat independent with his school work. So, during the summer months, I set an impossible goal for myself. I called the school in June and purchased every single textbook that he would use for the next year. I recorded every day, chapter by chapter, every text. This was a monumental task mostly accomplished in the wee hours of the night, or even while nursing and rocking the baby. Every minute of every day had to be utilized and maximized by multi-tasking. There was no free time, even to nurse a baby. This became an exhaustive pace. I feel tired just writing about it.

I began to feel almost as helpless as when Evan had gotten sick. We were trying to address four major issues: (1) Dyslexia. We switched schools, hired tutors, and read with him every day, without fail. It seems his life was always attaching reading to a prize. "You can swim for one more half hour, if you promise to read an extra half hour tonight." Often Evan would weigh the deal and decide that it wasn't worth it. (2) Undisciplined Behavior. Evan became so frustrated, that he turned red in the face. He couldn't control the pressure, and sometimes, it turned to a rage. At times, he became pathetically unhappy with himself, and it sickened me to see him so distraught. (3) Physical Weakness. Was this the result of chemotherapy? Or the result of his spinal cord compression? Was this due to poor eating? He wanted so much to be part of a soccer team or baseball team, but he simply could not keep up physically. I worried that it was affecting his self-esteem and his friendships. (4) Eating. Before, he would not eat at all. Now, he only wanted to eat junk food and refused to eat dinner at night. We elected to insist that he eat healthy, and he elected to starve and hate us.

(Lord! It's me again. I need direction and help in knowing how to deal with each of these challenges. Help me know if we are just about to turn the corner and if pushing forward is the way to go, or will things never get any better, and I am only making things worse. Please guide me because day to day, I feel like giving up.)

At a time when I thought there could be no more worries added to the list, Mike came to me with a grim face that called for a halt. Mike noticed a lump on Evan's right upper lip. Funny, I had not noticed it. That night we both entered his room together to say goodnight, and also to ask for a good look at the inside of his mouth. We were nauseated! Could this be a tumor? Is this a recurrence of cancer in a new place? The swelling that was puffing out his lip, ever so slightly, was not his tooth. The swelling was above, and to the left of, his bicuspid. We were scared, and from there, panicked! Was this the beginning ...?

In this situation, a weekend is a lethal time. After one night of absolutely no sleep, we played the waiting game. When the hands of the clock passed the hour of noon, and even though it was Sunday, I called Jim Brittain, a neighbor and pediatric dentist. Maybe he could relieve our fears and tell us what this could be. Graciously, he told us to meet him at his office at 1:00. In the meantime, Mike remembered that a friend of his, Dr. Rider, had evaluated Evan for orthodontia six months prior. Mike also called Dr. Rider and asked if he would be willing to meet Mike at his office to pick up the plaster cast of Evan's mouth, done at the first appointment. Dr Rider and Mike both examined the cast of Evan's mouth and noticed the subtle misshaping of the gum above Evan's tooth on the right. Upon viewing the cast from above, they saw that the swelling was already the size of a dime. Whatever this was, it had started to grow at least six months ago. (*Oh God, No!*)

We were sitting on Dr. Brittain's stoop a little before one. He examined Evan and confirmed that Evan's mass was not related to a tooth. He was cautiously optimistic that it was most likely a benign cyst. He also said that he hadn't seen anything like this before. He suggested that tomorrow (Monday) we return, and his technician would do a panorex (a surround x-ray of the mouth).

When we returned home that afternoon, Mike and I discussed whether or not to call Dr. Golembe today or wait until tomorrow, Monday. Filled with too much anxiety, I could not help myself. I paged Dr. Golembe and reached him immediately. He was making rounds at the hospital and offered to see Evan first thing in the morning at his office. Mike and I became paralyzed with fright. We decided that we would see Dr. Golembe first, before calling Murphy (Dr. Murphy at St. Jude Hospital), and then, I went upstairs and quietly packed our "Memphis bag," ... just in case.

Within a few hours, the doorbell rang. Dr. Golembe was on his way home from the hospital and probably felt guilty after my call, sensing the terror in my voice. When he examined Evan, he admitted that he did not know WHAT he was looking at. All that he would say was, "Well, there is definitely something there." We told Dr. Golembe that we were scheduled to have a panorex done first thing in the morning, and that we would bring it over to his office.

Mike and Dr. Brittain studied the xray film the next morning. They saw a semi lucent mass, about the size of a Vicks triangular cough drop, between the 2nd and 3rd teeth on the right. The point of the triangle lay in a position that pointed down, and the base pushed up against Evan's maxillary sinus. Dr. Brittain did point out that there were no other holes in the jaw, and that Evan's bones looked pushed aside, but not destroyed in any way.

By 9 a.m. we were in Dr. Golembe's office with the plaster mold from six months ago and the panorex from 30 minutes ago. Dr. Golembe was perplexed and asked an otolaryngologist in the clinic to see Evan, as soon as possible. This doctor incised the cyst and drained the cyst and started Evan on antibiotics. However, he called Mike and Dr. Golembe, to say that he had not ruled out a tumor. By Wednesday, the doctor called to say that the cultures were negative but perhaps Evan had developed a fungus infection, and that he wanted to culture the cyst again. More panic set in.

Another desperate call was made to Steve Hemming, an oral surgeon, whom Mike knew professionally. He offered to see Evan the next day. After a few prayers, we were in another waiting room to seek yet another opinion. "I think I can put your mind at ease," he said. (*Oh glorious sentence! thank you, God!*) "This is a classic globulomaxillary cyst." He had seen many of these, and the x-ray further confirmed the diagnosis. It was totally benign. (*precious relief for this time.*)

The emotional road that we had just taken mimicked our panic four years prior. Our sick guts were identical in quality, reaching level "extreme" in only a week. The sequence was the same: disbelief/denial, fear of the unknown, helplessness, solicitation for help, terror, non-stop prayer and finally, the relief of knowing something... sometimes, the scale tips good and sometimes bad. How many times would we live through similar scenarios? How many times would we travel a detour on Evan's road? This one episode stopped life altogether at our house. Was this a reminder that dyslexia was relatively minor compared to the recurrence of cancer? Was it really possible to live life under this sort of stress? Do other people live like this?

"Oh yes, not to forget, have you watched him walk today?"

CHAPTER VIII

"EVEN THE SIDE EFFECTS HAVE SIDE EFFECTS."

Despite the hopefulness surrounding Evan's last treatment, and following Staver's birth, life did not become easy. The pace at our house was overwhelming: the needs of an infant, the rigors of Evan's reading plan, the responsibilities at the office, and the demands of a teenager who now dared to rebel. But the biggest stress was watching, ever so closely, for a limp, lethargy, or loss of appetite. Similar scares, such as Evan's maxi facial cyst, would happen over and over.

One week, Evan had two nose bleeds. For most kids, this would be a passing interest. For us, it generated panic until we could prove that it was nothing. Sometime after that, Evan developed a dark blue bruise on his left arm near the elbow, without recalling any trauma. The worst part was that the bruise did not carry any soreness with it. What did that mean? (*"Oh God, What did that mean?"*) Did he seem to be more tired? This was a tense time; a time when tumor cells, that had been suppressed for so long, might come back if left unchecked by the weekly poison. How could we possibly ever return to non-stop vomiting, trips to Memphis, another protocol? How could we go back to the hospital to start over again, knowing that eventual success, the promise of getting off therapy forever, was greatly dwindled?

Evan's sweet disposition gave way to outbursts of temper; he could not contend with frustration, had difficulty dealing with disappointment and lacked confidence. I would ask myself: Is this a result of the cancer, the treatment (drugs and radiation), or the result of years of coddling Evan? If the academic stress became too much, Evan learned to hit verbally, where it would hurt the most: "Sorry I'm not a good son. Sorry I can't read like every-one else. Sorry I'm not what you want." We dealt with this, as best we could. I tried not to over-sympathize, and all I could think to do was remind him of how much I loved him, no matter what. I learned as a mom, that I should not over react. The reason for the behavior did not matter.

I would estimate that the "grapefruit" in my stomach began to dissolve slightly, ever so slightly and slowly at the one year mark of his last treatment. I was working so hard to achieve a normal life for Evan, that I completely lost track of an important first step for me: totally dissolving this rock in my stomach, becoming nor-mal myself instead of constantly jumping at every corner, think-ing: "the cancer is back!"

Evan was already different. He was nine, but looked seven, and in many instances, acted like a five-year-old. Then sometimes, his thinking was that of a seventy-year-old. He had not grown more than an inch in two and a half years of chemo, making him the shortest kid in the class. This was hard on Evan when he reasoned that he was also the oldest in the class. I decided to mention this to Dr. Golembe on our next visit.

Surprisingly, Dr. Golembe had planned to discuss Evan's growth pattern with me, even before I could introduce this as my next worry. According to the charts, Evan had a steady straight line growth since his radiation. Dr. Golembe looked at me with a seri-ous grimace and mentioned the possibility that the radiation had stopped the pituitary gland from producing an adequate amount of growth hormone. He recommended that it was now time to see a pediatric endocrinologist.

Dr. Parker performed a complete exam on Evan and affirmed Dr. Golembe's suspicion. Evan's growth hormone levels were low, and his growth was stunted. However, Dr. Parker was hesitant to consider treatment for Evan, given his history. He said that there was not enough data from child cancer survivors who develop growth hormone insufficiency, (due to lack of child survivors period) and he worried that injections of growth hormone might increase the risk of abnormal cell division, that is, increase the risk of a relapse.

Mike and I discussed this at length. Nothing could be so important that we would risk a relapse. In the end, we opted for a second opinion. Marc Drezner, an endocrinologist at Duke and close friend of ours from our days in Durham, referred us to Dr. Nan Friedman, a pediatric endocrinologist, for whom he had great respect. We had quite a wait for our first visit. Dr. Friedman was fresh from her sabbatical at Harvard and had a long waiting list of patients. Perhaps our appointment was squeezed in, but, on our day, she was three hours behind schedule. By the time we saw her, Evan was impatient and tired. Dr. Friedman, herself 4' 11", ordered x-rays and tests and told us that Evan was clearly two standard deviations below normal for his age. She confirmed that patients, who have been aggressively treated with chemotherapy and radiation, all have some subtle, to not-so-subtle, growth hormone deficiency. And then our discussion centered on the decision to chance a cancer reoccurrence. By measuring a bone in Evan's wrist, we learned that his real life height would have been 5'7" to 5'9". This seemed logical, given his two short parents. But because of his health history, his eventual height, untreated, would now be somewhere between 5'0" and 5'1".

Dr. Friedman told us that prescribing growth hormone injections was always optional. Unlike St. Jude Hospital where our doctors made all the decisions, the choice of growth hormone therapy was squarely in our court. An additional problem was that we could not delay the decision. After Evan entered puberty, the therapy would no longer be an option. Do we walk away and offer Evan one more dimension of being different forever, or do we go for broke and help him achieve his God-given height, with a dark shadow of possible cancer looming above? The weight of this decision would haunt every waking hour.

Evan made the decision more difficult. The idea of injections every day for years was all Evan had to hear. He was against this and was adamant that he was satisfied with his height. He did not want to see any more hospitals, any more needles, or any more doctors. Incensed, he pleaded his point: "I had to have chemo to get rid of the cancer problem. Now I have to have shots to get rid of the chemo problem. Even the side effects have side effects. When will this end?" (*My sentiments exactly, Evan ... my sentiments exactly.*)

After prayer, discussions, research, and blind faith, we started the first growth hormone therapy in the summer of 1989, only five years after our first chemo injections. At this time, growth hormone was not produced synthetically in the laboratory. The cost of Evan's human growth hormone would amount to over $10,000 per month, and he would be on this regime for the next four years. Our insurance company had now reached the $1,000,000.00 paid-claims mark. At this point, it would be necessary/crucial to research insurance options, if any were to be found. (*When will I find the time to do this????*)

Mike, who gave all the shots, went to great lengths to extract every last drop from each bottle. Evan would decide where the nightly shot should be given, arm or thigh, an attempt on our part to have Evan feel that he was in charge of something. The visiting nurse from the insurance company suggested that we teach Evan to give the shot to himself, but never would he agree to this. Usually, it was not a problem, but occasionally Mike would be out of town, and we were forced to impose upon our neighbor, and registered nurse, Elaine Griffin, to administer the shot.

We made a great effort not to have the shots interfere with Evan's life. For example, in sixth grade, his class was taking an overnight trip to the mountains. Fortunately, one of the teachers who had planned to go on the trip, had been a medic in the army, and agreed to give the shots while on the trip. Evan asked if this could be done in secret. Even overnights at a friend's house had to be dealt with creatively.

Perhaps, in one instance, I went a little too far. In the spring of Evan's first year of growth hormone therapy, he announced that he really wanted to go to Camp Thunderbird with his friend, Jason. The camp was located 45 minutes south of Charlotte on beautiful Lake Wylie. The boys would be sleeping in cabins, and their session would last a full two weeks. After signing up, I called the camp nurse to say that my son was on growth hormone shots, and that I would be supplying the medicine, needles etc. I wanted to discuss Evan's desire to take his shots in private. To my shock, she answered that she was very sorry, but Evan would not be able to get his shots while at camp. I could not understand why. Surely, someone at the camp was qualified to give the shots! She explained that due to some insurance liability issue, this was impossible. Not one to take no for an answer, I began to suggest solutions. She reiterated that the insurance guidelines dictated that only the camp doctor could give the shots. Thinking "no problem," I asked for the camp physician's name and number. The unfortunate answer was they no longer could find a volunteer physician. The camp clinic was staffed entirely by nurses who were not allowed to give injections.

How could this be? How could these shots stand in the way of Evan experiencing summer camp? Surely, I can come up with a creative solution here: Could we suspend these shots for two weeks? "No." Could Mike make the trip to camp each night to give the shot? (a solution that Mike did not favor) "No." I was left with only one possible solution: Mike "was volunteered" to be the new camp doctor for the two week session!

It took a lot of coaxing to convince Mike that this was a good idea. First, he had not seen the inside of a child's ear since a pediatric rotation in medical school, years ago. (And I must say that his track record was not very good, concerning our own children.) Second, this was not the way he wanted to spend his precious vacation time. Eventually, faced with the facts, he agreed, but in his conscientious, compulsive way, he asked Ray Swetenberg, our pediatrician, if he could shadow him at his pediatric clinic, look-

ing at sore throats, bee stings and painful ears of each little patient. In addition, he extracted a promise from him: that he would
stay near his phone so that Mike could call him with any problem
about which he was unsure.

It actually turned out to be a fun, family vacation, almost. Mike,
Staver, and I stayed in a rustic little cabin that had air condition-
ing and a stocked refrigerator. Evan loved inviting camper friends
to our cabin during free period. He loved camp, in general, and
was able to get his shot each night privately. Jenny was attending
the older camp, and she and her friends would surround "Baby
Staver" in the mess hall each night. Staver loved the swimming
pool and all the extra attention of the campers. The only person
without a smile was Mike, who was taking call for hundreds of
children, with only the help of a well-seasoned nurse and a PDR
(Physicians' Desk Reference). Mike was a good sport, but I had to
promise never to ask this of him again. Fortunately, it was the end
of Evan's camp experience while on growth hormone therapy.

In the end, taking the growth hormone was the right decision but
it surely required a lot of courage. For the most part, Evan got to
the point that he did not mind the shots. Usually, they did not
interfere with his life, and he began to grow. He seemed to take
great pride in his height, and also in developing leg and arm muscles. The first year was anxiety producing, as we watched for and
focused on signs of a relapse, but sometime during the last three
years, we began to relax just a little. On Evan's last follow-up with
Dr. Friedman, we fantasized that it was, perhaps, the last hospital
appointment for long-term treatment. Counting the chemotherapy
and growth hormone shots, Evan was completing 8.5 years of daily
medical treatments. Surely, life was going to revert to slow-paced
and worry-free.

On a good day, I would count my many, many blessings. Evan
seemed to have beaten the odds. We were hopeful that his health
problems had passed. He was a wonderful son. His teachers loved

his personality, his tenacity, his sense of humor. He had weathered the storm. We made it through.

On a bad day, I feared that his medicines and irradiation had robbed him of happiness in life. Would these be the childhood scars that Evan would carry for the rest of his life? I could not imagine what lay ahead and my imagination often turned dark. I was worn out. Could I continue this journey? Was there a choice? Was the course of his future path on my shoulders?

What if I fail him?

CHAPTER IX

WHAT LIKE TO HAVE A LEARING DISABILITY
In my own words by Evan Kaufman.

My third grade teacher was Ms. Johnson. She was tall, with red, curly hair. I remember work sheets. She would tell the students at 10 o'clock to read the directions and work through the sheets. Well, if you can't read the directions, you can't really work through the work sheets, so a lot of times I would still be trying to read the directions, when half the class had completed the task and turned in their papers. I quickly understood that there was something that I was missing. I did not feel stupid in the class. People didn't make fun of me. I wasn't ashamed. I just wasn't doing the work as quickly as everybody else; in fact, I wasn't doing the work at all! In order for me to survive in the class, I had to figure out a way to understand what I was supposed to do. Instinctively, I knew I better not admit that I couldn't read the directions myself, because I felt that I wouldn't dare let her, or anyone, know that I couldn't read.

I would walk up to Ms. Johnson and casually ask her a question about the directions, without asking her to read the entire direction paragraph. Usually, she thought that I was trying to get out of doing the assignment, and she would ask me to return to my seat and do the work myself. After I got no information from Ms. Johnson, I would ask a classmate beside me, or in front of me, something relatively simple, like, "Are you circling the right answer, or, are you crossing out the wrong answer? Are you underlining the right answer? How do you do it?" Sometimes I would be able to understand what was happening, what was going on, and sometimes I wouldn't. I always felt tense, as if someone might think that I was cheating. I knew I could give the right answer if only someone would tell me what the directions were! Sometimes the room was so quiet I couldn't ask questions out loud, and I would act like I was reading the directions, but my eyes would be anywhere but on the page: they would be on the page of the girl next to me, or the person across from me, or someone else, to see what they were doing, and then I would copy that. Ms. Johnson quickly caught onto this, and would say, "All right, eyes on your paper, everyone," and I'm pretty sure that she wasn't talking to everyone; she was talking to me.

So that was my first memory: trying to do these work sheets and not being able to, because I couldn't read the directions. I felt like there was just nothing coming out of my brain. If I didn't know a word, or I couldn't figure a word out, it was just blank. It was like, "All right, okay, where is my brain?" I felt like everybody else's engine was going, and mine was stalled. I knew I had an engine, I knew I had a brain, it just wasn't working. Those were my third grade thoughts (and fears).

I specifically remember when I had to leave Latin and switch to Fletcher School. My parents introduced the subject with "We know of a special school that could help you do your schoolwork better." That was code for: "we have decided to send you to another school, because you can't make it at Latin." I didn't want to lose my friends. I didn't want to lose the environment that I knew. I didn't want to switch schools. After going through chemotherapy and losing my hair, the last thing I wanted was to change schools. I was tired of being different. Not only was I going to be different health-wise, but now I had to have different friends, at a different school, with different teachers. It made me very angry. When they told me about this new school, I made them promise that, if I got better at my schoolwork, they would allow me to return to Latin. This promise motivated me. I resolved to get back to Latin somehow, where Jenny was, and where my friends were.

Fletcher was everything that a "regular" school was not. There were 28 students in the school. My class had 4 kids, and it was composed of 2 grades. There was no gym, no playground, and it was located in the back of a church. The recess area was a public park that was across the street from the church, and some days, we had people there who were sleeping on benches. When I looked around at Fletcher, it just didn't feel like a place where I was supposed to go to school. There is a certain smell a school has. Maybe it is the sharpened pencils, or chalkboards, or desks, but there is a certain smell with a traditional school. Maybe it's something in the soap they use to mop the floors, but Fletcher had a very stale smell. When I walked into my classroom, there were bookshelves, with hymnals and Bibles, used for Sunday school. I felt that Fletcher was for dummies. We started off in a math class doing addition and subtraction; whereas, at Latin, we had been doing complex word problems, much more difficult than addition and subtraction. I quickly got frustrated. I thought, "I'm not learning anything. I don't need remedial math." For the majority of my Fletcher experience, Linda Howell was my teacher, and she and I got along like peanut butter and jelly.

Mrs. Howell was there to teach me, and I was there to bargain. I always loved to say, "You know, Mrs. Howell, you wouldn't have to grade so much at home, if I didn't have to do so much work here. So I'll tell you what. I'll cut you a break. Instead of doing the full two chapters in our reading comprehension book, I'll do half of it, and we'll all benefit from that." Mrs. Howell was not an easy target. She saw right through me, and she always looked at me with a grimace, a smile, a smirk; she had a way of smirking. "Evan, don't mess with me, but good try. I really appreciate your trying to get away with something, but I'm no pushover." It was kind of a head down, eyes up grimace, with a little smile at the end. Mrs. Howell was my teacher for the remainder of my third, fourth and fifth grades.

I wanted to return to Latin so much, but I finally reasoned that I was not going to get there by a sudden break-through in my reading. Therefore, I decided that I would need to come up with a plan. I decided that, if I could convince Dr. Levine to recommend my return, it would happen. After all, my Mom and Dad always did whatever Dr. Levine said to do. This would prove to be a valuable lesson: There is more than one way to get where I wanted to go, and for me, the best way was to maneuver my way around a problem ... to talk my way through it.

Whenever we met with Dr. Levine, he would always have the four of us sit around the table, and then he would interview both of my parents to learn how my school work was coming along. Before ending the session, he would always turn to me and give me a chance to describe how things were, from my perspective. This was my chance. This was the moment that I had planned for. I tried my best to be convincing.

"Well, I have been giving this a lot of thought. I think that I have learned a great deal at Fletcher, mainly how to study, how to organize, and how to let the teacher know what I need. However, I don't think that I am EVER going to be the greatest reader. I think that I should return to Charlotte Latin, where I can learn a lot, just being around a lot of smart kids. I also want to return to Charlotte Latin because my friends are there, and I think I can learn best, if I am happy. And also, I think I should return to Latin, to try out my new study skills. I just need for you to give me a chance!

I couldn't believe the next part. Dr. Levine agreed with me!!! I really talked him in to this. And just that fast, I was returning to Latin. My parents were shocked, and so was I. It worked! All the way back to Charlotte from Chapel Hill, I could not believe that my plan worked. I was on my way back to Latin! Right there and then, I learned another valuable lesson. I have the ability to talk my way into most anything I want. This was a great thing to discover.

I don't think I was even nervous on my first day back at Latin. I just couldn't believe that I had made it back! I was there. I had overcome the Fletcher stay. Not that Fletcher was a bad place, but returning to Latin was another step toward normalcy. In sixth grade at Latin, I had four different classes, and I switched from class to class. I had four different teachers. We had our own lockers. We had a library. We had PE and a uniform for PE. Latin also had junior varsity sports. This was all very, very exciting to me. Little did I know that the work would overtake life.

The work at Latin was significantly harder. If the workload at Fletcher was comparable to Lake Norman, a small lake north of Charlotte, the workload at Latin was like the Atlantic Ocean. Not only did English, Social Studies, and Science require a great amount of reading, but math was that way, too! I had always been good at math, and now even math was over my head.

One day in sixth grade, I forgot my lunch. Jenny always had some money in her wallet, so I reasoned: if I could find her quickly, get some money from her, I would still have time to buy lunch and eat. At the same time that I was supposed to be eating lunch, I got a note to report to Mr. Dubick, about my science project. I was beginning to feel upset because I was hungry, I had to find Jenny, and I had to meet with Mr. Dubick. I went to my locker and felt overwhelmed. I couldn't do it all. I didn't know what to do first. I didn't know whether to go get lunch. I didn't know if I could find Jenny. I didn't know if I needed to go to see Mr. Dubick. I just didn't have time to get it all done. I simply sat down and tried to hold back the tears.

Ms. Harris, my home room teacher, was very direct, a strict teacher. She saw that I was feeling bad and asked me what was wrong. I was kind of gasping for air, and she said, "Come into the room," and I just lost it. I told her all the different things I needed to get done in only one class period. She looked at me and said, "Well, Evan, if you're gonna' get it done, you better stop crying and get your tushy in gear." That surprised me. She didn't say it would be all right or offer to take care of it. All of a sudden I stopped crying, shocked that she wasn't pampering me, and I left. What it taught me was: don't spend time crying for yourself. That's a waste of time. Just get going and get it done. Things will work out.

There were still worksheets to answer, just like in third grade, but since I had been to Fletcher and back, I was a little wiser, a little quicker, and a little better at figuring my way around my reading problem. I figured out my own method of "key words." If I had to read a paragraph and answer questions about it, I would not spend time deciphering the paragraph. I would search for the answer with the key word. For example, if the question were: "What did Kenny have for lunch?", I would look for the words "lunch" and "Kenny." She gave us a worksheet to do and I started using my method, matching the words in the question to the same words in the paragraph. Usually, the first question would be in the first paragraph, the second question, in the second paragraph. For the first time, I answered all the questions, even before some kids in the classroom. I thought to myself: "look at me... I answered all the questions all by myself. I didn't have to cheat from anybody. I did it." Important lesson: I learned to adapt to my learning disability. I found a way to use clues. That's what you have to do: if you can't read, you find a way to succeed. I learned to repeat to myself: "Set yourself up for success. Use all your resources."

Not everything worked out so easily. For me, the most difficult assignment was when they asked me to read a book and then write a report about it. For this, I had to use my mother as my secretary. I would dictate, and she would type. But my language skills were poor, and I couldn't dictate my thoughts logically. I would become so frustrated that, sometimes, I would lie right down on the floor and scream at her.

In the eighth grade we were asked to read Hamlet and write a paper on it. Trying to read Shakespeare was like reading Greek. I didn't understand it. I didn't know how to begin. I didn't understand what was going on. I didn't understand what the point was. Mom would start off saying that we needed to make an outline first. I refused! I just wanted to sit down and get it done. Writing an outline would take too much time.

Imagine Mom at the typewriter. She would say, "All right, Evan, what do you want to write first?" I had no idea. I answered: "I don't know." She replied: "Well, let's try to come up with a main idea." I had no main idea. So, by this point, I was feeling angry and in a bitter tone I yelled at her. I was mad at myself, because I had to have help, and I didn't have a clue how to help myself. Mom then turned the typewriter off. She would say: "We have to make an outline. That way, you can follow it and dictate paragraph by paragraph.

"Mom, outlines are stupid. Let's just write it and let's just get it over with." So Mom, frustrated herself, went back to the typewriter, turned it on, and said, "All right, I'm ready for you to tell me what to write." I was almost out of control: mad, defensive, frustrated. So I started to yell, "Give me the book! I'll figure out what we need to write." Grabbing the book of Hamlet, I opened it up to any page and tried to find some main word to give me a subject to write about. This was impossible! Mom turned off the typewriter again and tried to explain to me, "Evan, did you even read the book (on tape)? The tension was mounting. "I tried to listen to the book!" "Well, can you tell me about it?" "No!" Then the crying would start, and I would openly admit I had no idea at all about the story. It wasn't even in English! I was defensive about not being able to understand the book. I was angry about the fact that I had to have my Mom read and type the report for me. I was frustrated, because I couldn't even help her. All of this led to deep sadness. I was sad that I was inferior to the other kids and to Jenny. At this point, I needed to start the cover-up, because I didn't want Mom to know that Latin was too hard for me. This happened too often to admit.

I did not want my parents to know the depression, the anger, the frustration that was mounting up within me because of the amount of work at Latin. I would not give up. If I could just break through this learning disability, I would be all right. The thoughts that would bring me out of this were: "I am a survivor and I have to do this." So with all these emotions in me, when they would ask me, "Is it too hard? Do you want to leave Latin and go somewhere else, where the work would be less difficult? The answer was always, "No! I will not leave! I will not give up! I will not fail!" Through all of this tension and kicking, and all of this scream-ing, all I wanted to do was just break through, kick through it, break through the disability. Why couldn't I type the paper? Why couldn't I understand the letters on the page? Why couldn't I do my own work? Why did I need so much help? The tears were disgusting! My stomach hurt! My muscles were tense! Everything about me was just balled up in a knot. I was tied in knots.

In the end, at about nine o'clock at night, after the tears, I would admit to my Mom that I couldn't dictate the report. She would begin at Chapter One, reviewing chapter by chapter and telling me in English what was going on. We would pull together some paper that would barely pass the assignment. This went on for years. Through all the tears and gut-wrenching frustration, I would repeat to myself: "I am a survivor. I beat cancer, I can beat this. Failure is not an option. I have to do this!"

Considering the problems with reading comprehension, sen-tence formation and my writing, getting through Latin was looking impossible. My parents decided to hire a private tutor. I didn't like it that my friends saw me working with "this lady in the library," but soon I realized that it was the only way to get through the work. I reasoned that this was the means to an end. Mrs. Huntley was more like a teacher, and so I would bargain with her on my schoolwork. She really didn't have any power to change the amount of work load I had, so my bargaining was not too effective with her.

Working with an outside person, someone not in my family, cut down on the feelings of frustration, anger and sadness. I couldn't yell and scream at Mrs. Huntley. She could just walk away: have a nice day, thank you very much. She would not take my temper tantrums. My parents, on the other hand, couldn't leave. They were stuck! With my parents, I was more embar-rassed and frustrated.

Mrs. Huntley and I worked together for so many years that she almost became a second-mother to me. We worked together every day at Latin and also every day after school. She would always have a snack ready for me when I got off the bus. I couldn't give her any excuses, and I learned that we could get the homework done if I plowed right in, instead of wasting time complaining. A few times, I was so tired from all the work, that I told her that I didn't have any homework. But she could tell by the way I said it, that I was testing her and wanting to get out of the work. She didn't put up with anything, and our sessions were positive and helpful. Sometimes, she was also a therapist. If I wasn't having a good day, or if there was something that was bothering me, she always lent a kind ear and listened and told me that things were going to be all right.

Evan with his wonderful tutor and family friend, Terri Huntley.

In middle school, everyone had one period for an elective. I didn't want to be different from the others, so I, too, signed up for an elective. It was called "developmental music," which means that everyone learned to play a recorder. I learned that, even though I enjoyed listening to music, I couldn't do two things at the same time. Trying to read music was even worse than reading words. Needless to say, I could not read a note, AND play it on the recorder, or, for that matter, do either one separately. People who play instruments must be geniuses. Fortunately, we played in groups, and it was very easy to fake my non-talent. However, toward the end of the semester, the teacher surprised us and decided to have each individual student play for the rest of the students. For some reason, she called on me first. I was the lone ranger in front of the kids. As I "played," the kids were howling with laughter. I laughed at myself because it was the only thing I could think to do, but deep down, I wasn't laughing. I was humiliated. Even the teacher laughed out loud. I was devastated. When I went home, I was very discouraged, very depressed. I didn't want to tell my parents what had happened that day, when everyone laughed at me, even the teacher. By bedtime, my Mom sat on my bed and asked why I felt so bad. Then it all came out. I am not exactly sure how it all ended so fast, but, by the very next day, art was my new elective.

Art class was the best thing to happen to me. I found out that I had some talent in art, and I felt very comfortable with the art teacher. Art class was about showing up, and participation; that is, if you started a project and finished the project, it was all that really mattered, and that's how I got my grade. I loved the creative projects and was more than happy to work hard on them. I am proud to say that several of my pieces won awards. The art teacher would say: "What do you want to do next? What motivates you? What inspires you?" So I really liked the freedom I had with my art. I quickly developed some style. I liked drawing pictures of structures, buildings, scenery, things that are very concrete, things that have defined lines.

Every year at Latin was the same: I had trouble with schoolwork. The longer at Latin, the harder I had to work. By the time I was in my junior and senior years, I needed to spend between four and five hours of work at home per night, in addition to my session with Mrs. Huntley after school. I could not participate in any activity that met during the school week, and every weekend was 75% catching up on school work from the week before. I had learned to live with this, and working hard became a norm for me. I had absorbed a strong work ethic at Latin, out of necessity, rather than out of choice.

In my senior year, my biology teacher, Dr. Kneidel, was one of those teachers who assigned unusual projects, and it was fun to learn from him. For example: for our final exam, we had to describe how bacon, once ingested into the body, made its way to the hair follicle. He wanted us to describe the pathways in detail: eating it, digesting it, what proteins got absorbed, and then how it went through the bloodstream, how it got deposited into the hair follicle, and how the proteins form hair. I didn't know where to start. How can I memorize this? Then, I figured out a new system: charts. Basically, I broke down the different phases into chunks. The first part had to do with digestion, so I drew a chart with the human digestive system including the muscles in the mouth, the stomach and what acids were there, and the liver that forms bile, etc. It was more like a "chart formation" than a "paragraph formation."

The next chart had to do with just the hair follicles and what goes on, when the hair is being produced at the follicle. One chart was a picture of RNA and DNA and formation of the genetic sequence, the formation of protein, once it was digested in the body. I learned from those multiple charts. I discovered that this was my weapon against my learning disability. I had an artistic ability and my mind worked best if I could break information down and then "chunk it." I learned that, if I put the information into an artistic chart, I could learn it! And I could learn it much faster, if I could SEE it. So, when I started making these charts, I said, "Uh-ha! I should study this way for everything. This is great! I could be doing this with all my subjects!" This was a break-through discovery to all future study: making charts. It was almost like it was a flash picture in my mind, like "Boom!" When it was time to retrieve the information, I didn't retrieve words, I retrieved charts! When the charts popped up in my brain, I could search my photographic memory for the information I wanted. Incidentally, I got an A in biology.

All through high school, I had to work very, very hard. I learned that papers couldn't be written in just one night. I had to plan way ahead for all assignments and to work twice as hard as my peers. I had to learn how to ask for help. I had to find my way if I was going to be able to pass each course. I also learned that I needed every ounce of help that I could muster. I had to make each teacher like me. Every teacher needed to know that I would do anything in her class to do well. I discovered that teachers really respond to kids who are trying hard. There would be no clowning around in a class, no falling asleep out of boredom, no bad-mouthing a class or a teacher. There would be no cutting class. I had to maneuver in any way that worked.

My biggest regret was my wrestling career. I wanted to be an athlete. I didn't even try football or basketball. I was cut from the soccer team (out of 42 kids trying out, two of us were cut: the foreign exchange student and me). So I decided to try wrestling. My favorite art teacher doubled as the wrestling coach, so I thought I would give it a try. Unfortunately, I was a very poor wrestler, winning only 2 rounds out of twelve. I was short and kind of fat for a wrestler. I don't know why I didn't spend a lot of time working out and getting into shape. I think I simply did not have the time to devote to this. I just got killed, and then I started to give up. I did not give it one hundred percent effort, and that turned into a feeling that I hated: failing because I did not work hard enough. It was a regret; but, I learned from it. I would think about this failure, and whenever I was discouraged or about to give up, I would remember my wrestling career. It resulted in the most important lesson that I learned at Charlotte Latin:

It is OK to fail.
It is OK not to measure up.
The only thing that is not OK,
is to fail because I didn't give it my all.
That feels the worst.

CHAPTER X

Making it Back

Dr. Fox kept his word. When I called to say that Dr. Levine thought it appropriate for Evan to return to Latin, Dr. Fox replied that he had already received Mel Levine's letter, and Evan was on the 6th grade roster. We talked about the major step this would be for Evan, and the concern I had with this move. We reminisced about Dr. Fox's visits at the hospital, his sadness in recommending that Evan leave during third grade, and his one hundred percent support of Evan's return.

Before school started, I asked Dr. Fox if I could call a meeting of all of Evan's teachers and prepare them for a student who had a learning disability. I asked that they help preserve Evan's comfort level at school by promising never to call on him to read aloud during class. I also discussed with them that Dr. Fox had approved of Evan's taking his tests with the tutor, and that they could be assured that the honor code would not be compromised. I asked if it would be possible for the teachers to give Evan an advanced notice of any books that needed to be read, or papers written, or projects completed. This would give him just a little extra time to complete the assignment. I thought it would be a good idea if each of them met Mrs. Huntley and called on her to help Evan, in any way they found helpful. If possible, could they give Mrs. Huntley a copy of their notes to review with Evan before a test? I hoped that Evan would be given extended time on his tests. (Later, in high school, I asked for a foreign language waiver.) In public school, these accommodations would have been offered to Evan, by law, but at Latin, they were approved by a headmaster who wanted to see a highly motivated student succeed.

One particular week, Evan came down with flu symptoms and missed two days of school. When he returned to school, he became overwhelmed with the amount of work he needed to make up from class work, as well as, the homework from each class. Mrs. Huntley was immediately concerned that Evan became overwhelmed and felt like he would never catch up. She always remembered his statement: "I will NEVER get sick again. No matter how bad I feel, I will never miss school, because it is so impossible to catch up afterwards."

The pace and the academic rigor at Latin was similar to taking college courses. Evan used every weekend to stay afloat which also meant that every one of MY weekends was spent helping Evan write essays (after skimming the book), going over math equations, learning about the latitude of Iceland, understanding photosynthesis, identifying the causes of the French and Indian War, grasping what a recession is, and deciphering atom and molecular structure. Evan had to drop out of scouts because he did not have a week night to devote to scout meetings, nor did he have any weekend time that was not entirely devoted to keeping up with school work. We even had to negotiate the demands of his church confirmation class so that it didn't interfere with school homework.

Most parents of a teen would find it difficult to believe this: but one of my worries about Evan was that, as my mother would say, "He is all work and no play." Evan was taking his work ethic to extremes. He had a neighborhood friend whom he would see for small bits of time on Saturdays, and depending on homework, on Sunday afternoons. Evan was a kid who never got in to trouble. He once said, "If there is any chance of getting caught, while doing something wrong, I will be the one to get caught. That's just how it is for me." I began to worry that Evan wasn't enjoying life, that his drive to "make it through Latin," was coming at a very high price. Not that I wanted Evan to get into trouble, I just knew that the healthy stage of becoming a teenager involved a desire for independence, a need to spread his wings, a wish for a peer group ... and testing the rules, just a little.

Each fall, the school held a "Parents' Night." The itinerary was the same every year: meet in the auditorium to listen to an address by the headmaster. Then, follow your child's academic schedule, spending 10 minutes in each class to meet the teacher. In Evan's sixth grade year, I was already known to all the teachers because of the interactions we had had even before school started. On Parents' Night, Mike and I entered Mr. Dubick's room. He was the science teacher, and by this night, Evan was already having trouble in his class. I stayed behind after the other parents left to ask Mr. Dubick if he could suggest anything we could do to help Evan further.

He could easily see the desperation on my face and the anxiety in my voice. His response to me would ring in my mind for the rest of Evan's years at Latin: "There is no doubt in my mind that Evan will do fine in my class and in all of his classes. The degree of motivation and willingness to work hard is something I have never seen before. I doubt if there is a parent here tonight who wouldn't change places with you in a heartbeat." This was astounding to me... trade places with a student who had difficulty with a basic skill such as reading? Switch places with a student who desperately wanted to be independent and couldn't? I smirked to think of a parent wanting to switch places with ME? ... a mom who has virtually re-enrolled in high school classes again? Alas, I had missed Mr. Dubick's point. I was so deeply immersed in the struggle, so stuck in the trenches, that I didn't realize that Evan had the most important key to future success: motivation and a strong work ethic. And he had it in spades!

The only time that Evan got into "teenage-trouble" was mostly due to his innocence and not knowing the rules. It involved his friend, Seth. On this particular evening, the Charlotte Hornets basketball team was playing a home game at our coliseum. Tickets were somewhat hard to buy, since the team was having a good season. Fortunately for the boys, Seth's father owned four season tickets and could not use his tickets on this night. The two boys decided to use the two best tickets for themselves and keep the revenue they "earned" from the sale of the other two. This was the first time the boys had had this opportunity, and they were not apprised of the rules. (The most important rule was that you could not sell the tickets for more than what they cost originally.)

Unbeknownst to them, there was an important "slight difference" in the specific language used in the transaction. As the "customer" approached, it was allowable for the buyer to say, "I'll give you $100 for those tickets." But it was against the law for Evan to say, "I will sell these tickets to you for $100" (if that price was more than the original cost of the ticket). When Evan offered to sell his tickets (at a profit) to an under-cover police officer, the night ended abruptly. The boys were taken to the police office under the stadium and were detained and interrogated for most of the evening. Because neither boy had ever been in trouble before, the police discharged them with a warning, and with a threat that each of the parents would be contacted about breaking the law. Seth's father was called to come after the boys. Each left the coliseum in horror.

When Evan arrived home, he walked in as white as a ghost. With a few tears, he announced that he would not be leaving home for at least six months. Surprised we asked, "Why is that?" Evan answered that, when we hear what he had done, we would be grounding him. We braced ourselves for the story. When we all sat down and heard the night's events, we could hardly keep a straight face. In fact, Evan's behavior, and subsequent repentance, was nothing short of endearing. When the police called the next day, to be sure that we were aware of "what our son had been doing," it was hard to come up with the appropriate "concern."

The year Evan turned 15, he decided that he needed to have a summer job and wanted to earn his own money. He became quite frustrated when he found how difficult it was to convince a future employer that he should hire someone who was sixteen and had never held a job before. We tried to soothe the frustration by telling Evan that he really didn't need a job and would have plenty of time to work the rest of his life. He countered that he really DID need a job and then gave two reasons why: First, he needed to start a "retirement plan." He told us that it worried him that he did not have any money saved up for retirement and secondly, he needed to start saving for his kid's college education. I have NO IDEA where he ever came up with this. (Kids listen at the dinner table more than parents ever know!)

Evan applied his "hard work" ethic to his grocery store job at Harris Teeter.

"Baby Staver" was now seven years old but spoke and acted like she was seventeen. When we were checking out at the Harris Teeter on Park Road, Staver struck up a conversation with the bag boy, informing him that her brother REALLY wanted to be a bag boy too. The bag boy thought that Staver was so cute and earnest, that he called the manager over. Staver began talking without taking a breath, describing her responsible brother and not giving the manager a chance to speak. Finally, the manager suggested that Evan come over and fill out an application. Staver was beside herself with excitement and couldn't wait to arrive home and announce that SHE had found a job for Evan.

This is how Evan's grocery store career began. Later the manager would tell me that when Evan walked in to apply, it was the manager's lucky day. Evan was never a minute late to work and would often stay past his shift without extra pay. One day, a small child got sick in aisle #4, and Evan was the only one who would answer the overhead call for clean-up help. The supervisor also told me that Evan went out of his way to be pleasant to customers and offered to take bags out to the car for those who looked like they needed help. After some time, the manager changed Evan's hours. Evan was given the key to the store, and the manager asked him to "open up" each morning at 6:00 a.m. (What a wonderful promotion for me, too, since I was driving him to work each morning!)

One night, Evan called me into his room. Important (and painful) conversations usually took place at night there. It seemed easier to confront hard topics in the dark, without eye contact. This night, Evan was worried about college. He listened to many conversations at the dinner table regarding his sister's college choices, her anxiety about the SAT and about college applications, in general. It worried him that he would never be able to go to college. It worried him that I would not be there to help with all the assignments that I was currently doing with him each night. It worried him that no college would accept him, given that they would find out that he had a learning disability. It worried him that he would have to leave home. It worried him that he would take the SAT and get a "0" on it. He worried that, if he didn't go to college, he would never be able to support himself.

I immediately soothed his worries. I assured him that I knew all about colleges. There would be a perfect college for him and I will find it. I assured him that there would be all the help that he needed. I assured him that, when the time came, he would be ready and that he would do well. I told him to trust me, and that I would figure it all out. I would not let him down. When falling asleep that night, I, myself, wondered how a student, with Evan's learning disability, could possibly do college level work? How would Evan function with time management when on his own? How would I EVER deliver on these promises? I was at the base of the mountain, and it was time to start the climb.

Was it crazy to begin worrying about a career for Evan? (*Was there not enough to worry about?*) To this point in his life, it appeared that his strengths lay in the art world. If that were correct, I thought that I should begin researching art careers and art schools. And if not, it was time to begin researching careers and schools that would fit Evan's strengths and disability.

Having been through the entire college application process with Jenny, I was well aware of the many college counselors in Charlotte, but none of these folks were any help with the specific needs of students with learning disabilities. Were there schools devoted to this, I wondered? Were there programs that could help Evan make it through? Could we hire "a coach" at his college, much like Mrs. Huntley in high school? Would there be special admission policies for students with learning disabilities? Would it be better to choose a very small school, where professors might get to know Evan and, subsequently, be willing to work with him through the various courses? The problem with a small school was the limited number of majors. A major, such as history, might be appropriate when a student is applying to graduate school, but this broad major would pose a problem when looking for a job right out of college. Would it be better to choose a large school where there would be an array of majors leading to a specific job? I feared that Evan would be lost in a large school, a mere number in English 101, and where many courses were taught by "grad students," and professor contact was nearly zero. I had a promise to fulfill. I needed help!

I thought that the answer would become clear after spending days in the reading corner of Borders Bookstore. There were volumes of books with enticing titles like "Students with Learning Disabilities Go to College." Each school on the list included a write-up about the school, enrollment statistics, the admission process, and facilities for students with learning disabilities (LD). When I saw inclusions of schools like Princeton, Yale and Duke, I wondered just WHO was utilizing these programs and WHY these schools were included in the first place. The answer was that every school must comply with the Americans with Disabilities Act. Every school must serve their enrolled students-with-disabilities, but here's the catch: they do not need to accept the student in the first place. In the fine print, one learns that the problem the LD student faces is the competition in the admissions department.

I decided that I would write letters to anyone familiar with college-bound LD kids, for suggestions of colleges that might be a possibility for Evan. Dr. Levine's educational specialist was helpful. She gave me the names of some schools in the northeast like Curry College, Iona College, Hofstra, University of Connecticut, but also forwarded the name of Midge Lipkin. Mrs. Lipkin was a contact of Dr. Levine's from his days in Boston. She published a little known book about programs within large universities that served LD students. I wrote her a 25-page letter describing Evan, his history and his learning style. I was desperate to meet with her. Unfortunately, she was getting ready to retire, but she sent me a list of schools with her "A" rating. These included Muskingum College in Ohio, Rochester Institute of Technology, Davis & Elkins, and Marshall, to name a few. I took a cue from Evan and decided to buy a poster board to make a large chart. I would list all the schools that had been suggested and then, next to each school, all the factors that were important for Evan. In the end, I eliminated some schools by phone conversation. Between 9th grade and 12th grade, I visited 27 schools around the country that had special programs for students with learning disabilities.

Mrs. Lipkin also suggested that I look into boarding schools as a fifth high school year for Evan. Her thought was that it would be a good preparation for independent college living, but under strict supervision by teachers and administrators. I actually visited two such boarding schools in Massachusetts, but in the end, I was too worried about Evan's health issues to send him away. Every time he left the house, I was still watching for a limp.
One college recommendation came from the librarian at Charlotte Latin, Mrs. Kennedy. She, herself, had lived through the death of

her beautiful daughter, Anna. She was compassionate and empathetic and became good friends with Evan, who was in the library every day with his tutor. Mrs. Kennedy knew of a neighbor whose child had a learning disability and was in college. The neighbor's child was attending Southern Illinois University and enrolled in a program called "ACHIEVE." Following up on every suggestion, I called the school and had the good fortune to speak with Dr. Barbara Cordoni, the founder and director of the program. She was willing to speak to all of my questions and could give a reasonable solution to each scenario I posed regarding Evan's disability. She also connected with me on a "mom level." She had three sons, all of whom were dyslexic, and each had graduated from S.I.U. and was successful. She assured us that ACHIEVE would provide Evan with a tutor in all subjects, that he would take all of his tests at the center, and be assigned a reader and scribe, if necessary. The center was well aware of which professors were structured in their courses, and which professors were helpful to students with learning disabilities. Students at the center had priority registration and, therefore, were signed up for classes with handpicked professors. The center would provide Evan with his textbooks on tape, as well as ancillary books that were assigned. In summary, I could not describe an academic problem that they had not dealt with, or could not offer solutions for. I thought I had found a great school for Evan and I immediately arranged a visit.

The program would begin accepting applications in the student's junior year, and the process was laborious. One of the most important components was submitting an educational evaluation that described in detail the student's learning disability and his I.Q. scores, his achievement scores, and his educational history. It certainly did not hurt that Evan's evaluation was completed by the nation's authority on learning disabilities and that his personal recommendations from teachers were stellar. When we arrived in Carbondale, Illinois for our scheduled interview, we were ready to fall in love with the school. We checked in to the "best" hotel in town, an old Howard Johnson's motor lodge which was still waiting for renovations. Before leaving for the day, I stopped at the front desk to inquire about making dinner reservations for that night. I explained that Evan would be testing all day, that he would be exhausted at the end of the day, and that I would love to find a quiet restaurant, where we could relax and talk. The desk clerk asked, "Do you mean a restaurant, where they come to your table to take the order?" This summed up the town.

The campus was spread out. The older buildings were charming, dating from the turn of the century. The learning center was somewhat unattractive from the outside, but the program was peppered with good natured, helpful folks who impressed us from the start. The admissions process was encouraging. If Evan were admitted to ACHIEVE, he was automatically accepted by the University. Since Evan's learning disability was well documented, I was fairly sure that, if we wanted him to go here, Evan would be accepted.

Coincidentally, there was another student there, also going through testing. Simon was from Winettka, a suburb of Chicago. He was extremely handsome and looked like he had been living in the weight room of a gym for the last ten years. His grandparents lived in Australia, and he spent summers in the Outback. He had a delightful accent, and altogether he was very likeable. His parents shared the waiting room with us all day, and we liked them so much that we all decided to have dinner together. Evan felt very positive about the school, because he could picture himself receiving the help he would need. He and Simon joked at dinner. Evan laughed when he announced that he could not read, and Simon countered that he could not add. Simon joked: "Heh! We can go to the grocery store together, and I can read the labels, and you can count the change." They agreed to room together, and we left Carbondale with a college choice, a learning center that would replace me and Mrs. Huntley combined, and a roommate that would totally "get" Evan. Everyone was on a high.

Knowing that he was already in college (and even had a roommate), Evan's senior year was less stressful. It was miraculous that my college-finding job had been completed at a time when all the other parents were worried about this big step. After all, the private school tuition that everyone had paid all these years was supposed to pay off senior year with prestigious acceptances. The students, too, kept a steady stream of conversation about retaking the SAT, preparing for it, keeping up their grades, volunteering to "round off" their resumes, and the time consuming job of completing applications. Evan was so grateful to be out of this loop.

With the arrival of spring, most seniors knew their college fate, and everyone settled down with a sigh. Evan and another student volunteered to put together the senior video, and it was the first time that he was able to take on a project that wasn't part of a course that he would be graded on. He seemed to love the responsibility and the required interaction with the other students in the class. It was not surprising that Evan took the job seriously and that it was finished ahead of schedule.

Senior awards day was always the culmination of the high school years for all the students. It seemed like there were hundreds of awards called out, and it occurred to me, that, perhaps, they handed out this many so that, in the end, everyone was called up on the stage for something. This was not the case. There were about ten students who received every award they offered. I remembered attending Jenny's ceremony years before. It was so thoroughly enjoyable but now I wondered if that was due to Jenny's numerous trips to the stage. Now I wondered if there were other parents back then, thinking: "Why not spread out the awards among a larger group of students?"

This was Evan's senior year. I was truly thrilled just to be there ... awards or no awards. Evan had successfully completed the rigorous, competitive high standards of Charlotte Latin School, albeit paying a very high price with his self-esteem and the intense effort that was required. At this point, he had been off chemotherapy for nine years and off of his growth hormone shots for two years. He had a rich and exciting college experience ahead of him. What award could possibly compete with this?

Graduation took place on a hot, humid day at the end of May. Evan's allotted tickets were used by his 2 grandparents, his 2 sisters, his tutor, Mrs. Huntley, and Mike and me. I became tearful when we took our seats in the auditorium. As best as I could remember, we were sitting in the very same place when attending a meeting for parents of accepted kindergarten students. I became emotional just contemplating the long road we had travelled, the roadblocks that we had circumvented, the gratitude I felt for the basics: Evan was still alive!

I admit to having a wandering mind throughout Dr. Fox's address. My handkerchief from Pop was already in a moist, wadded-up ball. In fact, I wasn't even paying attention to the description of the only award to be given at graduation. It was called The Headmaster's Award, given to the one student in the senior class who embodied all the qualities of the ideal Charlotte Latin student. The award was voted upon by the teachers and the headmaster. I awoke from my melancholy daze. I was hoping it would go to Jason, one of Evan's friends who was outstanding and accomplished in every way. Dr. Fox described the award and in his exact words said: "Planning to attend Southern Illinois University next year, the award goes to Evan Kaufman." The gasp that I made out loud and followed by sobbing was embarrassing. Parents and grandparents sitting around me turned around to stare at this shrilled response.

As if this weren't enough, the whole senior class stood and clapped for Evan the entire time it took to make his way to the aisle, walk up the stairs, and walk across the stage to where Dr. Fox stood. The clapping did not stop. On his return, the parents and guests also stood and clapped until he made his way back to his seat. The message from this caring community was clear: "We've been with you all the way! Congratulations!"

As an aside, our local TV station, WSOC, had featured Evan several times over the years. Once, when they did a piece on local children who were being treated at St. Jude; another time, they featured Evan's fund raising efforts at the end of our driveway. On this graduation day, during the 6 o'clock news, they broadcast snippets from these past productions, and then featured a video of Evan accepting this award.

I still tear up, when I tell this story.

Charlotte Latin School graduation with Headmaster, Dr. Ned Fox.

CHAPTER XI

"I'M A COLLEGE STUDENT!
I'M INDEPENDENT!
I'M SCARED!"

Whenever anyone asked Evan what he was planning to major in, he would always answer: "I'm in pre-med." His long time dream was to go to medical school and become a doctor and then return to St. Jude Hospital and take care of children with cancer. His heart was in the right place, and his goal was admirable, but not realistic. When I would gently allude to the fact that medicine was a very long, hard road, he would answer: "I'm willing to work hard and anything can be accomplished if you just work hard enough." This mantra worked well during the "medicine years," but was now coming back to haunt me. I would gently remind him that students who go to medical school are the top students, the ones with all A's, and who have taken the most difficult subjects. Evan would answer: "I'm willing to work hard, and anything can be accomplished, if you just work hard enough." Have I wronged Evan by being too optimistic over the years? Have I given him an unrealistic view of the world? And worst of all, have I set him up for disappointment and failure?

There was hardly time to ponder this. It was time for the next step, and definitely no time-off. Evan needed a crash course in college preparation, on becoming an independent student. Earning a few hours of college credit in the summer would benefit him, as well. After researching programs and schools, I was lucky to find a summer program at Landmark College in Putney, Vermont. It is the only accredited school, specifically for students with learning disabilities. Many people know it as the school Bill

Cosby chose for his son, Ennis. It turned out to be the perfect summer program for preparing students with learning disabilities to go to college.

At Landmark, he signed up for several courses that were focused on the transition from high school to college. He also took a rigorous and challenging course: statistics. We reasoned that it was an ideal time to get this difficult course out of the way, when he could concentrate on it. Landmark was equipped to deal with any learning disability and all the issues associated with it. For example, students with learning disabilities often have difficulty with organization. At Landmark, each student has a yardstick-sized calendar on his desk. A resident assistant, whose job it was to check up on test/homework deadlines and scheduled meetings, made the rounds daily. Even laundry day was scheduled on the calendar, and Evan learned to rely on this organizational tool. There were courses on appropriate social interactions and seminars on self-esteem. Evan made friends, passed statistics, and left Vermont feeling confident that he could handle college.

We purchased our very own personal computer that summer and since Evan was attending school so far away from home, I hired a computer whiz to make a house call and teach me how to send English papers back and forth on the computer with revisions and without re-typing the document each time. It was amazing to me that we could send an edited assignment easily and faster than the US mail.

The end-of-summer was hectic in 1997. Jenny was packing up to spend the year at The London School of Economics where she was beginning her master's degree; Evan was packing up for his first year at S.I.U. As luck would have it, Evan's orientation day at college coincided with Staver's first day of 4th grade at Charlotte Latin, so Jenny became the volunteer mom that day, while Mike, Evan, and I drove to Illinois with a packed-full car.

Evan was rather quiet the whole 10 hour trip and I knew that he was intimidated by the distance from home and all that he was facing. I had made an exhaustive itinerary for our few days there. Evan needed to sign in at ACHIEVE (the learning center) and meet his new L.D. assistant. We also needed to wait in line at the housing building, to obtain a key to his new dorm room and unpack the car, along with 200 other sets of parents who were planning to do the same. Because we needed Evan to establish residency in the state of Illinois, we also needed to stop at the DMV to obtain an Illinois driver's license, and at a government building to register him to vote. There was a picnic for all new students on his floor, as well as a parent get-together of ACHIEVE students.

First day of college ... pretty scary!

It was so hectic that none of the three of us had time to consider that our departure time was upon us. When we pulled out of the parking lot, Evan was standing in the hot sun with baggy, un-ironed shorts and shirt, leaning on his new used-bicycle, facing a mountain of the unknown. I know he was feeling a little sick, as he was realizing that, now he was on his own.

All the way home, I kept listing in my mind all that we had done, all that any parent could do to assure success. I had found the program ACHIEVE; he was somewhat familiar with his new roommate, Simon; he had had the experience at Landmark and was somewhat prepared for organizing college work and the deadlines of college life; his classes had been chosen very carefully so that he had every chance to succeed; he had a check book, a credit card, and a phone card that he could use on the pay phone in the hall; he had two week's worth of underwear and the use of a computer to send work back and forth to home if need be. I was hoping that all of this was enough.

The folks at ACHIEVE formed a team to help Evan and the other students be successful. But the team was only available to those who helped themselves. In other words, there was no support for those who were too lazy to get out of bed in the morning or were too busy with social engagements to make it to class. Coming as no surprise, Evan became the favorite student of the team. He never missed a session, never missed a class, and was always the hardest worker of the group. Early on, back in grade school, he learned how to ingratiate himself and impress those who could help him, an attribute that, by now, was fine tuned.

On Evan's team were: 1) the test coordinator, the person who was in touch with all professors, knew when all tests were to be administered and arranged for these tests to be taken at the LD center with an available reader/scribe who would read the test and write down the dictated essay. She was in charge of obtaining the test, so that it was at the center at the appointed time; 2) the note-taking coordinator, the person who was in touch with each professor to arrange for a note taker in each course. She paid each of the note takers and made sure that the notes were in the student's mailbox within 2 hours of the class; 3) the media coordinator whose job it was to be sure Evan had all of his textbooks and outside reading material on tape; 4) the tutor coordinator, whose job it was to arrange for tutors in specific area classes; and finally, 5) the ACHIEVE learning assistants, Amy and Amanda.

Evan described these two very important people: "Amy was a graduate student at SIU, majoring in special education. Amy and I became very tight friends. She had an interesting sense of humor and was very sarcastic. But if I needed a scribe or someone to read my test to me or needed help with writing a paper, she was there unconditionally. She had her own work to do, but she never once let me down, saying that she had too much to do of her own work. She would drop everything to help me out. I don't know if that was a condition of working for ACHIEVE, or if she was always available because of the special friendship we developed. She became familiar with my thinking pattern, familiar with the speed to read the material, familiar with my learning style, and we worked together easily. She made me feel comfortable. She became as necessary to my school work, as Mrs. Huntley was in high school. If the work we needed to do was boring or mundane, she never once complained. Sometimes the work that we were doing lasted many hours past the allotted time, and again, she was never hurried or irritated. She was learning to be a teacher of students with learning disabilities, and she would say that she learned far more from me, than I from her."

"The second person to whom I owe so much was a very attractive, young woman named Amanda. She was so pretty and personable that I had a crush on her the whole time I was in college, but I would never spoil our working relationship with an inappropriate announcement of feelings for her. She came from a very small town nearby, and while she was very smart, she had not had such advanced courses from her high school as I had. She was pre-med and began looking for a part time job as soon as she arrived on campus. By serendipity, sophomore year we landed in three of the same classes together. We studied together for the first round of tests, mostly sharing her compulsively complete notes. Her notes were so helpful, that I suggested that she go over to ACHIEVE, where she could be hired as a note-taker. This was a win-win arrangement for us both. She ended up as my note-taker, a study-buddy and a friend until graduation. Since we were both taking the same science courses (Inorganic and Organic Chemistry, Physics, Biology, Microbiology, Physiology), we made a point of matching our schedules, so that we had the same professors, the same test schedules, and could study together for each course. Ironically, because of my superlative high school teacher and my advanced math background, I was a stronger student than she in physics. It was the most difficult class, and we logged in the most hours for the final exam. She would never ask what my grades were, because she did not want to make me feel that we were in competition with each other, nor did she want me to ever feel embarrassed. But she certainly told me how relieved she was with her solid B in physics. I told her I did OK, too. (Amanda, if you ever read this, I never told you that I got an A in Physics at SIU. Thank you!)"

When Evan signed up for his courses, the registrar at ACHIEVE always signed him up for six courses even when he planned all along to end up with four. Evan would attend all six classes for the week and was able to determine fairly quickly which two classes to drop. He made it a habit to introduce himself to the professor on the first day. He would explain that he was a member of ACHIEVE and could usually ascertain, immediately, if the professor understood that Evan would be eligible for accommodations. The professor's response was always invaluable in deciding whether this was one of the two classes he would be rescheduling for another semester with another professor. Evan commented: "Going through school was not easy, and there were a lot of times when I didn't know how I was going to make it through a certain course, but I had to learn to adapt. Mom always said, 'play to your strength,' and one of my strengths was that I learned that I could read people very quickly, and I could tell whether they would be advocates of mine or be detrimental to me. I had to adapt my study habits and set myself up for success. I grew to love that phrase: 'set myself up for success' which meant to me that I didn't need to overcome everything; rather, if I could just find another way to do it, I could make it easier on myself. I learned to analyze the situation and figure out another way, often a creative way, to achieve the goal."

Evan illustrated this idea from a freshman course called Design and Critical Thinking. It was taught by an engineer and was a requirement for students interested in graphic design. Evan recounts: "On the first day, the professor stated that students would be given one point for attendance, one point for completing a project, and one point for the design of the product. The only way to flunk the class was not to show up. The assigned project was as follows: he gave us two pieces of paper and a paper clip. We were told to design a 'system' that we could launch with one hand. He would measure how far the system traveled. Everyone in the class immediately began to think about paper airplanes. The students began experimenting with the position of the paper clip on the paper airplane and that location (of the paper clip) would enable the plane to have the longest projectile and flight. At this point, I was completely influenced by all the smart kids in the class and so I, too, followed along, designing a fancy paper airplane. However, I found out that it is almost impossible to get the aerodynamics of paper to be perfect. Usually, paper airplanes do not go straight; sometimes, they go straight up, stall, and then fall back to the ground. Sometimes, it just loops the loop and falls to another side.

The time came to go outside and test each student's paper airplane. There were only about fifteen students in the class, and, therefore, it was pretty easy to complete each person's demonstration in one class period. The first plane went about three feet; the record was ten feet. I was in second place at nine feet. The last student to go was a sorority girl. She had no enthusiasm, and I could tell that she really didn't want to be in the class, nor did she know how to build a paper airplane. She was bored with the whole process, probably because she could see no lasting value in making a stupid airplane out of paper. When it was her turn to step to the line, she turned to the professor to affirm that she would receive her one point for attendance, one point for making the product, and one point for completing it. He assured her that those were the rules and that she would be given all points. At that, she decided to depart from the group and, as a small rebellion, crumpled up her would-be airplane into a ball, put the paper clip in the middle, and threw it. It landed 20 feet out, and she won the competition. The professor was most happy with her departure from the airplane mentality. I learned how important it was to think outside the box. The entire class was caught up in airplanes, so much so, that no one thought of another way to use paper to launch a product, so that it flies a certain distance. A wadded up paper goes a lot farther, with the launching power of somebody's arm. Is it possible that a kid with a learning disability can go a lot farther, with the launching power of hard work and determination?

Evan and close friend, "Bink."

Part of Evan's enthusiasm for college life stemmed from the descriptions of college that his older sister, Jenny, brought home from Duke. She was a gifted student and, because of that, she found it easy to balance partying with good grades. We listened to her "Cameron Crazies" stories and reports of her Tri Delt parties-- escapades like swallowing a live fish still wiggling in her throat as it went down. (*Ugh! Glad we were paying tuition for THIS experience!*) Evan was anxious to experience fraternity life, but we shelved this idea until sophomore year when, hopefully, he arrived at a stable point in his college career. Evan purposely took a lighter load fall semester to accommodate rush, and, with fingers crossed, he entered the race for the perfect "frat." Evan had a wonderful time during rush, and it ended with his having a choice between two "houses." He frequently called home, excitedly describing his new social life and new friends.

After rush, the guillotine was lowered, and he became a pledge. Joining the fraternity required the pledges to be out running errands all night long. Each pledge had to memorize the names of all members, their home towns, the names of their girlfriends, their favorite foods, and on and on. Required study halls took place each evening but this was not helpful to Evan. Weekends did not include any time for study. I answered the phone a week in to this new schedule. Sadly, Evan was not calling for advice as to how the fraternity could overlap with ACHIEVE. Instead, he was calling to say that he had submitted his resignation. He went on to admit that he had received an "F" on two different tests. He had concluded that either he could continue as a pledge and enjoy frat life for one semester after which he would flunk out of school, or he could drop out of the pledge class and stay in college for four years. I would have loved to have talked him out of this decision, knowing how much he wanted to be a "brother," but I knew, as well as he did, that he had to make a choice; he couldn't do both. He ended up becoming best friends with five non-fraternity guys. As with many things in life that cause such disappointment, the end result is often a wonderful surprise.

This five-some group of friends, all of whom lived in Felts Dorm, was known as "Felts Five," and they really made college a lot of fun for Evan. For the first time in his life, Evan felt as smart as his friends. Evan later wrote: "I got in with a group of guys that made me feel really normal. The setting was still difficult; the learning disability was still prohibitive to some degree. But the time I spent relaxing with my friends made college life fun and memorable. In the group, I was known as the hard-working guy who studied too much. My best friend, Bink, was kind-hearted, loyal and relaxed. He could always come up with a joke at a serious, stressful time. He would kid me about my learning disability, but coming from him, it did not hurt my feelings; it made me laugh. He taught me not to take myself too seriously. Dave was the funny one; Roman, the talented one (athletic and artistic); Watty was the goofy one; and Bob, the serious one."

"One time, Bink came into my room and said: 'Kaufman, why are you studying for that test? You're gonna' fail it anyway.' This was his idea of prying me away from the books, when he realized it would help me more to take a break, than to sit there and stare at the words. Another time, he reasoned: 'you know what you need, Kaufman? You need a beer to study better. You read things backwards, right? Well, sometimes when you get alcohol in your system, it changes the way you see words. This beer will make you see things differently, that is, it will straighten out your reading.' He simply made me laugh. He also taught me that I couldn't study all the time; I'd burn out. Bink taught me to study hard and to play hard. When he knew that I really did need to study for a test, he would leave me alone and not let the other guys disturb me. But he was the first person at the door to insist that study time was over. I needed to learn this, and he was more than happy to teach me."

This group of friends became Evan's family. They ate dinner together and enjoyed a ritual "loaf-day" on a weekly basis. Evan began to "feel intelligent" as the guys began to refer to him as "the smart one."   For Evan, the fun of college life was wrapped up with this group who still get together 15 years later. These fellows reminisce about putting a restaurant out of business because it offered an all-you-can-eat-crab-legs-night for an entire semester. They still laugh over the time that they dismantled the automatic doors at Wal-Mart and watched from afar as people walked IN to the doors.

It is said that, many students enter college as pre-med but change their career path after taking organic chemistry. Notably, Evan made it through both organic chemistry and inorganic chemistry. However, chemistry lab almost changed his career path. Every chemistry class included a lab, and the labs were extremely difficult for him. It required him to read directions carefully, understand the directions, and have a general idea of the purpose of the experiments. If the directions were to boil 2 ml of water in a 5 ml beaker, Evan easily could have read "boil 2 grams of water in a 5 liter beaker." Even as a little boy putting Legos together, he would throw away the directions because it was impossible for him to go back and forth between reading directions and building. As a young adult, whenever he bought a piece of furniture that needed to be put together, he would throw away the directions and piece it together by using common sense and the picture on the front of the box. He had a sense for how things fit together.

Chemistry lab was different. He could not throw away the directions. The directions were crucial, and exact measurement was also crucial. Carefully following directions was the only way to obtain the exact result. Unlike third grade, students did not tolerate anyone looking over their shoulders and copying what they were doing. Not only was it difficult to execute directions, but he had a certain allotted time to complete the experiment. Evan had to work on the premises, and therefore, he could not take the lab experiment to ACHIEVE. He felt that this was a problem with no answer. Evan called home and told me that he was dropping out of chemistry lab. He could not do it! He was done! Further into the conversation, I learned that his lab partner requested a new partner after Evan had made a mess of the first experiment. I knew immediately that he felt exposed and humiliated. Evan outright refused to go to another lab. It was simply too painful! As he put it: "I cannot take the abuse."

I wasn't sure whether or not there was any hope of saving the situation, but before hanging up, I made him promise not to drop the lab until he met with Dr. Cordoni. He HAD to give ACHIEVE a chance to step in. And they did. After hearing Evan's predicament, they hired a senior chemistry major to be Evan's new lab partner. They also changed lab days. The students of the new lab simply assumed that these were two sophomore students who switched their lab days. Evan's new chemistry lab partner had a good suggestion. He insisted on meeting with Evan before each lab. He went over the experiment as a whole, explaining the purpose of the experiment, and what it was that they were trying to prove. He tried to make sense of the experiment.

On the first new lab, Evan and his new lab partner walked in without a question from the other students. The lab partner would read the directions, and Evan would follow through with whatever he said, step by step. Evan hated that he needed someone to stand there and walk him through the experiment, but the lab partner delivered the directions in such a way, that the other students just assumed that this pair was doing the experiment just like everyone else. The lab partner would not do any of the experiment. His only job was to read the directions. Interestingly, one day, the new partner was unable to attend the lab. However, he went over the directions ahead of time and did his normal explanation. Though nervous, Evan went in to the lab alone that day and did the experiment. He attained the correct result. Herein was another valuable lesson: no one really cared about what Evan was doing, or who the new lab partner was; likewise, no one really cared who needed extra help or who completed the lab differently from anyone else. He earned a B in lab and a new mantra: Don't worry about what others are thinking! No one really cares!

Evan wrote down the many lessons he learned in college. He made some very interesting observations: "I have failed more tests, quizzes and papers than anyone else I know. But failure is not a bad thing, because you can only go up from failure.

"I am no stranger to failure. For me, the more that I fail, the harder I work. I am never mad at myself for failing. I will only be mad at myself for quitting. I don't mind failure, because I will look at the challenge, figure out a way, and then feel the high of 'making it.' Failure is one more chance to prove to myself that I can find a way. Therefore, I am not afraid of failure. I am only afraid that I will not have a chance to overcome my failure."

Halfway through Evan's college experience, I realized that I had dug an enormous hole for myself. Evan was highly motivated, and the team at ACHIEVE certainly sang his praises. He was very proud of his accomplishments (and so was I) and dead set certain that he was headed to medical school. The staff at ACHIEVE would refer to Evan as their poster child, and they would use Evan's good grades and accomplishments as proof positive that a student with a learning disability can succeed in college and graduate with an impressive record.

I had instilled a "can do" attitude early on as part of his will to live. This spirit conveniently worked through high school and college. However, this work ethic and this motivation, alone, were not going to be enough to secure a space in any U.S. medical school. Retreating to a dream world where I can fix everything, I even researched the idea of going to medical school in the Caribbean, where you can enroll, if you can pay the steep tuition. I dropped the idea when I found out how difficult it would be to pass the boards and return to this country to practice.

Surely, there was something in the medical field that he would enjoy and could train to do! I began researching careers: physician's assistant, physical therapist, occupational therapist, podiatry, chiropractic physician, anesthesiologist technician, radiology technician, osteopathic physician, nursing ... The list was long.

Evan had already volunteered, during college, to ride in the ambulance alongside the EMT people. He loved it and was hoping that it might be a good activity to list on his medical school application. He also took a First Aid course and Advanced First Aid. I was thinking about a career as a paramedic; and therefore, I took him to visit Western Carolina, where there was a program that led to certification in the field. Evan visited and then, refused the idea.

I had Evan take an aptitude test that showed that he had a strong ability in "spatial relationships" and therefore, might make a good dentist. I became very excited about this possibility. My brother, Joel, was a full professor in the dental school at The Ohio State University, and he arranged for Evan to visit him and shadow dentists in many different sub-specialties, so that he could get an idea of the wide variety of possibilities open to those who choose a career in dentistry. Evan was appreciative of this effort. But upon his return he said that he simply did not want to work in general dentistry. Oral surgery looked intriguing but he was afraid that he would not achieve a top position in the class, a necessary feat to continue training in oral surgery. That put an end to that idea.

My research continued and once more I became excited about another field for which I thought Evan would be well suited. That summer, Evan worked part time with two local optometrists, two part-time jobs that added up to one full-time internship. He earned certification as an optos technician, and evenings were spent with a Central Piedmont Community College physics professor who was helping him prepare for the national optometry test, a part of the optometry school application.

We were on a roll. Evan was excited about this career, and now our major challenge was how to be accepted into optometry school. Evan asked a favorite college professor to write a recommendation for him. The professor was so delighted to write this, that he sent Mike and me a copy of what he submitted to the school. It was a real emotional high to read this letter that stated that in all of his 40 years as a professor, he had never had a student who tried harder, worked harder, and who was more diligent than Evan. The optometrists for whom he worked also wrote stellar letters. Evan's transcript was average making it all the more important to do well on the entrance exam. This created enormous pressure. I wrote a letter to the national testing board, under Evan's name, to request a reader and extended time when taking the test. Because the board had never had an occasion or a request to award accommodations to any test-taker, it was necessary to educate them about the Americans with Disabilities Act. The board learned that Evan had a right, by law, to have a reader and extended time. Susie, his faithful test coordinator with ACHIEVE, was finally approved and was willing to read the whole test to him and track the time used.

In the meantime, I wrote to all of the then fourteen optometry schools in the U.S., hoping to find one that would offer some LD support program for its students. The answer was always the same: we do not serve any LD students! I guessed that we were breaking new ground. In the end, we eliminated three schools in the west and applied to eleven schools. Even though the applications were all similar, each required just a little something different, often an additional essay. It was a monumental task.

Based on the submitted materials and recommendations, Evan was granted an interview at five schools. The first interview was in Birmingham, Alabama. Because of the stress, the interview went poorly, and Evan returned home discouraged. Uncle Joel was visiting over the Christmas holiday and listened intently, as Evan described the questions posed at the interview, and how he froze while trying to answer them. Evan explained to the panel that he had a learning disability, and that revelation seemed to seal his fate.

Uncle Joel explained to Evan that he had spent the last 40 years interviewing dental school applicants and tried to clarify for Evan what the interviewers were looking for: hard workers, talented, and motivated students who would stick it out, even if the course load became very difficult. They were looking for self confident students who were well spoken. Joel suggested that he give Evan a mock interview at our house, and he even insisted that Evan change into a suit, to create the right kind of environment for this practice-run.

"Hi! I'm Dr. Weaver and I will be interviewing you today." At first, it was awkward but Joel had a reason for the actual exercise. As he asked Evan questions, he began to count the number of "ums" and the usage of "like." This was a first-hand look at run-together sentences that needed to be changed to clear and precise. He insisted that Evan do his homework about the school, showing his interest in the latest and greatest aspects of the school. Lastly, he and Evan worked on a catch phrase that needed to be inserted throughout the interview and definitely at the end of the interview in order to separate Evan from all the other candidates. He needed something to be remembered by!

The next interview was scheduled in a few weeks in St. Louis. Evan carried a small piece of paper that Joel told him to review right before going into the interview room. This time Evan was calm and pensive. He paused after each question, to give thought to how he would answer. Although nervous inside, he remained composed. As Joel had suggested, Evan did his homework about the school and had prepared questions about a special program that was started there. His catch phrase described his work ethic and stated "that while he was sure that other candidates may have higher GPA's, no candidate could out-work him" (which actually is more than a phrase... it was true!). When asked, at the end, if there were anything else he wanted to say, Evan closed with a story about the "Woody Hayes work ethic"* and compared himself to this coach's most successful run in the college football world. He ended with a plea to "give me a chance. I will make you proud."

When Jenny heard this story for the first time, she just shook her head, because she said that what happened next simply never happens during a panel interview such as the one just described. The head questioner of the group looked at each member of the panel one by one, and Evan detected a nod given by each member.

The head of the panel looked at Evan and ended by saying: "Well, Evan, we ARE going to give you that chance. We hope that you will start in the fall, here at St. Louis." Evan was taken completely off guard. In fact, he wasn't sure he had heard right. He asked for a clarification of what he thought he heard. "Yes, Evan, we hope you will join us as a first-year optometry student in the fall."

Evan cannot remember what he said or did next, but he thought he shook each member's hand and thanked each for his time.

---

*The famous football coach of Ohio State University, Woody Hayes gave an interview once when he described his success: "I am not the most talented coach, nor am I the smartest coach in the country. But I can out-work anyone out there, and it is only through long hours and hard work that I have been successful."

Maybe he just left dumbfounded. But he did know one thing; he was a kid who had beaten all the odds. He was alive. He was a kid with a learning disability who had graduated from high school and college. And this kid was just accepted to optometry school! Oh my God!

It was time to call home.

Some people remember January 20, 2001 as the day George W. Bush was sworn in as President of the United States. But more momentous than an inauguration was the news that Evan Kaufman had been accepted into optometry school. Screams of disbelief and sobbing engulfed me. Just when I calmed down enough to dial a family member, someone would say "hello," at which point I began sobbing again. More than once, the family member heard this weeping on the phone and asked if one of the grandparents had died? This was an emotional high that would last my lifetime.

Evan's last interview took place at Indiana University. There is nothing like an acceptance from another school in your back pocket to help the self-confidence. Perhaps Evan changed his closing remarks to include the "Bobby Knight Work Ethic," but whatever he said, it produced one more acceptance. Upon visiting this beautiful campus, especially in the spring, when the red tulips were blooming on every walkway of the campus, Evan made the decision that this was the school for him. The die was cast. Evan was proud of himself beyond description.

Optometry school at Indiana started at the end of May rather than the fall. In fact, it started one week PRIOR to Evan's college graduation at SIU. So Mike and I spent the weekend before his college graduation helping to move Evan from Carbondale, Illinois into his very first apartment in Bloomington, Indiana. After his first week of optometry school, Evan returned to Southern Illinois' graduation exercises, under the watchful eyes of 19 extended family members who came out in full force to help celebrate. The irony of the situation was that, instead of partying with friends, or relaxing with his family, instead of a moment to enjoy this monumental achievement, he chose, instead, to retreat to the empty library with Mike. The two of them started to review his first week's work in microbiology. Would this young man ever have a chance to bask in his own sunshine?

Not today.

Graduation from Southern Illinois University:
Staver, Evan, Jenny.

CHAPTER XII

BEATING ALL THE ODDS

Throughout his school years, Evan had total academic support from us, from Mrs. Huntley, and from the teachers at Charlotte Latin. Everyone worked hard, as did Evan, to be sure he was successful. As an undergraduate, Evan was fortunate enough to have been accepted into a comprehensive program called ACHIEVE, for learning disabled students at Southern Illinois University. There, Evan was given a host of accommodations for which he qualified, and with guidance through the center, he came into contact with professors who were well acquainted with learning disabilities and who believed that, by leveling the playing field, these students could compete favorably with other students. Although college was still difficult, Evan had a team of people who were always standing by, to smooth any rough edges. Until he left for Indiana, Evan reached a level of success in most everything he tried. His reality check to this point was: work hard, use your resources, accept help, and you will achieve your goal.

Everything changed in optometry school. His support system was totally different; there was none. Subsequently, his recipe for success changed, as well. There was no ACHIEVE program to run interference; he was totally on his own. There was no priority registration, because everyone took the exact same courses. Everyone had the same professors whose expertise was challenging gifted students. There were no books on tape, no readers. There was no such thing as taking a reduced course load during the school year and making up for it in the summer. There were no extra points given to students who were willing to do extra credit projects. There was no impressing professors when a student was willing to work hard and go the extra mile because all the students were willing to work hard. The class was full of very bright students, all of whom were motivated, albeit some worked harder than others. Indiana was one of the highest rated optometry schools in the country, and the students there were handpicked, competitive, and competent. There were certainly no other LD students.

The courses were highly sophisticated and specific. Therefore, no one outside of the field could meet with Evan for review. Paid tutors were not available. Students did group together and study together but these groups developed dynamics all of their own.

First day of optometry school.

All groups who studied outside of the classroom were informally organized. Even though professors were not used to teaching students with learning disabilities, most had an accommodating attitude and allowed Evan extra time, as needed. The truth was that Evan had experienced such success in college that he, himself, began to think that he had outgrown his learning disability and that he might not even need help.

Evan got off to a good start with his first course (Optics) at Indiana. Optics was all about numbers; more specifically, all about decimals. It was mandatory that every answer be placed to the fourth decimal point, i.e. the ten-thousandth of a point (.0001). Evan would explain: "An image is light passing through a lens and then focused. One millimeter off is significant in relation to your vision." The equations dealt with positive and negative numbers, making it easy to make a mistake. There was no room for sloppiness or inaccurate mathematical equations. Evan found the subject matter to be very precise, and because his personality was precise and careful, he did very well in this course. This first "A" bolstered his confidence.

Evan noted: "they were more concerned about making me a good doctor than they were pushing me though the system." On the first day, Evan attended orientation by Dean Lowther. As Evan recalls, he started his lecture:

There are three types of students who graduate from Indiana University School of Optometry. The first type is my base students. They got straight A's in college, and they will continue to get straight A's here. They are awkwardly smart and, in fact, sometimes have difficulty socializing with the other students. They become the researchers. They will write papers, get grants, and probably won't spend much time in the exam room. They are the smartest students, and it is they who will discover new cures, new information, and will be on the leading edge of optometry. These students are sitting here in the auditorium right now.

The second type of student is the B student. These students will get an A every semester in something, but mainly will be B students. They are smart enough to get the A in every subject, but they do not live and breathe by the book. They will take a practical problem, apply their superior knowledge, and come up with the right diagnosis. These are the students who become professors and clinicians. They will become specialists in their fields of interest. This very fact is what makes them a B student: they are not interested in everything, but what they are interested in, they will work to achieve at a superior level. They will be teaching at the universities, and they will be great teachers in your class. Look around you, because these students are sitting right here in this auditorium.

The third type of student is the C student. Usually these students did not get all A's in college, but they are here, because they know how to work the system. They are bright, bright enough to sift through an ocean of material and concentrate on what is pertinent. These are the students who are well rounded. These students become excellent clinicians because they enjoy seeing patients. These are the doctors that I would choose to care for my own children. They are also the group of doctors to whom I turn, when asking for donations for the school. They are excellent in figuring out how to make optometry practical in the real world and who realize why it is important to financially support their colleagues. These students are probably sitting in the back right now, tuned out of this speech because they deemed it unimportant a while ago.

"So what type of student are you going to be?"

"I began to ponder this question," thought Evan. "Clearly, there was a part of me that was here because of wanting to emulate my father. He was the #1 type, the "all A's" student, the researcher. I needed to try to separate out that which I thought my father wanted me to be, with a future that suited me. I wanted to be the careful, thoughtful, and compassionate doctor who gives my patients as much time as they need. I wanted to be the teacher and help students achieve a hard-fought goal. I suppose that these two needs stem from my doctors at St. Jude Hospital and from the teachers with whom I have had contact. Regardless of why, I concluded that my dream career would be to blend the university academician/teacher with the private practice clinician."

In the fall, Evan started on the initial rigorous course load. The four years of optometry were set up with stringent rules and milestones that had to be met satisfactorily before the student was allowed to proceed through the maze of the curriculum. The first two years were classroom work in applied basic science. For example, required courses included: Cell Biology, Anatomy, Histology, Pharmacology, Ocular Anatomy, Immunology, Neuroanatomy, Physiology, and on and on. To stay on track, it was necessary to take six courses per semester. Evan had never taken more than four. The third year consisted of clinical work that was overseen by professors at the school. In order to reach this level, the student had to pass a practicum that showed competence in clinical ability. The fourth year consisted of rotations in clinics offering a glimpse of pediatrics, ocular disease, and geriatrics.

By second year, Evan seemed to be "burning out" due to the extreme stress. He simply did not have the time to "get his bearings" and learn to study differently. He was on the steps of the library when it opened, and was the last person to leave at night. Still, he was spinning his wheels. Even though he was working every weekend and every night, it was recommended that he repeat several of his first-year classes. This "recommendation" was made, not because he failed the classes, but because it was so important to have a strong foundation in the sciences. He was devastated. This meant that he had to drop back to another second-year class. It was humiliating in front of his new friends. It was discouraging after working so hard. It was worrisome since he felt that he had given it his all.

The worst part of this crucial situation was that Evan was facing the hardest course of all as part of the second year curriculum. The course was called pharmacology. It was the only course that was worth five credit hours, instead of three. The upperclassmen agreed that it was the most difficult course of optometry school. Poor performance in pharmacology was the most common reason that students were asked to leave. Evan was scared to death.

Sometimes good luck appears at just the right time from faraway places. My brother, Joel, happened to have a Ph.D. in pharmacology and, among other things, taught pharmacology to dental students at Ohio State. Having won many teaching awards, Joel was known as an excellent teacher whose explanations were crystal clear. He was able to bring the most complicated subject matter into understandable concepts.

Given his fondness for Evan and his acumen as a teacher, it was no surprise that Joel insisted on becoming Evan's new pharmacology tutor. Early in Evan's illness, Joel learned magic tricks expressly to entertain and encourage his six-year-old nephew. What an unbelievable trick it would be if somehow he could work more magic and help Evan master this course!

Before the semester started, Joel asked that the course syllabus and textbook be sent to him and then he set up a phone appointment for each night of the entire semester. He would not even let up while he was on a camping trip in Sanibel Island, Florida. Because of poor cell phone reception, Joel stood in a hot telephone booth each night of vacation, reviewing pharmacology to stay on schedule. He was unwilling to let Evan get behind. In addition, before the end of the course, and right before the final exam, Joel donated his entire weekend to Evan's critical course. Evan drove from Bloomington to Columbus and spent two 14-hour days covering a summation of the entire course. Only two "A's" were given out in Pharmacology that semester. One of them was Evan's.

Five credit-hours-worth of A raised Evan's grade point average very nicely. His outstanding performance in this difficult class was proof positive to the school that Evan had what it takes. Even though he had an excellent tutor, he was still the test taker, and it affirmed my belief that Evan was a capable student, if only the information could be delivered to him in the right way. Also, this stellar performance lent Evan temporary confidence about his ability.

Third year consisted of the last of the basic science courses. Evan seemed to be holding his breath for this part of optometry school to be over. He would say over and again how much he couldn't wait until the clinic year, the last year, because he knew that he would enjoy seeing patients and that it would be his forte. However, in order to be eligible to go on to the clinic year, he had to pass Diagnostics. It was the end of the third year, and Evan was nervously staring down the final exam.

Evan recounts this stressful time: "Diagnostics was a course that tested your critical thinking when examining the patient. This is

Uncle Joel, the consummate teacher, with his most motivated student.

very important. The class was graded on a bell curve, so all the tests were scored, and then everybody's grade was plotted on a curve. Therefore, I was not only graded on how I did on the test, but also how I did in relation to the other students taking the test. I thought this was a miserable way to grade.

"I decided to go in to speak with the professor. He was a very fair man, and he told me outright that he could not grade everyone on a curve and then grade my paper on a straight right/wrong answer line. So, in one scenario, I might get a good enough grade to pass but if everybody else aced the test, if my score were significantly off the curve, then I would get a failing grade. When I heard this explanation, when I considered the gifted students in my class, I simply felt defeated. After I walked out of the test, I counted up how many questions I knew for sure, how many I was not sure about, and then I listened to the feedback from the other students. I guess that I had so much on the line, and felt so discouraged, that I talked myself into thinking that I would fail Diagnostics. If that happened, I would not be allowed to continue on to the clinic.

"After the test, I got in the car and began to drive, even though I had no destination. I was very upset, and as I drove I seemed to melt away in every way possible. I became a bit disoriented. I just kept driving and picturing all that I had done to get through high school, to get through college, to somehow get in to optometry school. And now, as close as I was, I thought I was going to fail. I kept picturing packing up and leaving. How would it feel to give up after all of the work? I kept thinking about how many people would be disappointed with my failure. I began to be angry and then felt a huge wave of sadness. And all the time I just kept driving. I actually drove until the road ended. It was fitting for the mood. I began to think about how the drive was a one-way road to nowhere, similar to my career path. It was very symbolic. I pulled the car over and got out. As I sat by the side of the road, it occurred to me that, however it turned out, it was going to be: what was to be. I asked myself if I could deal with the worst-case scenario. Answer: yes. I asked myself, if I failed Diagnostics, would I be able to look at any and all options? Answer: yes. I thought about how I was, first and foremost, a survivor. If I had to leave, would I simply start over again? Answer: yes. I would somehow re-apply to schools. Somehow, I would get in somewhere. I would start from the beginning, but I WOULD make it at some point, maybe not here, maybe not now. Maybe next time I would learn from my mistakes and insist on using accommodations. My future was a matter of determination, of resolve, of backbone. Did I have the will? Answer: yes.

"I turned the car around and drove straight back to Bloomington. I lived through a stressful weekend, not knowing whether I passed Diagnostics or not. On Monday, I learned that I had passed with a high enough grade that I could go on with my clinic year. This was the turning point, the point at which I would truly begin to enjoy my work and my career."

Amidst the extreme stress of taking courses in the basic sciences, another miracle was in the making. Carter Robinson, Evan's closest friend from high school days, was a student at Austin Theological Seminary, and the two friends would talk frequently. Carter was worried about Evan, as he had never seen him so discouraged, and under so much pressure and strain. One evening, Evan picked up Carter's phone call with a memorable and surprising declaration: "Evan, I met your wife today!" Carter introduced Evan to a fellow student and good friend of his, Kelly, and a long distance but close phone friendship developed. Studying to be a Presbyterian minister, Kelly was able to calm Evan's frazzled nerves by being a good listener and offering insightful wisdom. She was able to paint the big picture and helped Evan realize that, having a learning disability was not failing as a person. Kelly could soothe Evan far better than I, and I thanked God that she had come into his life. Carter was right. She would later become his wife.

During the summer before Evan's last year, it was time to begin preparations for taking the National Board. Passing the board was imperative, since it led to licensure. Without a license, one cannot practice optometry. Part of Evan wanted to study for it himself and not accept help; another part of Evan acknowledged that he needed "to use all of his resources." Mike offered to take on the preparation for this test despite the fact, that most of the material was unfamiliar to him. He began plowing through Evan's books, making up questions that he thought were reasonable. As Mike would sigh, "the easy part is thinking up the questions ... the hardest part is coming up with the multiple choice answers." Of course, one of the choices was the correct answer. But Mike had to familiarize himself and understand the material enough to structure three other choices that would be close, that would be logical, and that would make Evan think it through.

Mike labored each night of the week preparing the questions that he and Evan would review by phone on the weekend. On our annual "beach week" vacation at Isle of Palms, S.C., Evan and his task master would only enjoy the ocean from the desk on the porch of our cottage. Both realized that this one chance had to count.

My part was to engage in battle with the National Board. By law, Evan qualified for a quiet room and extended time, but because he was the first student EVER to take the National Board as an LD student, i.e., asking for accommodations, they needed a little help to "understand their obligation." My efforts paid off for

Evan. We both hope that, in a small way, we have paved the way for other LD students.

On the day of the test, Evan's anxiety level reached an all-time high. His cold, sweaty hands shook; he was sporting a dull, low-grade headache; his digestive track was thrown out of whack; his appetite gone. All he could say when he finished was, "I tried hard and did the best I could." As always I would answer, "this is all that anyone could ever ask of you." But Evan held himself to a different standard. Unless he passed, it wasn't good enough.

The way we learned the results of the exam was rather unorthodox, and for sure, memorable. Mike and I had been pacing the floor of the maternity waiting room at New York Hospital all night, along with the other grandparents. We were awaiting news of the birth of Jenny's first child, our first grandchild. At daybreak, I could only fathom what the day might bring. Jackson was born in the early morning hour and after my first real look through the nursery window, after checking on Jenny to be sure that she was resting, I needed just one more miracle to make the day perfect. I set out to find a "computer for patient use." One was located in each waiting room, on each floor.

Arriving in the waiting room out of breath, due to the intensity and importance of the mission, I obtained the password from the desk clerk, but the computer had no internet connection. Because the elevator took too long, I was sprinting down the stairwell with Mike running at my heels. Again, we faced the frustration of locating the waiting room, begging for the password, only to find out that this computer was not working either. We then learned that, unfortunately, the internet connection was not available for any of the patient computers throughout the hospital that day.

Pleading, I asked the desk clerk if she would allow me a few minutes on the computer that she was using to look up the do-or-die edict from The National Board. The answer was no, because her computer was networked only with the hospital patient base.

Emotionally drained, and speaking with no sleep, I begged the woman to direct me to SOMEONE who had access to the internet. Pointing to the left, she mumbled something about the business office, and without directions, I was on the run again. Probably embarrassed to be related in any way to this crazy woman, Mike called out that he was going back to Jenny's room.

I was cold and numb, but I was determined! I must have landed in the business office somehow, because there were small cubicles lined up next to each other, each manned by a lady staring at her computer screen and talking on the phone. I remember standing by one of the cubicles and calling out "I am having an emergency. Can someone please help me?" Instead of just one lady pausing from her work, about nine women peered into the hall to see WHAT was happening. "Please, I desperately need a computer." I am not sure why I said the following but in one breath, it spilled out, "my son beat cancer and now he must pass the board in order to practice and the pass/fail list has just been posted. PLEASE someone! Let me use your computer." (I realize that the explanation, just given, made NO SENSE.) A kind lady closest to me, looking rather frightened, stepped aside and motioned to me to sit down. When I saw the score, I collapsed in a flood of tears.

Running down the hall, sobbing, I had to calm myself enough to remember how to return to Jenny's room. When I arrived there, everyone was aghast at what had to be terrible, awful news. Jenny's mother-in-law, Renee, spoke first, "Helen! WHAT is the matter? Are you OK?" Mike added, "Oh God, this must mean that Evan flunked the boards." But my sweet "Jenny-girl," my little soul mate, the person who could read everything about me by looking into my eyes, interrupted, "No, Dad, this means that Evan PASSED!"

(I wonder, if the nice ladies one floor up, still tell the story of the day that a crazy woman appeared out of nowhere.)

In the fall, Evan started his last year of optometry school, called "clinical rotations." Each student was assigned a rotation, most often outside of Bloomington, and the student saw patients in a clinic setting each day under the watchful eye of a designated clinician who had a joint appointment with the optometry school and who would give the student a grade at the end of the rotation. Evan was assigned to Wright-Patterson Air Force Base in Dayton, Ohio for his first rotation. By request, Evan's second assignment was Charlotte Eye, Ear, Nose & Throat Group. This rotation was a stroke of luck for three reasons. First, it was thrilling for Mike and me to have Evan live at home and Evan enjoyed home-cooking, if not our company. Secondly, his rotation was under a most competent clinician, Dr. Ron Melton who was as good a teacher as any at the optometry school. Lastly, it was during this rotation that Evan almost lost his life.

I have already established Evan's work ethic and his determination to do well. He has always been willing to put in the energy necessary to do a good job. On this particular weekend, Evan was living the bachelor's life at home because Mike and I were on a trip out of the country that had been planned for some time and could not be changed. By Sunday night, Evan curtailed his eating due to significant stomach pain. He decided to go to bed early thinking a good night's rest was needed to be up and ready for work the next day. Unfortunately, when he awoke, the pain was worse. Evan decided to ignore this and was at work on time but as the pain got worse, his enthusiasm and cheerful personality were gone. After working up the first two patients, Evan's pain was so bad that, between seeing patients, he had to sit down and take a deep breath while looking for more determination to keep going. Mid-morning, Dr. Melton noticed the color of his face and his demeanor and suggested that Evan go home. "I'll be OK," came the reply. One patient later, Dr. Melton ordered him home. Without a fight, Evan hobbled out to the car and on the way home, called Jenny's husband, a gastroenterologist. Jon asked some probing questions and then told Evan to call him back as soon as he arrived home. In the meantime, Jon called Jenny and told her that he thought Evan was having an appendicitis and promised to call Jenny back as soon as he heard back from Evan. When Evan arrived home, he crawled on all fours to the house with excruciating pain. Luckily, Evan had the good sense to call our next door neighbor, Hannah Wilson, before passing out. Hannah rushed over to the house and somehow got Evan in to the back seat of her Suburban. On the way to the hospital, she called her husband, Hadley (a physician) and asked that he meet them at the Emergency Room. Evan was in surgery within the hour.

When Evan's ever-protective sister, Jenny, could not reach Evan, and knowing that Mike and I were out of the country, she rushed out of her law firm on the 82nd floor in midtown Manhattan, flagged a taxi and called for a flight reservation en route to the airport. She also phoned her cousin Laura who lived in Durham, N.C. to alert her to the emergency. Without a request from Jenny, Laura jumped in her car and drove the two hours to the Charlotte airport in time to pick up Jenny and the two of them formed their own version of EMS on the way to the hospital. I still marvel that all of this could happen by the time Evan was in the recovery room. His appendix had not ruptured and we will never know how close it came. Dr. Melton visited Evan in the hospital the next day. Kidding Evan about his never-wanting-to-take-a-day-off-work ethic, he instructed Evan to make a full report on each drug he had been given. Jenny stayed in Charlotte until Evan was discharged and able to begin eating ... starting with jello and crackers. I will never forget the phone call in the middle of the night in Greece that started out: "Hi mom. First of all, Evan is all right."

Graduation was May, 2006. The optometry school had its own ceremony, apart from the graduation of Indiana University's undergraduates. However, the two ceremonies were on the same weekend, making it difficult to find lodging for a large group. Though it was monumental for the whole family, we arranged ahead of time that the extended family would attend in absentia and throw a party for Evan at our annual Isle of Palm's "beach week." The graduation roster would include only Mike and me, Jenny and her husband, Jon, Evan's younger sister, Staver, Evan's good friend, Bink and Evan's fiancée, Kelly.

The graduation concluded in a teary moment, as the entire family watched our Evan take his own incredible walk across the stage. For me, this electric scene appeared as a reverie, mixing past and present, in slow motion. His formal name was called: Evan Joel Staver Kaufman. But what I heard was his name being called by the pediatrician's intercom: "Evan Joel Kaufman: proceed down the right hall to exam room #3." Though he was sporting the traditional navy blue cap and gown, in my mind's eye, he was wearing his small, worn out tennis shoes and his Adidas shorts, while the pediatrician carefully watched his walk for any trace of a limp. As Evan took a few sturdy steps toward the Dean, I could see him on another walk, stopping at the bench, because the kindergarten door was too far away to make it all in one effort. The family stood up, I among them, clapping non-stop. The noise level was high, but I could still hear Dr. Murphy's words reverberating in my ear ... "if the cancer ever comes back, the first sign will be in his walk, just like it started." Evan had a huge grin and extended his hand to the Dean for a warm handshake. Simultaneously, I saw the handshake extended by Dr. Fox at Charlotte Latin, after announcing that "the headmaster's award goes to Evan Kaufman." I was teary, just contemplating the courage it took for us to decide that Evan should undergo growth hormone therapy. He was walking tall now, 5' 9" to be exact. Here we were, our little family, joyfully standing at our seats, watching and cheering the last few steps of this victorious walk. My! There had been many critical crossroads and stumbling blocks in this journey, from a one percent chance to this day of triumph! Even though Evan had the enthusiasm to run, he had been restrained always to the walk: slow and steady, one step at a time. We witnessed Evan cross the finish line in grand glory. I whispered to myself: "Thank you, dear God, for this moment." And then the Dean handed him his diploma.

Evan was now a Doctor of Optometry.

Left: Evan's sisters and cousins all had some fun "focusing" on his new career.
Right: Evan and Kelly celebrate graduation.

Dr. Evan Kaufman and his proud mom.

St. Jude Children's Research Hospital® Today

St. Jude Children's Research Hospital opened on February 4, 1962, with the mission to find cures for children with cancer and other deadly diseases through research and treatment. Since its opening, treatments invented at St. Jude have helped push the overall childhood cancer survival rate from 20 percent to 80 percent today. Over the years, patients have come to St. Jude from all 50 states and around the world.

When we first walked through the doors of St. Jude with Evan, we felt devastated and hopeless. Evan's cancer, that had been so difficult to diagnosis, acute lymphocytic leukemia (ALL), is now the most common form of childhood cancer. About 3,000 children each year are diagnosed with ALL nationwide, most commonly in children 3 to 5 years of age. St. Jude has increased its survival rates for ALL from 4% when the hospital opened to 94 percent today – the world's best. Thanks to research done at St. Jude, radiation therapy can now be safely eliminated for the majority of children with ALL. This vastly improved survival rate is truly one of the great success stories of St. Jude.

Several years ago, St. Jude completed an extensive expansion program that bolstered the hospital's research and treatment efforts and more than doubled the size of the original hospital. The campus now has more than 2.5 million square feet of research and clinical space, and a new tower under construction will expand the hospital's research and care programs and include the world's first proton radiation therapy center dedicated solely to the treatment of children.

Today, St. Jude is the global leader in finding cures and saving children from cancer and other deadly diseases. On average,

7,800 patients come to the hospital per year and most are treated on an out-patient basis as part of ongoing research programs. St. Jude invents more clinical trials than any other children's hospital. Research is focused specifically on cancers, acquired and inherited immunodeficiencies, sickle cell disease, infectious diseases and genetic disorders. Everyone associated with the hospital is proud of the fact that St. Jude freely shares its discoveries, and every child saved at St. Jude means doctors and scientists can use that knowledge to save thousands more around the world. In fact, St. Jude has an International Outreach Program with 20 official partner sites in 14 countries, whose mission is to improve survival rates of children with cancer and other deadly diseases worldwide, through the sharing of knowledge, technology and organizational skills.

It is now known that cancers are genetic diseases, triggered by harmful changes or mutations in the DNA of normal cells. These mutations occur among the three billion DNA base pairs of the human genome. In 2010, St. Jude launched the Pediatric Cancer Genome Project, in collaboration with Washington University, to find clues to the causes of childhood cancer and potential new treatments and cures. Until that time, not even one whole pediatric cancer genome had ever been sequenced, and the project's ambitious goal was to sequence the complete cancerous and healthy genomes of 600 childhood cancer patients in three years. They exceeded that goal, sequencing the paired genomes of 700 pediatric cancer patients, and have made ground-breaking discoveries in a number of different aggressive childhood cancers. St. Jude is now in Phase II of its collaborative Pediatric Cancer Genome Project with Washington University. In addition, the hospital plans to sequence the normal and cancer DNA of every St. Jude cancer patient beginning in 2014.

Despite the tremendous progress that has been made in overall survival rates for childhood cancers over the last half century, the outlook for some types of pediatric tumors remains poor. In fact, childhood cancer continues to kill more children in this country over age 1 than any other disease. St. Jude is working to drive the overall survival rate for childhood cancer to 90 percent by 2020.

While much has changed since Evan was treated at St. Jude in the 1980s, several things have not changed. Thanks to generous donors, families never receive a bill from St. Jude for treatment, travel, housing or food. Also unchanged is the energetic and caring manner of the staff who attend to each child, the reassuring expertise of the physicians and the thoughtful details spent on making sure that the children come first, always. Everybody at St. Jude projects an optimistic, nurturing attitude that one can see on their faces and observe in their meticulous skills. One can actually feel hope in the air. Today, more than ever, these young patients feel, as Evan so eloquently said, "I think this is going to be the perfect hospital for me."

ADDENDUM II

THE FLETCHER SCHOOL TODAY

The Fletcher School opened its doors in August of 1982 with only six students, one principal, one teacher and high hopes. When Evan attended Fletcher in 1986, it was located at St. Mark's Lutheran Church with an enrollment of approximately 28 students and several teachers. A lot has changed since those early years. Today, The Fletcher School enrolls about 265 students each year in grades K-12. An 82,000 square foot classroom space on a 13 acre campus has replaced the church basement.

It is astounding to those of us who remember how Fletcher started out: with a mimeograph machine, a telephone answering machine and donated books. Facilities today include: two art studios, a Technology and Learning Center, two Upper School Science Labs, interactive projectors in all classrooms, and a cafeteria. When Evan was a student, parents took turns carpooling classmates to the local YMCA for physical education once per week; Fletcher students now enjoy a state-of-the art gymnasium with a weight room and locker rooms. In addition, there are track and soccer fields.

Academics come first, and the school is very proud of the academic success reached and measured by achievement testing administered at the end of each school year. The Fletcher School is based on the Orton-Gillingham approach to teaching. This means that the program is individualized, structured, and multisensory. The student to teacher ratio is 6:1. The high school boasts a college preparatory curriculum and every year our students are accepted by a wide variety of schools. To name a few, students have gone to various in-state schools in the UNC system, art schools such as Savannah College of Art and Design, and small liberal arts schools such as Elon University, High Point University, Brevard, Gardner Webb University. The class of 2013 was awarded $582,950.00 in scholarships.

Unlike Evan's experience at Fletcher in the 80's, Fletcher now offers after school programs such as drama, piano lessons, science club, art, chorus, karate and others. Fletcher also boasts an extensive athletic program that includes basketball, cheerleading, cross country, golf, soccer, swimming, tennis, volleyball and ultimate Frisbee. In 2012, the boys' soccer team was conference champion and the girls' middle school cross-country team was also named conference champion. If only Evan could attend today!

I credit Fletcher for teaching Evan how to advocate for himself and for helping him establish a superior work ethic. He learned how to remember information in a different way allowing him to feel successful. For the first time, he felt self-confidence. He also learned time management skills and the importance of being organized. All of these tools continue to help him today.

The Rankin Institute is a newer component of The Fletcher School, founded in 2004. It is the community outreach and professional development leg of Fletcher. Through the Rankin Institute, educational programs for parents, teachers and professionals in Charlotte and the surrounding region are offered. In addition to inviting nationally-ranked speakers and holding workshops for teachers and parents, an Orton-Gillingham training course is offered to teachers at The Fletcher School and teachers from the community.

From a very small program in 1982, The Fletcher School has developed into a comprehensive educational opportunity where "performance meets potential" for students with specific learning disabilities.

Epilogue

The author lives in Charlotte, North Carolina. She is a graduate of The College of Wooster and holds a master's degree from Duke University. She is the Director of Assessment at The Fletcher School, a school serving students with learning disabilities.

After graduation, Evan was accepted into a residency in ocular disease at The University of Kentucky. He married Kelly, and they moved to Virginia where their first child was born in 2012. She is a Presbyterian minister. Evan is on the staff at Medical College of Virginia. He has been an examiner for the Part III of the National Board. He is the founder of an association of optometrists at academic medical centers, and is also on the Board of Richmond Optometric Association. Recently, he was honored for a second time by being voted onto the list of "Best Docs" in Richmond, and featured in the magazine by the same name.

"Big sister, Jenny," is married to a physician. They have two children. She is an attorney in the Northeast.

"Baby Staver" graduated from Wake Forest University and from Parsons New School of Design. She is a designer in California.

Mike is a neurologist and continues to work at The Multiple Sclerosis Clinic in Charlotte. Sadly, Mike and Helen parted in 2007, but remain friends and continue to rejoice in the family that they created.

Made in the USA
San Bernardino, CA
19 March 2014